Many happy returns
of the 16ᵗʰ and welcome home
all my love
Mary.

16/4/1981

THE BOOK OF
FRANCE

THE BOOK OF
FRANCE

Consultant Editor
John Ardagh

WINDWARD

Windward

An imprint owned by
W. H. Smith & Son Limited
Registered No 237811 England

Trading as WHS Distributors,
St John's House,
East Street,
Leicester, LE1 6NE

First published 1980
Copyright © 1980 Adkinson Parrish Limited

ISBN 0 7112 0059 9

Designed and produced by Adkinson Parrish
Limited, London

Managing Editor	Clare Howell
Design Manager	Christopher White
Editor	Corinne Molesworth
Designer	Peter Saag
Maps	Ingrid Jacob

Phototypeset in the United Kingdom by
Servis Filmsetting Limited, Manchester
Colour illustrations originated in Italy by Starf
Photolitho SRL, Rome
Printed and bound in Italy by L.E.G.O.,
Vicenza

Contributors

Catherine McLeod
Region Introductions

Rupert Swyer
Towns and Villages

Nina de Voogd
Châteaux and Churches

Michael Schwab
Cuisine

Steven Spurrier
Wines and Spirits

Jeanne Brody
Paris

Special Contributions by

Tim Albert
David Paton

Illustration, title page View from Notre-Dame,
Paris.
Contents page The church of Saint-Jérôme,
Toulouse, Midi-Pyrénées region.

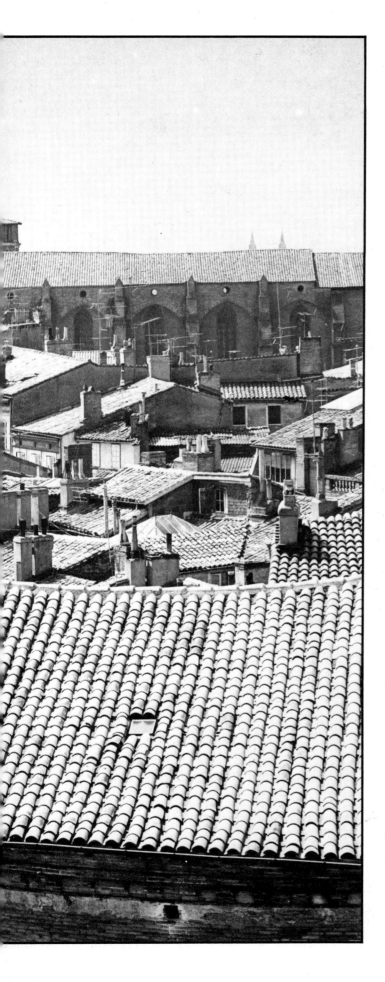

Contents

LA MANCHE

Calais
Boulogne
Lille
NORD
Amiens
PICARDIE
Le Havre Rouen
Beauvais
Oise
Reims
Metz
Meuse
LORRAINE
ALSACE
Caen
Seine
NORMANDIE
PARIS
ILE-DE-FRANCE
Seine
CHAMPAGNE-
ARDENNES
Marne
Moselle
Strasbourg
Brest
Rennes
Mont-St-Michel
Vilaine
BRETAGNE
Sarthe
Orléans
Loire
Yonne
Saône
Belfort
Besançon
FRANCHE-
COMTÉ
PAYS-DE-LA-LOIRE
Tours
CENTRE
BOURGOGNE
Dijon
Angers
Loire
Indre
Nantes
Creuse
L. Léman
Poitiers
Allier
Rhône
Ile de Ré
Ile d'Oléron
POITOU-
CHARENTES
LIMOUSIN
Limoges
Clermont-Ferrand
RHÔNE-ALPES
Lyon
BAIE DE BISCAYE
AUVERGNE
Loire
Rhône
Grenoble
Bordeaux
Garonne
Lot
Durance
PROVENCE-
CÔTE D'AZUR
AQUITAINE
MONACO
MIDI-PYRÉNÉES
Nîmes
Toulouse
Montpellier
Marseille
Biarritz
LANGUEDOC-
ROUSSILLON
Perpignan

MER MÉDITERRANÉE

Introduction John Ardagh

The joy of touring in France is a thousand things. It is to drive at sunset through rolling vineyards, then find a simple village inn with true country cooking, trout from the stream, richly casseroled chicken, local wines, and to chat with the jovial patron while at a nearby table a family party are boisterously celebrating some birthday. It is to watch a *son-et-lumière* display in a Loire valley château, gently floodlit; or to stumble on some festival of medieval music in a Romanesque church in the Pyrenees. It is to wake in a chalet on the pine-clad slopes of the Dauphiné Alps, where the air is crisp, then drive for miles past the ancient, sleepy red-roofed villages of upper Provence, to descend finally into an utterly different world – the crowded, sophisticated resorts of the Riviera, and there enjoy the bizarre parade of cosmopolitan youth in the bars and discos of Saint-Tropez, or the élan of Dior and Gucci on the promenade at Cannes. All this is France, and more.

The delight of France is its ever-changing diversity, welded by French genius into a subtle harmony. Landscape and climate vary hugely, so do accents and dialects, even customs. Yet everywhere there is a unifying Frenchness, easy to identify, hard to define. Its roots lie deep in French history and society, and it has something to do with a sense of style, a brisk competitiveness, a hedonistic zest for living, a strong feeling for tradition allied to a love of novelty.

The term 'sense of style' may cause a raising of eyebrows among some visitors, for it is true that France has produced its share of modern consumer ugliness. In Paris and other cities, the post-war high-rise suburbs are rarely lovely; new factories, pylons and skyscrapers have been allowed to disfigure some beauty-spots; and even gastronomy, that supreme citadel of French style, has come under assault from the rash of new snack-bars and fast-food eateries. But these are mostly the excesses of a too-successful commercial boom, and the French *know* they are ugly or trashy. Individually, they still preserve a greater concern for quality and elegance than most peoples. Insofar as they can afford it, they will always go for quality rather than cheapness: in any street market or supermarket, watch the care with which a housewife selects her cheeses and fresh vegetables.

The French may not always be the most tolerant or open-hearted of people, but their stylishness, their desire to do a job well, is a constant source of pleasure to the visitor. In the smallest café or restaurant, a waiter serves you with brisk professional skill. French women rarely score the highest marks for natural beauty, yet they do live up to their

CORSE

ajaccio

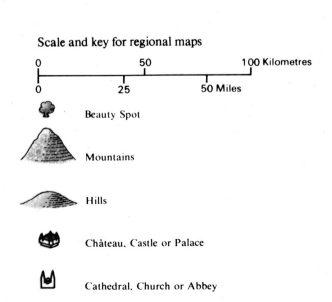

Scale and key for regional maps

0	50	100 Kilometres
0	25	50 Miles

🌳 Beauty Spot

⛰️ Mountains

⛰️ Hills

👑 Château, Castle or Palace

🏛️ Cathedral, Church or Abbey

Introduction

reputation for carrying themselves with elegance, for making the simplest clothes look chic. On holiday – at a woodland picnic, even on a camping site – the French again show a flair for style, and it is no surprise that the Club Méditerranée, most original and sophisticated of modern holiday ventures, is a French invention. Here the back-to-nature rituals of the noble savage are performed with a careful concern for elegance – and, in the French scale of values, few epithets rate higher than *élégant*. To be a success in France, you must do things *avec élégance*, whether it be writing a thank-you letter, laying a dinner-table, flirting with your neighbour's wife, or drawing up a business memo. Even being rude and arrogant – and the French can be experts at that too – must be done with elegance.

The sense of style and harmony is enshrined in France's history, and embodied in her art and architecture. More than any other country in Europe, save possibly Italy, she exudes a sense of continuous civilization, from the Roman ruins and Gothic cathedrals to the latest *haute couture* boutiques and futuristic culture-palaces – and this diversity and contrast are often exhilarating. In a city such as Toulouse, Romanesque churches and pink Renaissance palaces co-exist with modern space-laboratories and mammoth aircraft factories; on the Riviera, the Roman Trophy of La Turbie towers on its hilltop above the half-derelict Victorian villas of Menton and the new skyscrapers of Monte Carlo.

The lover of history can begin his journey in palaeolithic times, with visits to the prehistoric cave-paintings of the Pyrenees and the Périgord (the finest, at Lascaux, have had to be closed to the public, alas). Then the visitor must make a big leap in time, for France has no Greek remains: but the Roman penchant for the colossal is well represented, mainly around Nîmes, Arles and Orange. The Middle Ages have also left mighty monuments in this area, notably the Palace of the Popes at Avignon. But the greatest glory of medieval France is her legacy of majestic cathedrals and abbeys, many of them in the northern half of the country – Chartres, Reims, Amiens, Notre-Dame de Paris, the Abbey of Mont-Saint-Michel, and many others. One of the delights of touring France is the immense richness of her past, the fact that even the smallest village or remotest valley can yield some historical treasure.

The Renaissance and post-Renaissance periods have bequeathed the loveliest of the Loire châteaux, as well as many charming towns such as Sarlat (Périgord) and the old seaport of La Rochelle. In the seventeenth century, Louis XIV built the great palace of Versailles, while the eighteenth century is seen at its best in the Place Stanislas at Nancy and the graceful avenues of Bordeaux. As in other countries, the nineteenth century added little of value, even if the Eiffel Tower and Sacré-Coeur in Paris are follies we have somehow learned to love.

The French love all their historic buildings and look after them with careful pride: since the war, hundreds of abbeys, castles and mansions have been beautifully restored at great expense, by the State or private owners.

The French love tradition: but since the war they have also, rather surprisingly, fallen in love with modernism too. The two co-exist, everywhere – and there are many who believe that the old France is being spoiled. The economic boom of the 1950s and '60s gave a huge impetus to new building, such as France had not known for decades, and the results are very noticeable. The French have moved in one swoop from the little corner-shop to the largest hypermarkets in Europe, some with forty or fifty check-outs: you see them on the edge of every big town. Silent valleys fill up with giant new factories and power-stations, and new motorways have bulldozed through country lanes. Some of the architectural innovations are extraordinary: for example, the futuristic resorts along the Languedoc coast, (notably the bizarre pyramids of La Grande Motte), the Manhattan-like clusters of skyscrapers at La Défense in western Paris, and in central Paris the new Beaubourg cultural centre, a weird building of glass and steel, covered with red and blue pipes – 'the arty oil refinery', its critics have called it. But the popular success of Beaubourg shows that the French, though creatures of habit in much of their daily lives, are also excited by novelty and new ideas. They do not mind the co-existence of the old and the new, the modern and the picturesque: in fact, it stimulates them. Some foreign visitors may be less enthusiastic.

The new, brash successful France may not be to their taste; they may be irritated by an assertive modernism that might seem more inspired by Texas than by old civilized French values. But there are two answers to this. First, if France had not modernized, she would remain decadent, as she was before the war. Second, the old picturesque France still strongly survives, for those who care to seek it out – the France of old men playing dominoes in backstreet bistros, of open markets in ancient city squares, of grape-harvesting in isolated vineyards, of peasants going to Mass in Romanesque churches hidden in silent valleys.

Diversity of landscape is as strong a feature of France as complexity of history and architecture. More than any other country, France belongs both to north and south Europe. Paris itself is a Latin town somehow strayed into a semi-northern climate. France has some of the highest mountains in Europe – the Alps along the Swiss and Italian borders, the Pyrenees bordering Spain – where the skiing is excellent. She also has some of the best Atlantic beaches (west and south-west of Bordeaux) and some of the widest expanses of wheat-growing plain (on every side of Paris). The bare rocky headlands of Brittany, lashed by Atlantic gales, are utterly different from the little coves of Provence, backed by pinewoods and olives. The Alsatian vineyards are flanked by the mountain forests of the Vosges; those of Languedoc rise gently from a flat coastal plain, under a scorching sun. Normandy, with its apple-orchards, hedgerows and half-timbered farmsteads, will remind the visitor of Kent or Sussex; in

Provence, he might think himself in Tuscany; in Savoy or the Jura, he could be in Switzerland; the Lille area looks and feels Belgian; the sweeping uplands of the Massif Central may recall the central Scottish Highlands.

The diversity of France is human as well as scenic. This is one of the most centralized of western countries, yet it is formed also of a marriage of many different peoples and cultures, welded into unity over the centuries by a powerful and determined State. Not all Frenchmen are Latins by any means: some are Celtic, Germanic, Basque or Flemish. The Bretons in the north-west are France's Celts: seafaring, religious, inclined to mysticism and even whimsy; they proudly keep up their own traditions and festivals, and some still speak Breton. The Alsatians in the east are Germanic, cousins to the Swabians and Swiss-Germans: Alsace is the least 'French' part of France, and so German in style are the buildings, the food and drink, the dress, the dialect, that often it is hard to believe one is not east of the Rhine. And yet, the Alsatians would much rather be French than German: having been twice annexed by Germany in this century, they have emerged as staunch French patriots. In the far south-west, France's 120,000 Basques are brothers to the far more numerous Basques across the Spanish border. They have a strong individuality and are proud of their special sports and folk-dances, their costumes, their flag, and their strange ancient language, all 'x's and 'z's. In the north, around Lille, are a small minority of Flemish French, similar to the Flemish of Belgium.

Even among France's Latins, the differences are

Introduction

great. The big gulf is between north and south. A fiery, wayward Corsican, or even a Provençal, has more in common with an Italian, by temperament and tradition, than with a cautious, phlegmatic Norman (who, anyway, is Scandinavian by remote origin). Similarly, the volatile and easy-going city of Toulouse has a very different ambiance from reserved and industrious Lyon – though both find common cause in their historic resentment of Paris, the 'enemy' that for centuries stifled the provinces. Provincials' scorn for haughty Parisians is just as great as the contempt that Parisians often feel, or claim, in return.

The post-war economic revival of the provinces has led, as in other parts of Europe, to a growing revival of regional cultures and a new regional awareness. The tourist in summer will find himself assailed by local folk-dancing, folk music, craft displays, even poetry readings in local languages – especially in such regions as Brittany, Languedoc, and the Basque and Catalan lands. These activities are often a little contrived, but they do spring from a real need for more local self-expression. However, except perhaps in Corsica, this rarely goes as far as a yen for separatism. Even in Brittany, true nationalists are few: people may want a little more regional autonomy, or a better economic deal, but they also want to remain part of France. The French nation remains firmly welded, after all these centuries, and the basic unity outweighs the diversity. A strong centralized education system has played a large part in the process.

France is ideal country for the motorist, most of the time. The network of ordinary roads is about the best in Europe: they are well-surfaced, and in mountain areas exceptionally well-engineered, as witness the famous scenic *corniches* of the Riviera. After a slow initial start, the French have now been building motorways fast as well. Most of these radiate from Paris, but some now link provincial and foreign cities, for example, Lyon to Geneva – and high time, too.

France is often regarded, wrongly, as an expensive country for the tourist. It is true there are plenty of tourist-traps, on main roads and in big resorts. It is true too that Paris can be pricey for the unwary: a cocktail or a coffee in a smart boulevard café can cost twice as much as elsewhere. But go to the provinces, especially rural areas, and you will often find remarkable value-for-money. For those with simple tastes, a double room in a decent country hotel need not cost more than fifty francs. And in little local restaurants you can still get a good meal with wine for thirty-five or forty francs. It is best to consult a good guide book, such as the red *Michelin* or the *Gault-et-Millau*.

In hotels, cafés and restaurants, in shops and garages, service is generally swift, helpful and efficient. It is true that in Paris service is not always with a smile, it may come garnished with brusqueness – but that is Paris. If there is one generalization to be made about French niceness, it is that provincials have more of it than Parisians. Foreigners are wrong to suppose that the French as a whole do not invite to their homes. Most Anglo-Saxon horror-stories about French inhospitality are based on stays in Paris: go to other towns, and you will find a people as welcoming as almost any in Europe. Even Parisians are hospitable when away from the Parisian rat-race. In frenetic Paris, they work so hard, and life is so hectic, that they do not have time to be kind and friendly except to a small circle of relatives and intimates.

As a result, visitors sometimes think the French xenophobic, but this can be misleading. Faced with Parisian sharpness or unhelpfulness, many foreigners at first take it personally: 'They're so anti-American', thinks a US visitor; 'They must still hate us', thinks a German. But Parisians tend to be just as prickly with each other as with foreigners. And elsewhere in France, visitors are generally welcome, with a few exceptions. Among older people who suffered in the war, some anti-German feeling persists, but it is seldom found among the young. American visitors will discover that the anti-US hang-ups of the Gaullist era have waned. After all, the French have now fully recovered their national pride, so they hardly need to resent the Americans any more. If they do so, it is more political and economic than personal, and the same applies to attitudes to the British.

The French have become less insular than in the days of de Gaulle. Increasingly they travel abroad, for business or pleasure; and many of the young are internationally-minded, almost unaware of frontiers in Europe, however sceptical of the EEC as an institution. The French feel part of Europe, but also French. They are not so much insular as, very often, chauvinistic; or rather, highly competitive towards other peoples. But at least they are eager to make contact, to take part in the game. Witness how, in the decade since de Gaulle's death, they have been abandoning their arrogant refusal to speak anything but their own distinguished language. They have seen it massively outstripped by English as the world's main vehicle of speech, and so they have decided, reluctantly, 'If you can't beat 'em, join 'em.' In order to promote their commerce and diplomacy, they have little choice but to utilize the world's new *lingua franca*. Thus the learning of English, in adult courses as well as schools and colleges, has been making astounding progress, and an educated young Frenchman is far more likely than ten years ago to speak good English. This will ease the path of many tourists. And yet, the Frenchman remains proud of his language, and will respond warmly if you can speak it with him. If you wish to be more than a tourist, and to penetrate the subtleties of French life, then at least try a few words in French.

Brittany

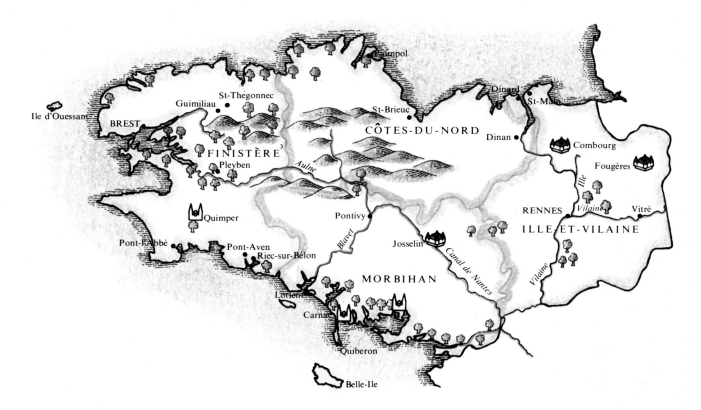

This is a land of mysticism, moorland and sea coast, a fiercely independent-minded Celtic province set on France's north-westerly peninsula, its climate tempered by the changing moods of the Atlantic. Stories of Merlin and Arthur lie buried in its folklore; memories of the Druids persist in the megaliths. Raised between 3,500 and 1,800 BC, these presumably were dedicated to some ancient sun-cult, and were placed with extraordinary astronomical precision, scratched with the strange symbols of a vanished faith. Thousands of these still stand north of the town of Carnac, some over six metres (nearly twenty feet) high and weighing up to 350 tons. As old as Stonehenge, some theories link them together, but little is known of the pre-Gallic race which raised them and worshipped or sacrificed here. More is known of the Celts who arrived from the British Isles in the sixth century BC. The area became known by their

name for it – Armor or Armorica, land of the sea. The interior was called Argoat, land of the woods.

The Celts who settled near the Gulf of Morbihan were the earliest Breton sailors. Five tribes populated the region, kinsmen to the Irish, Scots and Britons. Like the Scottish clans, the five tribes retained separate identities. The Veneti, or Morbihan people were decimated by Julius Caesar but on the whole the Romans succeeded in making little headway, just as Gallo-Christianity found it hard to leave an impression on these stubborn, moody individualists who merely reshaped their Druidic beliefs and redecorated their menhirs to render them more acceptable to the new faith.

Settlers from Britain began to arrive about AD 460. Gradually Armorica admitted Christianity, then embraced it with a passionate fervour that resulted in the creation of hundreds of saints, many of them peculiar to the country or even to a single village, few of them formally recognized in Rome. Later, in the sixteenth and seventeenth centuries, elaborate calvaries were erected at cemeteries and crossroads, humanized descendants of the menhirs. Christ and the Passion are depicted with touching naiveté around these granite bibles for illiterate villagers.

Four departments (*départements*) make up this region: Côtes-du-Nord, Finistère, Ille-et-Vilaine and Morbihan, but rebaptism did not alter the natural geographical delineation of the country. Upper Brittany (Haute Bretagne) lies to the east of Saint-Brieuc, Pontivy and Lorient. Here the old customs have disappeared and Breton is rarely spoken. Lower Brittany (Basse Bretagne) is the coastal region with its towering seas and violent storms alternating with sunlight and gentle rain. The stormy season is in autumn. An inconstant sun illuminates seaweed strewn rock, gorse, stone wall and pastureland with that ineffably pure light which sent Impressionist painters to their easels. Along the south coast, the climate is kinder and Mediterranean vegetation flourishes. Even in the north there are warm areas, pampered by the Gulf Stream. Off the coast lie the islands. Ouessant (Ushant in English) is the most westerly, as its name indicates. Belle-Ile, eight miles (thirteen kilometres) south-west of Quiberon, is the largest, a great slate plateau. Grainfields alternate with patches of reed, sheltered valleys with windswept 'highlands', all with a scattering of white-washed villages.

In Basse Bretagne the old customs and the old language are slowly dying out among the peasantry, but some intellectuals and students are now making efforts to revive them. There are many ancient dialects. Diversity is expressed in the Celtic proverb, '*Kant bro, Kant giz, Kant parrez, Kant iles*' – 'A hundred regions, a hundred manners, a hundred parishes, a hundred churches.' Key words are often contained in the place-names. *Pou* or *ple* indicates 'parish' and is found in Ploudaniel (the parish of Saint Daniel). *Loc*, 'place of penitence', gives Locmaria (Mary's place). *Traon* or *trou* means 'valley' and the word is encompassed in Tromelin, 'valley of the mill'.

The inland area was once dense forest, reduced now to rough patches of gorse, butter-yellow, nutty-smelling and sweet when in flower, the pods popping open in the sun. A few beech trees, a few oaks. Not much vegetation at all. The great old mountains have been eroded away and their stones gone to build granite walls that travel the arable landscape.

In the tenth century the Norman Vikings enjoyed two decades of power before being driven out. A long period of independence continued even after the marriage of Anne of Brittany with Charles VIII of France in 1491. Her daughter, Claude, inherited the duchy and it was part of her dowry when she married François I of France. Her name remains sweet in French history since she bequeathed it to a

delicious strain of plum, known as Reine Claude, when she died, aged twenty-five.

Brittany has been French since 1532, the date of the death of Queen Claude. But in mood it remains apart, passionately Catholic, preserving and fostering its Celtic tongue with a self-regenerating desire for regaining its old independence. Most Bretons hanker after internal autonomy, rather than centralized government.

A hardy, silent people, these Gallicized riders to the sea, dour and whimsical by turns, imprinted with the image of the cruel and fruitful ocean at their threshold and of highlands where the wind wakes through brush and stone, not unlike parts of Scotland or Ireland.

In the end, it is the sea which has shaped the people, even as it has shaped the long, dramatic coastline of churning water and looping white sand. The naval bases of Brittany suffered heavily in World

War II. The harvest of the sea – oysters, mussels, lobsters, clams, scallops, shrimps – is the area's pride. Even inland the smell of salt hangs in the air from the seaweed used to fertilize the fields. It nourishes fine vegetables: potatoes, beans and artichokes and those Brittany onions which you can still occasionally buy in Britain from the few Breton onion sellers who still hawk them around on their bicycles.

It is by the sea or in the old quarters of the towns you find the true atmosphere of Brittany. Here picturesque houses with overhanging rooftops give onto open courtyards. Inside, if they have not been relinquished to an antiques dealer or made their way to the Hôtel Drouot (the Paris auction rooms) are massive, carved pieces of furniture such as the characteristic *lit clos* or enclosed bed, and carved wooden chests. The family possessions, in true peasant style, are kept within surveillance of the joint conjugal eye, in these typical Breton coffers.

The sea, which has shaped Brittany's wild and rugged coastline (**above left**), rewards its people with a rich harvest of seafood (**top**).

Above An atmosphere of mystery and otherworldliness lingers round the standing stones at the prehistoric site of Carnac.

Towns and Villages

The Pardons

These festivals which take place all over Brittany are unique to the region: an expression of fervour by a deeply religious people. Even today, following the tradition of a thousand years, believers gather to ask forgiveness for their sins in 'pardons'. Banners, candles, images and processions pay homage to the local saints of towns and villages. Sometimes they even bless the sea, like a sop to the

old gods who alternately punish and reward them, widow their women and nourish their children.

One of the most popular pardons takes place at Sainte-Anne-la-Palud on the last Sunday in August. The traditional costumes: the lace-edged aprons, the high head-dresses or *coiffes* and exquisite lacy collars are brought out and shaken or starched into a sinless state in keeping with the occasion. Afterwards there is a village fête and the men may lock together in a *lutte* or wrestling match, pitting their strength against each other in silence watched by a spellbound crowd. Here bagpipes are in, and the traditional folk music has even been transmuted into a new Breton pop. Songs are linked to sea-going and legend.

The sea is the all-pervading motif of Brittany. The wealth that stemmed from trade and privacy helped to build her towns, and the life and death of her fishermen have shaped her everyday life and her annual festivals. Towns and villages lying inland and along the coast at the numerous small harbours are characteristically Breton: buildings are made of the stern local granite and are often medieval in feel, with their well-preserved old quarters.

The region has long been popular among holiday-makers who come for the quiet, unspoilt charm of her fishing villages; for the brisk ocean climate of La Baule; for the health cures at Quiberon's vast thalassotherapy institute. (It was at Quiberon that Monsieur Hulot enjoyed his momentous holiday.) Other resorts, like Dinard, founded by an American in 1850, were fashionable from the mid-nineteenth century, when the Empress Eugénie came here, although Dinard today is gently decayed.

Across the Rance estuary from here, beyond the world's first tidal power station built in the 1960s, the attractive resorts of Saint-Servan and Paramé yield pride of place to Saint-Malo, the old pirate town huddling behind massive walls. Heavy fighting in the last war left

Above An aerial view of Saint-Malo shows the massive walls protectively encircling the old town.

but a few of the attractive shipbuilder's houses. Their heavily-studded front doors conjure up an age when bold, marauding seamen lived here, and lived by harassing the shipping of England, Spain and Holland.

The naval base of Brest is modernity's answer to Saint-Malo. The old town was flattened during a forty-three-day siege by the Allies in 1944, and has since been successfully rebuilt. The huge natural harbour is one of the finest in the world, and today the port survives as a naval base, although its great military days are past. Today it is important more as a repair centre for mammoth tankers; a shore station for offshore oil-men (as yet unsuccessful), and the site of a major oceanographic research unit.

The commercial port of Lorient owes its name to a naval base established there in 1766 by the statesman Colbert. This base was the headquarters of the French India Company ('L'Orient'), moved to this stretch of the Atlantic coast so that the company's ships would not be so easily pursued by the British in the Channel. A submarine base established by the Germans during the war is used by the French today.

Right in the heart of Brittany is Rennes, the capital, one of the loveliest cities in France and now a flourishing industrial centre too, with car-assembly plants and electronics factories. Before the Revolution this was the seat of the Parliament in Brittany, which often gave the French monarchy sleepless nights. The independent-spirited Bretons have never fully accepted their attachment to France, and the parliament building, now the region's chief law court, is the scene of frequent trials of the more extreme Breton separatists. Of all the cities of Brittany, Rennes is the liveliest and the most outward-looking, where the latest ideas from Paris fuse with the strivings of a people to revive its ancient personality. Its atmosphere is due in part to its geographical position mid-way between Paris and the far reaches of Finistère, where Breton traditions survive most strongly. Rennes has a large university, and active cultural life, and is a centre of the current Breton cultural renewal.

Quimper, capital of the old kingdom of Cornouaille, still encapsulates much that is traditionally Breton, with its Brittany museum of folklore and history relating to the region. Many old costumes can be seen at the Great Festival of Cornouaille which takes place on the fourth Sunday in July, lasting three days.

Top Typical carved Breton dressers and cupboards of heavy wood lined up at a quayside market. The medieval, half-timbered houses in the background remain little changed.

Above The river Rance winds through Dinan, one of the most picturesque towns in Brittany, with its old quarter surrounded by impressive ramparts.

Châteaux and Churches

The essence of Brittany is embodied in her 'calvaries', those strange and enigmatic monuments that hauntingly link piety and prehistory. Hewn from great granite rocks, these rustic sculptures representing episodes of Christ's passion are the successors of medieval crosses and ancient menhirs that dot the countryside. The oldest calvary, at Tronoën near Pont-l'Abbé in the Finistère, rises mysteriously from the surrounding fields. Many are found in the 'parish enclosures', those groups of buildings so typical of Breton communities, consisting of a church, ossuary, triumphal arch and calvary set around the parish cemetery. Competition between villages such as Guimiliau and Saint-Thégonnec led to the building of beautiful closes; Pleyben and Lampaul-Guimiliau also have fine examples.

Brittany's earliest monuments are the megaliths, set up between 3,500 and 1,800 BC. Some stones stand alone, up to twenty feet high; others are set in lines, the most impressive being the vast arrangements in the Carnac area in the Morbihan, where more than 3,000 can be seen. The lines of menhirs appear to have some astronomical significance, being precisely set in relation to the sunrise and sunset etc., but their exact purpose remains a mystery. At Carnac you can visit the Tumulus of Saint-Michel, a fascinating subterranean network of prehistoric burial chambers.

The menhirs have long been linked with the mystic life of Brittany. The Romans carved pictures of their gods on some of them; the Christians later added their crosses and symbols. Numerous crosses and sacred fountains can be found throughout the region.

Although most of the Breton artistry was employed for religious works, there are many other architectural riches to be found in the region. A great number of towns have quarters preserved exactly as they were three or four hundred years ago, with half-timbered houses overhanging narrow, winding streets. Stern fortresses built of local granite and fortified manor-farms are characteristic of this region, rather than grand châteaux. An excellent example of these medieval fortresses can be seen at Fougères, where the massive curtain walls of the castle, with its thirteen towers, follow the contours of the land. Another formidable stronghold looms above the medieval streets and houses of Vitré, an ancient enclosed town and the best-preserved in Brittany.

The magnificent Château at Josselin began as a twelfth-century fortress, but was later renovated in the Flamboyant Gothic style. The wealth of carvings and ornamentation of the dwelling-house façade contrasts with the massive outer walls. Other châteaux, with literary associations, are those of Combourg and Les Rochers. The sombre but imposing castle of Combourg was for some time the childhood home of the writer Chateaubriand, who slept in the haunted 'Tower of the Cat'. Madame de Sevigné, whose vivid letters give such insight into life at the time of Louis XIV, lived in the Château of Les Rochers, with its curious polygonal chapel, and gardens by Le Nôtre.

The medieval flavour of Brittany lingers in the ancient quarter of Vannes, with its ramparts and old houses grouped around the cathedral. Dinan, with its winding, cobbled streets overhung by tall, ancient houses, is dramatically situated on a rocky crag above the Rance estuary. At the estuary's mouth is Saint-Malo, a unique and picturesque town surrounded by massive medieval ram-

parts, bordered on three sides by the sea. Much damaged during the war, this town has regained its former character after careful restoration. Dignified, classical houses line the central square of Rennes, the capital of Brittany. The seventeenth-century lawcourts (formerly the Houses of Parliament of Brittany), were designed by the architect of the Luxembourg Palace in Paris. Churches and chapels were built, like the fortresses, from the hard local granite, and ornate belfries and porches are characteristically Breton. The curious church at Carnac is dedicated to Saint Cornély, the patron saint of horned cattle, and has coloured figures of the saint and two bulls on its façade.

Quimper has a fine cathedral, and an important Fine Arts museum, containing works by Fragonard, Boucher and many others, as well as the Breton museum of local folklore and the traditional Quimper pottery. Not far from Quimper is the town of Pont-Aven, made famous by Gauguin, who formed a school of painting here in 1888. The Breton women with their picturesque head-dresses were a favourite subject for the artists of the Pont-Aven or syntheticist school.

Above The Calvary at Tronoën, one of the finest examples of these rustic, religious carvings which are unique to the region.

Opposite The Ménec lines at Carnac consist of 1,009 menhirs stretching from a semicircle of seventy stones partly surrounding the village.

Top right Gauguin used bright, flat colours and decorative lines to depict his Breton subjects.

Right Well-preserved medieval ramparts enclose the ancient town of Vannes.

Cuisine

Indifferent to the whims of man, the grey Atlantic Ocean dominates the angular peninsula of Brittany, and though the soil is fertile and the climate equable it is fish which takes the central place in local cookery. Deep-sea trawlers now take the fishermen to distant waters for sardines, tuna fish and cod, but most restaurants still concentrate on shellfish: lobsters, crawfish, oysters, clams and crabs. These, with tangy salt-marsh lamb, poultry, pancakes and abundant vegetables, make up much of the Breton diet.

In prehistoric times the peninsula was connected to Cornwall and where the Channel now separates the two was once – they say – the fabled land of Armorica. Today the name alone survives, a label for the infamous lobster sauce *à l'armoricaine*. A zany preparation of shallots, tomatoes, brandy and white wine, the sauce is sharply flavoured with garlic and cayenne pepper. Lobster with this sauce (*homard à l'armoricaine*) has been described as 'a gastronomic cacophany' and it detracts from the exquisite flavour of this deep-sea crustacean. Nevertheless it remains high on the tourist menu. Any Breton chef will recommend you have your lobster grilled or *à la mayonnaise*. At the restaurant Chez Mélanie in Riec-sur-Bélon, where the famous Bélon oysters are farmed, lobster and crawfish are served as hors d'oeuvres, there is an excellent crab soup (*bisque d'entrilles*), and those tiny shellfish called *pétoncles* are sometimes available, stuffed with garlic butter then grilled (*pétoncles farcis grillés*). Under the guidance of the original Mélanie's daughter, this little restaurant is a bastion of traditional cuisine.

Every town has its *crêperies*, sometimes no more than a street stall where a bowl of pancake batter stands beside a griddle stove, ready to be quickly grilled and filled for a passing customer. Cheese, ham, eggs and sometimes jam are ready to garnish the finished product. Together with the traditional crisp, buckwheat pancakes called *galettes* – often filled with anchovy paste or sliced fried onions or mushrooms – *crêpes* are the bread of Brittany.

Onions and mushrooms thrive in the heavy soils, along with carrots, cauliflower, potatoes and cabbages, but – thanks to the warm winds which the Gulf Stream brings – there are also less humdrum vegetables: artichokes, asparagus, cucumber and courgettes. Globe artichokes (*artichauts*) are trimmed and cooked then eaten leaf by leaf, dipped in a vinaigrette or mayonnaise; cucumbers are stuffed with chopped cooked carrots, peas and egg (*concombres farcis*); potatoes are boiled with onions, butter and salt pork (*pommes de terre au petit salé*) as well as playing a leading role in two local soups: the thick vegetable soup (*potée de Bretagne*), with cabbage, de-salted breast of Breton version of a *bouillabaisse* (*cotriade*), containing all sorts of odd seafish thrown up in the catch. *Cotriade* can be delicious, as at the Hôtel Barbu in Paimpol; but it can also be disgusting – so treat with caution!

Brittany is France's leading pig-breeding area, but the best of the region's meat comes from the flocks of sheep that graze on the salty coastal plain. Two popular ways of preparing the meat are leg of mutton with white beans (*gigot de pré-salé aux haricots blancs*) and lamb chops with tarragon (*côtes d'agneau à l'estragon*). The poultry too is good, especially the Nantais duck, traditionally served with cherry sauce (*caneton nantais aux cerises*): this is a speciality of the Moulin de Rosmadec in Pont-Aven, an old mill restaurant near the Aven mouth, where you will also find authentic Breton pastries like apple doughnuts (*pommes beignets*) and a delicious, light, toffee-streaked cake called *kouign-amann*.

Top The many varieties of shellfish, seen in abundance on this market stall, are a staple of the Breton cuisine.

Above Many vegetables, from cabbages to artichokes, flourish in the heavy soil of this region, which supplies the rest of France with much of its produce.

The Fish Museum

The fish museum (Musée de la Pêche) in Concarneau is splendid tribute to the generations of Breton fishermen who have plied these coastal waters. Situated in the old arsenal, which is part of the town's seventeenth-century fortifications, it contains a fine collection of model boats and fishing equipment which illustrate the evolution of fishing techniques in this region. There are also maps and charts which demonstrate both the shifting nature of the fishing grounds, as well as the growth of Concarneau itself.

Second in importance after Boulogne, Concarneau is a major landing port for many shallow and deep sea varieties of fish. Tuna is particularly important, and canning factories in the region are responsible for its export throughout Europe. Sole, mullet, turbot, ray, mackerel and bass are the most important coastal catches though from June to November, sardines are also important. The museum contains a large aquarium in which these, and a wide range of shellfish, may be viewed.

Above Young and old partake in a village feast at Plédéliac.
Left In this major pig-producing region, sausages are excellent and highly-flavoured, ranging from black puddings and Quimperlé chitterlings to the smoked sausages of Guémené.

Wines and Spirits

There is not a single drop of wine produced in Brittany, although a great deal is consumed. Most of this is the *gros rouge*, the most ordinary of French *vin ordinaire*, but in Brittany, as elsewhere in France, consumption of this is dropping in favour of *vins d'appellation*.

Probably the most common sights in the restaurants and bars along the coast are signs for Muscadet shellfish, and *crêpes bretonnes*. Muscadet also goes well with the excellent Breton *charcuterie*, but maybe the light red from the Coteaux d'Ancenis is better. Then a *pot-au-feu* or something in a cream sauce which used to be accompanied by a *vin d'Algérie* (the Bretons were the largest market for Algerian wine) and is now usually washed down with cider: the principal alcoholic produce of Brittany. Fermented from the juice of the local apples, Breton cider is generally dry and non-sparkling. It is also quite high in alcohol, being 7° to 8° by volume. Brittany also produces a little sweet cider, lower in alcohol since the sweetness is left by unfermented sugar, which is given to the children. The sparkling version is generally cloudy, since the fermentation continues in the bottle, producing the sparkle but also a deposit. Commercially produced sparkling cider is carbonated rather than naturally fermented.

With the *crêpes*, one can drink the local *eau-de-vie* distilled from the lees after cider-making, but when these pancakes are served *flambé*, they are probably best on their own. The spirit most commonly used for *flambé* dishes is Cognac from a hundred odd miles down the Atlantic Coast and then the sweet *eaux-de-vie*: Curaçao, Cointreau and Grand Marnier. These last three are liqueurs made from the skins of oranges, originally in the case of Curaçao from the island of that name off Venezuela. Cointreau is made in Angers and is a little drier (its original name being Triple Sec White Curaçao) than Grand Marnier, which is brandy-based and comes in two types: Cordon Rouge and Cordon Jaune. The latter is generally used for cooking, the former, more spirited, for drinking.

If you want to drink an imported wine with your meal (anything from outside Brittany is 'imported'), the best wine to choose is Côtes du Rhône.

Local apples provide the basis for Brittany's traditional drink, cider, which is generally dry and non-sparkling.

Normandy

Think of Normandy and the image is of a humane landscape, rolling green pastureland, placid cows, flowering apple trees, cream the colour of ivory. And Deauville, that combination of French hard-headedness and French frivolity, near where the Seine finally makes its way to the sea.

This is a large province, stretching on the coast from Le Tréport to Mont-Saint-Michel. To the south-west the boundary is marked by the river Couesnon. A waterway of fickle loyalties, it shifted course from the east to the west of the Mont-Saint-Michel, so this province consequently acquired one of the wonders of France, the tide-washed island, town and monastery with its nineteenth-century spire topped by the reassuring presence of a statue of the Archangel himself. The Bretons then made up a jealous little rhyme: '*Le Couesnon, par sa folie a mis le Mont en Normandie*', ('The Couesnon, in its folly has put the Mount in Normandy.')

Five *départements* make up Normandy: the Seine-Maritime, Eure, Calvados, Manche and Orne, and all but the last touch on the sea.

The province falls into two economic 'regions', Upper and Lower Normandy. Rouen, where Joan of Arc was burned, is the capital of Upper Normandy, Caen of Lower. Divergences are revealed by a coastline which begins as chalk cliff in the east, changing to low sandy beaches, followed by the aggressive granite of the Nez de Jobourg, ending as a rocky edge down to the Brittany coast. The part of the Seine valley area known as the Vexin Normand is rich agricultural land, and so is the Pays d'Auge, where Upper and Lower Normandy meet. South lies the Perche, home of the Percheron horses whose high-stepping forebears carried the Crusaders to the Holy Lands. The Cotentin peninsula is moorland, beaking

Introduction

to a land's end of perilous grandeur, while behind it lies the *bocage* country, named for its multitude of hedges, green, pleasant and bushy.

The province owes its name to the Norsemen whose longboats raked the coast in the ninth century. They even followed the Seine all the way to Paris. France and Ireland trembled before these Nordic plunderers, who alternated savagery with politic baptism and repentance. It took Charles the Simple, no victim to his name but a crafty negotiator, to do business; in 911 he signed a treaty with one of their leaders, Rollo, and quietened him down by presenting him with the area he already occupied. This land became the Duchy of Normandy and Rollo its first Duke. Rollo was followed by an unmanageable band whose names are thumb-nail sketches of their characters and physiognomy. There was Richard the Good. There was William the Bastard, who was later to become William the Conqueror (although Harold of England no doubt found the original name more fitting). Robert Short Hose was followed some time later by his sartorial descendant, Henry Short Mantle. The last of them was defeated by France in 1204 and Normandy became properly French.

Many Normans still carry traces of their Nordic ancestry in their fair hair, blue eyes and tall figures, thickened by the good eating in this part of the world and their appreciation of local cider.

Much of the story of the Norman Conquest of Britain lies stitched into the muted colours of the Bayeux tapestry, possibly the world's first comic strip. It would be a shame to allow the heroic action in the central portion to dim your appreciation of the erotic goings-on in the upper and lower bands.

Apples, cows, horses and fish. The Norman cow is bred for milk production and meat and is a tri-coloured animal of white, dark brown and cream, with whitish rings like spectacles around the eyes. These rings are characteristic of the breed. Any animal not so marked is denied entry to the Norman Herd Book, a kind of bovine *Who's Who* for the locality, first started in 1883. Interestingly, the English word 'cattle' comes from the Norman-French, *catel*. Near Caux the peasants tie their livestock to a stake and the fields are marked with regularly cropped circles. One steer with his mind on the job can eat up to sixty-five pounds of grass and put on two pounds a day. A cow of equal commitment gives from twenty to thirty quarts of milk. Linen flax is also grown near Caux and the valleys where it is retted retain a characteristic odour.

Half-timbered farm houses set amid lush green fields and abundant orchards are a familiar sight in Normandy.

Sophisticated Deauville on the Côte Fleurie was founded in 1860 by the Duc de Morny and has never lost its patrician elegance, although it also submits to visits from film stars, pop stars and other international celebrities. In the old days, wives, nursemaids and children took the air at Trouville, just around the bay, leaving mistresses free to stroll along *les planches*, the Deauville boardwalk. Here Claude Lelouch made that popular film *Un Homme et Une Femme*. Deauville stands for business as well as pleasure. The casino is famous and so are the horse-races and annual yearling sales. Normans are passionate horse-lovers, so the polo fields and race courses are well placed. Contentin and Orne are favourite breeding areas for horses and superb pastures lie around Merlerault.

Apple trees fill the soft Normandy air with foaming blossom from mid-April to mid-May. Apples lie in piles before the countryside doorsteps, the first tender fruits maturing in September and October, the hardy, lasting varieties still being picked after November.

For many people, though, the name Normandy is linked with war. On 6 June 1944 the invasion of Europe by the Allied Forces began.

The landing took place in the early hours of the morning along the coasts of lower Normandy between Saint-Vaast-la-Hougue and the mouth of the Orne near Caen. There were five main groups of beaches, code-named Sword, Juno, Gold, Omaha and Utah. The overall attack was code-named 'Operation Overlord'. More than 185,000 men were involved in this culmination of top-secret preparations. The Americans aimed at capturing Cherbourg from their landing points at Omaha and Utah. The British and Canadians aimed at Caen. Artificial ports, the largest one known as 'Mulberry Harbour', were towed across the Channel by tugs. An undersea pipeline for fuel had been laid from the Isle of Wight to Cherbourg to be set in use after the invasion. Charming, now, in its luxuriant verdure, the *bocage* area beyond the beaches offered a nightmare of attack and counter-attack with its deceptive hedges and ditches. The Museum at Arromanches is especially interesting.

Museums, commemorative plaques, steles and monuments mark the struggle. North of Saint-Laurent-sur-Mer are the graves of nearly 10,000 American servicemen. At Sainte-Mère-Eglise begin the first of the symbolic milestones marking Liberty Highway (Voie de la Liberté), the route followed from Utah Beach across northern France to Metz.

Towns and Villages

Many of the towns and villages of this region were the setting for important events: Rouen, where Joan of Arc was burnt by the English; Caen or Thury-Harcourt, arisen from the ashes left by the Allies' advance through Normandy in summer 1944; Bayeux with its famous tapestry telling the story of the Norman conquest.

Its long history of Viking invasion has left Normandy with many place names with Norse suffixes: -*bec* signifies stream, giving us Orbec, Briquebec, Bolbec or Caudebec, villages of brick and timber-frame dwellings that seem to play hide-and-seek between hill and vale, from the Pays de Caux in the East to the Cotentin in the West.

The capital of Upper Normandy, Rouen, luckily preserved many of its fine old quarters with their timber-framed houses, from the ravages of the last war. The market place where Joan of Arc was martyred on 30 May 1431 remains little changed, and but for the array of contemporary consumer goods behind plate-glass shopwindows, one might almost say that the centre had preserved its medieval atmosphere. Of course the influx of new activities, the growth of the big port which daily unloads cargoes from all over the world, the new petrochemical plants and the burgeoning administrative sector have inevitably diluted the authentic atmosphere of Rouen; but the light still plays on the cathedral façade as it did for Monet in 1894. (His paintings of the cathedral capture it in changing moods and light.)

Caen, the capital of Lower Normandy, lies in the heartland of the province, in the rich and charming Pays d'Auge, famous for its cider and Calvados, not forgetting, of course, its pungent cheeses, Camembert, Livarot and Pont-l'Evêque, all bearing the names of the villages whence they sprang.

Caen itself took an awful battering in the last war, and much had to be rebuilt. The 1950s architecture, around the Avenue du 6 Juin, is sober and a little austere. But the fighting somehow left intact the magnificent Abbaye-aux-Hommes and the Abbaye-aux-Dames, reminders that William the Conqueror once ruled this city. Nearby is the Pegasus bridge over the Orne, scene of bitter fighting on D-Day and after.

One of the two main cities of Lower Normandy is the port of Le Havre, at the mouth of the Seine Estuary. Today this is France's largest commercial port after Marseille, with long piers where giant oil tankers berth; oil refineries and storage tanks line the shore by the river-mouth. The *France*, former pride of the French passenger fleet, rode at anchor in the harbour until 1978, when it was sold to foreign interests. The people of Le Havre had adopted the ship as their own and valiantly fought to keep her afloat under the French flag, but in vain. For more than a century Le Havre was, with another Norman port, Cherbourg, Europe's port-of-embarkation for the transatlantic run.

Before the rise of Le Havre, the main port at the mouth of the Seine was Honfleur now declining gracefully on the opposite shore of the estuary. This picturesque fishing town had been a prosperous and important port in the days when Samuel Chaplain set sail from here in 1608 to found Quebec (note again the Viking suffix). Tall, narrow slate-roofed houses huddle protectively around the old port. The effect is most captivating, and many Impressionist painters came here, in particular Boudin, Monet and Sisley, to live and work.

The road climbs steeply out of Honfleur westwards up the coast. In summer, Parisians like to weekend here in their apartments and holiday homes, which have mushroomed in and around the twin resorts of Deauville and Trouville. These have been popular since the Second Empire, when the Duc de Morny, Napoleon III's half-brother, frequented the Promenade des Planches (boardwalk) at Deauville. The spacious, flowering esplanade is now lined with shops sporting internationally-known trade names, and the atmosphere is opulent rather than refined. Trouville, across the harbour, is more compact, homelier, less ostentatious. Westward along the coast lies a string of smaller though popular resorts: notably Houlgate and Cabourg (the model for the town of Balbec in Proust's vast novel *A la recherche du temps perdu*).

Tourists travel east of Le Havre less frequently. Yet Etretat, where the cliffs are gouged into curious arches by thousands of years of battering by wind and waves, is attractive, and so are fishing villages such as Fécamp. Most of the Norman fishing villages abandoned their traditional festivals when they switched from sail to steam after World War I. Only Fécamp still celebrates its 'Pardon de Terre-Neuve' (Newfoundland), for fishermen, annually in mid-January. Fécamp was also a major goal for pilgrims, who came to see a relic

The seaside towns of Normandy, where fishing is a major industry, vary from attractive old harbours like Honfleur (**left**) to the tanker-filled port of Le Havre to elegant resorts like Etretat and Deauville.

Far left The long and varied coastline changes character from steep, chalky cliffs in the north to rugged granite towards Brittany, with sandy beaches in between.

enshrined here: a container, supposed to contain some of Christ's blood.

Further along the coast to the west lies the great artificial port of Cherbourg. A trading centre since the Bronze Age, Cherbourg has been a key port. Destroyed by the Germans in 1944, it was rapidly rebuilt by the US forces, and became their main supply port.

On the far western side of Normandy, where the Norman *bocage* merges with the Eastern marches of Brittany, Mortagne-au-Perche too has preserved its traditions, and holds an annual fair to celebrate its most famous product, *boudin* (black pudding) – delicious fried and eaten with stewed apples!

It is in this frontier territory that the Mont-Saint-Michel stands, claimed by Normans and Bretons alike, yet beyond the reach of earthly concerns. It has been a place of worship since the earliest times, but it was Saint Auber who 'christianized' this strange, solitary rock; the 'Charitons', a brotherhood founded in the Middle Ages to see that the dead were given a Christian burial, still walk in procession through the streets below the abbey each year, wearing embroidered costumes and carrying banners. As one looks out towards the Mont-Saint-Michel from the shore, it is easy to forget the Normandy of the fertile Lower Seine or the well-fed herds of the Pays d'Auge; one forgets that the favourite saying of this prosperous people is a non-committal 'Maybe, and then again, maybe not', as one contemplates this uncompromising lone rock stranded on the mudflats at low tide, man's last earthly gesture as land meets sea – a lighthouse of the spirit.

Above Old buildings along the quay at Honfleur. Samuel Champlain, founder of Quebec, set out from here on the first of his voyages to Canada.

Far left Caen, mostly destroyed in 1944, but now rebuilt with a thriving port, still has pockets of historical interest.

Left Men playing *boules* in Rouen. This is a typical scene in towns and villages throughout the country.

Châteaux and Churches

The traveller leaving the Ile-de-France to enter Normandy along the Seine valley could hardly wish for a more eloquent introduction to the region's rich architectural heritage than the towers, keeps and ramparts of Richard the Lionheart's twelfth-century Château Gaillard. Its massive ruins loom impressively above the town of Les Andelys against the soft Norman sky.

This region is one of the birthplaces of the Romanesque style, and here many fine examples of these great churches with massive walls supporting huge barrel-vaults can be seen, such as the Benedictine Abbey of Jumièges, the churches of Saint-Etienne at Caen, Saint-Georges at Saint-Martin-de-Boscherville and Cerisy-la-Forêt. The Gothic style which originated in the Ile-de-France was brought into Normandy gradually. Using crossed, pointed arches and flying buttresses, the master masons developed a style of incredible grace and lightness; the Saint-Romain Tower of Rouen Cathedral and the Cathedral of Saint-Pierre in Lisieux are excellent examples of Early Gothic. In the thirteenth century the Gothic and Norman styles were fused, Coutances Cathedral being the best example of this. Pure Norman proportions and simple lines blend harmoniously with the Gothic geometry and reaching spires.

The Church of Notre-Dame at Louviers is the quintessence of the Flamboyant Gothic style: a mass of intricate details, its fantastic ornamentation seems hardly to be carved from stone. Rouen is rich in Flamboyant Gothic buildings, including the Church of Saint-Maclou, Saint-Ouen, and the splendid Cathedral of Notre-Dame, which spans four centuries of Gothic architecture, and was the subject of a major series of paintings by

Monet. Particularly famous are the elaborate Butter Tower, and the Gros Horloge, a large and colourful clock mounted on a Renaissance arch.

Other major churches of the region include the Benedictine abbeys at Caen, the Abbaye-aux-Hommes (or Saint-Etienne), built by William the Conqueror, and the Abbaye-aux-Dames (church of the Holy Trinity) which was built by his wife Matilda. The Cathedral at Bayeux is an impressive blend of Romanesque and Gothic. The museum here contains the famous Bayeux tapestry, a unique medieval document recording the Norman conquest of England.

Most of the great châteaux began as military fortifications but from the fourteenth century, courtyards appeared and living quarters became more aesthetic and comfortable. The remains of several châteaux in Normandy show this transition from fortified dwellings, such as the Castle of Falaise and Dieppe Castle. Coupesarte near Livarot is a fine example of a Renaissance manor house

built of wood and varnished brick. The Château d'O, near Mortrée, is a hybrid work combining late Gothic and Renaissance. Surrounded by a moat, this building with its decorative turrets seems to rise majestically from the water.

In the village of Balleroy the seventeenth-century château designed by Mansart stands amid grounds landscaped by Le Nôtre. The magnificent Château of Fontaine-Henry also spans both Gothic and Renaissance, fine ornamentation contrasting with elements of classicism.

Besides its rich heritage of châteaux and churches, Normandy is associated with more recent artistic achievements. The town of Honfleur conjures up the names of Eugène Boudin, Claude Monet and the school of Impressionist painters, who lived and worked here, and were followed by the Pointillists Seurat and Signac. Many of their works are hung in the local Musée Eugène Boudin. At Giverny you can visit Monet's garden, where he painted the magnificent 'Waterlilies' series. This house is now a museum.

Left The imposing remains of the Château Gaillard, once a mighty fortress, where Richard the Lionheart defended Normandy against its French invaders.

Opposite A place of worship since Celtic times, Mont-Saint-Michel rises out of the sea like a mirage. Climbing up through successive buildings, one goes from Romanesque to Gothic splendour.

Left Rouen Cathedral was the subject of a major series of paintings by Monet. He lived for many years in this region, and his house at Giverny, with the famous waterlily pond celebrated in many of his works, became a museum in 1980.

Far left The Château Victot at Cambremer, with its attractively patterned, varnished brickwork, is surrounded by a peaceful moat.

Cuisine

Right This chef is justly proud of two specialities of the region: *le chantecler*, a layered coffee cake, and *terrine de caneton*, a coarse duck pâté.

Below In Normandy, as in Brittany, pancakes or *galettes* are served with sweet or savoury fillings, often from little stalls in the street.

Normandy is a prosperous and fertile land, where cows graze in rich clover, assuring the Norman of his rich cream and many cheeses; where apples grow in abundance, the raw material for the Norman's favourite beverage, cider, and that fiery liqueur, Calvados; and where fish markets offer a dozen types of Channel seafood. Whether you dine in a graceful manor-restaurant or at the red-checked cloth of a simple country inn, the service and the food are nearly always good.

Some restaurants are ancient, like the fifteenth-century Hostellerie Aigle d'Or at Pont-l'Evêque, a little town which has given its name to one of France's noblest cheeses. Here you will find sweetbreads, chicken, veal and fish prepared in the traditional style: the chicken liver *pâté* (*terrine de foie de poularde*); the fried prawns (*crevettes poêlées*) and the fried sole (*sole meunière*), swimming in butter, are excellent.

Other restaurants, like the Hôtel Malherbe in Caen, are brand new, lacking in rustic charm but efficiently designed for the many discriminating diners who come to sample grilled salmon with

anchovy butter (*saumon grillé aux anchois*) and the casserole of tripe cooked with ox feet, cider, and Calvados (*tripes à la mode de Caen*), which is tender, aromatic and delicious. The omelettes are also splendid – whether filled with lobster, kidneys, cheese or simply fine herbs – as good as any served at Madame Poulard's famous omelette shop in Mont-Saint-Michel, of which it has been said 'her omelettes have attracted more tourists to Mont-Saint-Michel than the famous Gothic abbey or the dramatic sight of the inrushing tide.'

Along the coast, there are many excellent fish restaurants. In the town of Villerville-sur-Mer, lobsters are prepared in many simple ways; crawfish are grilled or flamed in Cognac and the mussels drenched in cream. Further on, at Honfleur, the Ferme Saint-Siméon provides turbot, sole and salmon which are beyond reproach, as well as the traditional fish stew (*matelote honfleuraise*), flavoured with cider and herbs (Normandy's answer to *bouillabaisse*).

Normandy is the home of Camembert, that fine, moist cheese, tasting vaguely of mushrooms and smelling of – how can

one put it? The surrealist poet Léon-Paul Fargue likened it to 'the feet of the Lord' (*les pieds de Dieu*), a double-edged compliment! In the old days, the ripening of Camembert was left to nature, but the cheese often caught some foreign spore and turned blue. It was not until 1910, with the introduction of the penicillin mould, that a reliably consistent cheese could be made. Some of the best known Camembert-type cheeses of the region are the pungent Livarot, Pont-l'Evêque and Gournay.

Camembert takes its name from a village in the *département* of Orne. In nearby Alençon it is at the Restaurant Au Petit Vatel that the gourmets gather. Here you will find lavish *haute cuisine* at its most splendid and complicated. The dishes include melon with port (*melon au porto*); veal sweetbreads with grapes (*ris de veau aux raisins*); double fillet steak with mushrooms (*chateaubriand aux cèpes*); and veal kidneys in port ˘(*rognons de veau au porto*). The apples with Calvados (*pommes à la normande*) and the layered coffee cake (*le chantecler*) are splendid, the cheese board suitably Norman, and the prices outrageous.

Above Turbot cooked in cider and *crêpes* served with apple are among the appetizing dishes laid out at this country restaurant.

Below The mussels, oysters and other shellfish of Normandy are excellent. Here fishermen sell their catch at Saint-Valéry-en-Caux.

Wines and Spirits

Normandy is the country of cream, Camembert, cider and Calvados. No wine is produced, but, like Brittany, large quantities are consumed. It is best to avoid the *vins de table* or *vins du patron* in the bars and restaurants, and to ask for Bordeaux or Côtes du Rhône red and, of course, white wine from the Nantais region. The nearer you get to Paris, the more you come across Burgundy in the restaurants, particularly at La Couronne in Rouen where it is served with the pressed duck. But generally the Normans drink cider, for which they are even more famous than the Bretons.

The drink which is most associated with Normandy, however, is Calvados. From the *trou normand*, a shot of young Calvados served in the middle of a lengthy lunch and supposed to aid the digestion, to the finest examples which can rival the oldest Cognacs and Armagnacs, all true Calvados is made in

Normandy. Calvados, the department, owes its name to the galleon *El Calvador* which sank off the coast at the time of the Spanish Armada. Calvados, the *eau-de-vie*, owes its existence to the distillation of the fermented juice of Normandy apples. As Cognac is the distillation of the tart, low-in-alcohol wines from the Charente, so Calvados is distilled cider. For centuries, cider was drunk on the farms since it cost nothing to make, hence Calvados became the traditional *eau-de-vie*. Legally, the Calvados du Pays d'Auge is the only one with an *appellation* (and the best); all other Calvados are *réglementés*, meaning that the origin of the apples and the method of distillation are controlled.

The best Calvados is aged in wood for many years, losing its raw apply-spirity taste for a complex roundness from the cask while still retaining the tang of apples. Calvados still has the right to put vintage dates on the label, but this is not

always reliable. As with many wines, the plainer (and more explicit) the label, the more genuine the product.

In case the visitor should want a sweeter *digestif*, there is Bénédictine, first made at the Benedictine monastery at Fécamp. This is made from Normandy herbs on a brandy base. A higher brandy mix is sold under the name of B and B (Brandy and Bénédictine), drier in taste than Bénédictine.

Below left Testing the brew at the Rumesnil cider *caves*.

Below Normandy's most famous drink, besides cider, is Calvados, an apple brandy which although raw when young, can later rival the oldest Cognac and Armagnac. Bénédictine, developed in the sixteenth century in the monastery at Fécamp, contains a blend of many local herbs.

Nord Pas-de-Calais

These flat lands are windy and often mournful. The winter fogs when they descend are thick, chilly and greyish-white. Yet the area is often the first part of France that a visitor sees, whether travelling south from Belgium or across the Channel to the ports of Dunkirk, Calais and Boulogne. It is made up of two departments: Nord and Pas-de-Calais.

In the north, lying seaward, is the Blooteland ('naked land'), unmistakably Flemish in feeling, rendered even more so by the work of engineers from the Netherlands who applied their expertise to the draining of the marshes with the help of dykes and canals. Windmills dot the landscape. One of the oldest in Europe is here, the Nordmoolen, built in 1127 and still going strong until as late as 1959. The cultivated marshes reach on into Belgium, fertile land, still prone to flooding, its canals filled with fish, some of its farms covering huge acreages that stretch as far as the horizon with waving fields of crops.

The interior area known as the Houtland ('wooded country') measures up to its name. Trees that like to spread their roots in wet country thrive here. The poplars stand in rows, brushing at a watercolour sky, willows cheer on the northern spring with optimistic green and the elms stand majestic and apart. Chicory, cauliflowers and leeks grow well. Flemish cows graze the rich, damp pastures.

In spite of some attractive areas such as the sandy beaches stretching from Boulogne, the *nouveau-riche* animation of Le Touquet-Paris-Plage with its pine woods, nightclubs, casinos and expensive hotels and the Houtland with its quaint air suggestive of a very large Flemish painting tacked across the landscape, the North has few apparent claims to touristic interest. Yet dig deeper, and you will find it a fascinating region, not beautiful, but full of sturdy, hospitable people, and rich in historical reminders of past industrial glories and fearful battles.

Introduction

Even the produce of the sea and land is diverted into manufacturing. Boulogne-sur-Mer, the biggest fishing port in France, transforms vast quantities of its catch into frozen and canned foods. It is also the second passenger port of France. (Napoleon who, like Elizabeth I, seems to have slept everywhere, spent some time in Boulogne in 1803 planning invasion of England. He had second thoughts after Trafalgar.)

Grain goes into the manufacture of flour and biscuits. Barley and hops feed the breweries and almost a quarter of French beers come from produce grown in the North where the hops, supported on tall frames, are supposed to have an especially aromatic quality. The presence of large quantities of beer and the lack of vine-growing areas has naturally affected the area's cuisine. There is even such a thing as a beer soup. Chicory has given rise to its own industry and sugar beet represents a large proportion of the total French sugar production.

Linen, synthetic fibres, jute, cotton and wool spill onto the European market, reasonably enough, considering Flanders' long-standing tradition in weaving. Tapestries from the town of Arras were already famous in Shakespeare's time. (Hamlet, in one of his recurrent moods of oedipal depression, stuck a dagger through one to kill Polonius.) Twenty-two per cent of France's wool passes through Roubaix, Tourcoing or Fourmies. But the textile industries are today in crisis, and many have closed. Steel mills, chemical industries and their offshoots, the petrochemical and carbochemical industries, account for huge quantities of the national production. Dunkirk has a big ship-building industry and is the third largest port in France. Although steel mills around Valenciennes are closing, modern car and electronic component factories are arising in their place. Coal was the basis for the beginnings of some of industry. The coal basin is the western part of a carboniferous belt extending into Belgium and on into Germany. This is the 'black country' where slag-heaps and blast furnaces have created a huge industrial zone. Ten electric power stations work on low-quality coal. Large quantities of gas are also produced. What the area lacks in picturesque tourism it makes up for with the technical interest of its installations, many of them open to the public. But the coal mines are nearing exhaustion and many have now closed. Modern industries are taking their place.

Lack of natural eastern defences has laid the Nord open to numerous attacks. Vauban, Louis XIV's military engineer, constructed a good many forts in an effort to protect it. Both world wars have left

their scars and memorials. Dunkirk, Calais and Boulogne, for all the brave attempts to reconstruct after World War II, still seem like uneasy replacements for the towns that went before. Dunkirk itself was almost completely destroyed during the gruelling battle that took place from 25 May to 4 June 1940. The long beaches saw the embarkation of half a million British and Allied troops. Cemeteries and memorials are especially numerous between Lille and Arras, with row upon row of white crosses.

The sombre and magnificent monument at Vimy is dedicated to 75,000 Canadian soldiers killed in France in World War I. German and Canadian trenches are preserved nearby. The land is still pitted with shell-holes. From the foot of the memorial the view stretches over the grim mining valley – centre for coal. Nearby is the important French military mausoleum of Notre-Dame-de-Lorette. A light burns at night in the huge lantern tower, to commemorate the French who died in the bitter battle of 1915.

In World War II, the Nord suffered under a particularly harsh German occupation, owing to its strategic importance so close to Britain. Much courageous Resistance activity took place; especially heroic were the Communist-led strikes in the coal mines, forced to work for the German war effort.

Densely-populated as this region is (surpassed only by the Ile-de-France), with its busy ports and industries, there are still wide stretches of open countryside and green fields and meadows.

Towns and Villages

Visitors are sometimes surprised to find green meadows, forests and open countryside in this densely populated region (surpassed only by the Ile-de-France). Its industry and its major car-ferry ports distract people (Frenchmen and foreigners alike) from its remaining splendours, from the fact that real people live here and love the place. The region has a bad reputation, which is the trouble: the dust from the coal mines (now settling as the industry is phased out), the sulking clouds and inclement weather. Small wonder most Frenchmen would rather live in the Midi!

What the tourist knows of the region is probably limited to the Customs at Calais or Boulogne, and the endless roads filled with cars heading in procession southwards. How many stop to visit Montreuil, inland from Etaples, to stroll along the shady fortifications, parts of which date from the thirteenth century, with their magnificent views? How many take the trouble to discover the whereabouts of the 'horrible' battle of Crécy in 1346 (where 30,000 died), or that of Agincourt? In fact they are barely a swerve away from the main road to Paris.

Boulogne is worth more than a passing glance itself. It is France's largest fishing port, and its maritime terminal and port facilities are an imposing sight, whether seen from land or from the stern of a cross-Channel ferry manoeuvering to its berth. On the right bank of the river the houses rise in terraces up the hillside, hemmed in by a medieval wall and belfry. Caesar is presumed to have set sail from nearby Wissant to conquer England, and Napoleon camped here in 1803–5 planning to repeat the performance. Unluckily for the Austrians and Russians, he did not, trouncing them instead at Austerlitz in 1805. Today the tide has turned, and the English yearly pour through this city of herring-canners and pencil-makers.

Calais is the largest passenger port; the town centre was completely destroyed in the last war, and architects have made a brave job of building a homogeneous, brick-and-concrete town in its place. Rodin's monument to the *Burghers of Calais* is worth a pilgrimage, and on a fine day, when you have a few hours before sailing, you can while away the time on the magnificent beach.

The climate is cool and windy along the coast, but the air is so pure doctors recommend it to people suffering from bone disorders, to children and people feeling generally rundown: the air at Berck is said to contain only four bacteria per cubic metre, compared with Paris's 900,000! From here the fine sandy beach runs unbroken right to Le Touquet, one of the smartest resorts along the North coast of France. Its spacious checkerboard layout and domesticated forests surrounding; its slightly English atmosphere, and its luxurious Normandy-style and modern villas give it the look of a film-set resort of the thirties vintage.

Right at the far end of the littoral just before reaching Belgium (which you can reach by walking along the beach) is Bray-Dunes, where World War II bunkers are beginning to blend, however obtrusively, with the tall dunes. Like most of the coastal resorts, this is a 'thick-sweaters-in-summertime' place, and the climate demands a certain oblivious strength of mind. The rows upon rows of typical North-Coast holiday homes house windswept families who are determinedly *en vacances*.

Industry is the lifeblood of the region, though, and the capital, Lille (which, with its satellites Tourcoing and Roubaix, has a population of 1,000,000) is the leading textiles city in France: four-fifths of all wool produced or imported

Above A street scene in Dunkirk, the town best known for the World War II evacuation of thousands of men by a motley flotilla of small boats.

Left A view of the impressive marina at Boulogne, France's largest fishing port and terminal for cross-Channel ferries.

into France is spun and woven here. Lille is an important cultural centre too, with a fine symphony orchestra, a big university, and each year the *braderie*, a massive, popular event that spreads through the streets and squares of the town centre, held in September, when people come to buy and sell everything this side of the sun. Though outwardly dour, Lille is a town full of activity, if you take time to explore it.

Textiles have long been a staple activity in towns like Douai, Valenciennes or Cambrai too, and in some places, such as Valenciennes, efforts are being made to revive the traditional lace-making crafts. But the main source of the region's wealth had, for centuries, been the coal upon which it rests: it is from this that the slag heaps dominating Béthune or Bruay-en-Artois have grown; that the steel industries of Valenciennes or Dunkirk, which now light up the night skies for miles around, or the chemical plants, have arisen.

The Nord Pas-de-Calais region's past industrial growth also lies at the root of its present problems: its coal industry is being phased out as more profitable seams are discovered elsewhere in the world; foreign competition and the world crisis is closing down steel mills at

Denain, for example, while workers are even being laid off at the giant Dunkirk mill. Unemployment is likely to blight the region for years to come, after centuries of growth.

The outlook is not uniformly bleak, however. The region lies across the routes that link Paris, London and the Ruhr, placing her right at the heart of the Common Market. And she has picked herself up from the ruins of other disasters. Each year, the people of Douai wheel giant figures known as the *gayants*, through the cobbled streets; these figures represent folk heroes who fought against the Spanish occupiers in the sixteenth century. Many of the region's fine buildings and monuments have been damaged or destroyed in two world wars, and yet the towns have been rebuilt, twice in the case of the lace-making town of Bailleul. Much still remains to remind us of the glorious past of Arras, with her seventeenth-century brick-and-stone gabled houses keeping dignified watch over the Grande Place; or of Lille's prosperity as the capital of French textiles or earlier as the brilliant capital of the Dukes of Burgundy in the fourteenth and fifteenth centuries. Dominating French politics and wielding immense power, the Burgundian court was a centre of arts.

Top The tiled roofs and shuttered windows of canal-side houses at Saint-Omer. A network of canals intersects the surrounding marshlands, providing easy transport to local market-gardens.

Above During the spring and summer months, several northern towns hold carnivals, at which huge plaster giants are paraded through the streets. These figures are *Les Géants du Nord-Viguier*, from the port of Dunkirk.

Châteaux and Churches

Flat, industrialized, uninteresting at first sight, Nord Pas-de-Calais repays a closer look. Here there is much of architectural interest, often Flemish in aspect, a characteristic of this region.

In Arras, the birthplace of Robespierre, the two spacious squares – La Grande Place and La Petite Place (or Place des Héros) – are bordered by fine Flemish-style houses with arcades and ornamental gables, dating from the seventeenth century. The splendid *hôtel de ville* has a sixteenth-century Flemish Gothic façade and tall belfry. The former Benedictine Abbey of Saint-Vaast, a grand eighteenth-century building, now houses an important museum including paintings of many periods and the famous Arras tapestries, the craft that brought prosperity for centuries.

The old citadel at the edge of the town is one of several fortifications built in this vulnerable area, close to the Belgian border, by Louis XIV's great military engineer, Vauban. Other examples can be seen in Calais, Lille and Le Quesnoy. The fortifications at Le Quesnoy served their purpose until 1814–15, and were even used by retreating French and British troops in 1940.

The Flemish tradition is evident once more in Calais, in the fifteenth-century town hall with its impressive belfry.

Rodin's powerful statue of the Burghers of Calais stands in front of the town hall, commemorating a siege by the English.

At Boulogne-sur-Mer, the sturdy thirteenth-century walls of the old city remain virtually intact, encircling an ancient castle. The Museum of Fine Arts and Archaeology houses one of the best collections of Greek vases in all France.

Further inland, Saint-Omer, with its aristocratic streets lined with seventeenth and eighteenth-century townhouses and their carved bay-windows, has an air of quiet elegance. The Notre-Dame Basilica, a splendid thirteenth to fifteenth-century church, teems with sculptures dating from the thirteenth to the eighteenth century; a library known for its ancient manuscripts and incunabula, as well as a museum housed in the elegant eighteenth-century Hôtel Sandelin containing Dutch and Flemish paintings and a collection of ceramics.

War-ravaged Dergues, to the North, reminds one of Bruges once again, now that its old streets and houses have been beautifully restored; besides Vauban's important fortifications, there is also the seventeenth-century Mont-de-Piété, or state-owned pawnshop, the first of its kind in France, built of bricks and white stone, severe yet ornate in true Flemish fashion. This now houses a small

museum containing, among other works of art, works by Georges de La Tour, and Breughel the Elder.

Lille, a vast urban metropolis, has at its centre an old quarter, containing a wealth of landmarks inherited from its opulent past, such as the beautiful seventeenth-century Flemish Baroque Bourse; the many old streets and houses; and the Hospice Comtesse, a fine brick-and-stone fifteenth-century hospital now used as a Flemish Folk Museum. Most notable, however, is the Fine Arts Museum, one of the three most important French provincial museums.

In the vicinity of Roubaix, to the North, stands the Chapelle d'Hem, with its glorious stained-glass wall and tapestry from a design by Rouault. At Seclin, to the south of Lille, one can admire the inner courtyard of the seventeenth-century Flemish hospital built of brick and stone, a haven of peace and harmony.

In Douai, one cannot escape the

brooding presence of its square Gothic belfry-tower topped by turrets and pinnacles, immortalized by Corot in one of his best-known paintings, to be seen in the Louvre. Here, too, is a good museum housing, among its wealth of Flemish paintings, a sixteenth-century polyptych by local artist Jean Bellegambe, whose works are an unusual blend of traditional Flemish and Italian Renaissance art.

It is hard to reconcile the dreary industrial town of Valenciennes with the delicate shepherdesses of Watteau's pastorales, but this is his birthplace, and his work can be seen in the museum here. Also paintings by Rubens, Bosch and Breughel, and sculptures by Carpeaux.

The most important archaeological excavations in Northern France are being conducted at nearby Bavay, which have uncovered a large Roman city, as well as a number of remarkable objects, some of which are exhibited at the Douai Museum, which must be visited.

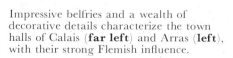

Impressive belfries and a wealth of decorative details characterize the town halls of Calais (**far left**) and Arras (**left**), with their strong Flemish influence.

Above and **top** Valenciennes was the birthplace of Watteau, one of the great French painters of the early eighteenth century. The somewhat bleak landscape of this northern region contrasts with the courtly figures and dreamlike settings of Watteau's paintings.

Cuisine

The French are a proud people, jealously guarding their traditional ways, and in no walk of life is this more evident than in the kitchen. The many tourists who pour across the Straits of Dover (Pas-de-Calais) every year are met at the quayside by the sights and smells of a nation that enjoys its food. The streets of Calais and Boulogne are lined with restaurants and cafés, where even on the coldest day there are one or two tables outside – to remind us that here eating is a public as well as a private affair. There is a smell of freshly-ground coffee from dawn to dusk, mingled with the yeasty aroma of baking bread, and – from the port – the salty tang of fish.

Fish is central to the gastronomy of the Nord, and shellfish in particular deep blue lobsters, spiny crawfish, crabs, clams and mussels, prepared in sauces that would astonish those used to less adventurous cuisine. A visitor to the remarkable Atlantic Hotel in Wimereux will be met by vast platters of these crusty delicacies (*fruits de mer*), heaped on a bed of ice and garnished with parsley; crab-meat baked in pastry (*chausson de crabe*) and crawfish, often called scampi nowadays, serve in a cream and white wine sauce (*langoustes à la crème*). Nor need you stop at that, for after an entrée of shellfish, there are the fresh sea-fish to sample. See with what imagination a simple sole in prepared: in Dieppe, for example, there is a traditional sauce of mussels, prawns and cream which transforms the fish into a gastronomic treat (*sole dieppoise*). Herrings (*harengs*) are smoked and salted; cod is baked in white wine (*cabillaud*); even the harbour fish are used – not for petfood as in England, where the idea of fish nourished on sewage is a little gamey – but to make a delicious fried dish (*friture du port*).

Inland, the mines and factories take up a large proportion of the land; yet in between, the heavy, fertile soil is covered with crops: cereals for the daily bread, sugar beets for the confectionery factory, and chicory which adds its particular flavour to the Frenchman's morning coffee. In the east, where dairy cattle are pastured, there are some interesting cheeses, like Maroilles and Sorbais, which come in a range of sizes and degrees of saltiness, which have been made here for centuries. Some – like Vieux Lille – are pungent with ammonia, which is an acquired taste: be guided by the patron, who is familiar with tourist palates unused to such sensations.

The cookery of this region, like the local dialect, strongly bears the mark of Flemish influence. Here the French meat-and-vegetable stew (*pot-au-feu*) is called a hotpot (*hochepot*), while the more sophisticated dish of beef in wine (*daube*), found in every region of the country, is known as a grilling (*carbonnade*); instead of the wine, mushrooms and tomatoes that are used for this dish further south, we find here onions, turnips, potatoes and beer. As in Belgium, many interesting dishes are cooked in beer. Other specialities include rabbit cooked with prunes (*lapin aux prunes*), Flemish veal (*veau à la Flamande*), served with a rich cream sauce, and beef tongue salad (*museau de boeuf*). The chips (*pommes frites*) are almost – but not quite – as good as in Belgium.

Lille is an important centre for the confectionery and biscuit industries and, though many of their products are lacking in any charm, one or two hark back to older recipes. Butter biscuits (*petits beurres*), simple and slim, and the thicker layered biscuits (*gauffres fourrées*) make a pleasant afternoon snack, while those with a sweeter tooth may enjoy the caramels of Berck-sur-Mer (*chiques*).

Above Windmills add a Flemish flavour to the sweeping northern plains, where vast acres of farmland are intensely cultivated.

Right Fine regional cheeses on display in a *fromagerie* in Boulogne.

Left The cone-shaped cheese Boulette d'Avesnes, from the district close to the Belgian border, is blended with herbs and sharp in taste.

Wines and Spirits

This heavily industrialized area has no room for vines, even if they could grow at this latitude. The most northern vineyards in France, in Champagne, are a great deal farther south; however, the inhabitants drink as much if not more than the average Frenchman, most of it in the form of *apéritifs* and beer. The beer comes from the great breweries in Alsace, from the *brasseries* along the Meuse and from just north in Belgium, and a good deal of the draught beer is imported from England. The *apéritifs* are more widespread. The classic is *pastis*, a hold-all name for the aniseed-based spirit which began life in the south of France and came to Paris known as Absinthe. Illicit Absinthe, with its horrific after-effects, has long been banned, but *pastis* still holds many *apéritif* drinkers in thrall, who consider it the only *apéritif*. Ricard and Pernod have become brand names, but there are hundreds of other brands. It is drunk mixed with two or three parts water added (which makes it cloudy).

While *pastis* takes care of the 'hard' *apéritifs*, there is a wide range of wine-based *apéritifs*: Byrhh, a *vin cuit* from the Pyrenees, the *vins doux naturels* (although they are not natural in the sense that they are fortified wines, like Port) like Muscat, Rivesaltes and Banyuls, and the imported Cinzano and Martini. All these are very popular but the most common *apéritif* in France, after *pastis*, is Port. France is by far and away the largest importer of Port and she likes it before a meal. Thus it is a Tawny Port of medium sweetness. Vintage Port is unheard of. In the bourgeois households in the Pas-de-Calais, the ladies will drink Port and the men whisky. If *pastis* still rules in the *café du coin*, whisky rules in the home, a revolution which has happened in the last twenty years. To offer a glass of white wine as an *apéritif* is not really acceptable, and to ask for one is considered strange, since there will be wine at table.

The north of France is the big market for the heaviest and cheapest of the blended wines from the Midi, so perhaps this is why it is still *apéritifs* and beer country. The traveller is usually in a hurry anyway to get farther south. In a couple of hours, he could be in Paris for '*un bon p'tit Sancerre, bien frais*'.

Right *The Absinthe-Drinkers* by Degas recalls the time when Absinthe, the forerunner of *pastis*, was the favourite drink of Paris café society. Absinthe was banned many years ago, but aniseed-based spirits such as Ricard and Pernod are available and extremely popular today.

Picardy

Roses still bloom in Picardy, as they did in the World War I song. And shell-cases are still turned up by the harrows of the farmers who work these wide, flat plains. In late summer grain burnishes the land as far as the horizon. In autumn the sugar-beet crop lies in knobbed piles at the sides of the road and the rumble of sugar trucks is heard from early morning. Winter brings mist. The soil freezes. Crows are black in a sky billowing grey and white. Spring hazes the furrows with green. Summer brings poppies to the fields and the roses to country gardens.

This old province of France has three modern departments: the Aisne, the Somme and the Oise, named after three rivers. Many of the villages were rebuilt after World War I and consist of red brick houses strung along highways which still conserve all the quirks of the bombarded roads they replace.

Little of Picardy has its face turned to the sea, although Berck-Plage is a sizeable watering-place. From Boulogne to Le Tréport there are miles of beaches and sand-dunes. Channel tides have deposited them there and in so doing have extended the coastline westward. This Opal Coast, as it is called, with tangy sea breezes and a cool climate, attracts a good many tourists, especially those in search of a health cure. Thousands of water-birds flock around the estuary of the Somme river.

Mostly the area looks in towards its centre. There is a dense population. Huge areas of cultivable land with a scattering of flint stretch right to the edge of the road. Even in the Middle Ages just about every square metre of soil was put to use. Driving from the coast or north from Paris this may seem a monotonous landscape. The long roads are edged with poplars. Innumerable war cemeteries and their identical white monuments seem to weight the soil. Picardy is lacking in natural defences and multitudes have marched through it. There are too many memories for it to lie easy.

Yet everything is not grain and beet. Around Amiens are market-gardens known as *hortillonages* where vegetables, flowers and herbs grow on

Introduction

rectangular islets separated from one another by canals, rather like the 'Venise Verte' of Poitou but decidedly more scruffy and down-at-heel. Shopping is done from little boats with tilted prows known as *bateaux à cornets*. You can hire one for a punting trip around this 'market-on-the-water'.

Amiens and Saint-Quentin are the commercial pulse of Picardy but Amiens is the spiritual heart. It would be difficult to better Ruskin, who put so much power into his description of the old town and the poetic miracle of its Gothic cathedral when he wrote *The Bible of Amiens*. This building is a sublime expression of northern France, built of stone from the Somme, seeming to express all the luminosity and airiness of Picardian skies. Beautiful in a different way are the carved choir stalls of Flemish oak 'living oak', says Ruskin especially grown and seasoned for the purpose, containing over 3,000 biblical scenes from the pious to the preposterous. Old Amiens lives on still in the city's manufacture of fine velvet, celebrated since the time of Louis XIV.

All the kings of France (or a good proportion of them) had a soft spot for Compiègne and its forest. It was Louis XIV who remarked: 'At Versailles I live like a king, like a prince at Fontainebleau and at Compiègne like a peasant.' Here the dauphin destined to be Louis XIV first encountered Marie-Antoinette, his future bride: he was too timid to look at her. Joan of Arc was taken prisoner by the English in the vicinity in May 1430.

Out of the town, broad Armistice Avenue leads towards the clearing where the Armistice was signed on 11 November 1918. Hitler insisted on accepting France's surrender in the same railway siding and carriage in 1940. Both the carriage in which Marshal Foch had travelled and a memorial plaque were destroyed by the Germans in World War II and have been replaced since.

The people of Picardy are as reserved as the land, slow to enter into friendship, capable of maintaining it for a lifetime. There is something spiritual about the true Picardian which you cannot quite put your finger on, product of the prairie and the sky. Perhaps that is why one has to refer to the architecture: intellectual, aerial, corporal, attempting the impossible union of earth and heaven with the grey bones of the soil. The spire of Beauvais Cathedral expressed it, rocketing with unreasonable faith towards the clouds. It collapsed only four years later, but the choir, the highest in the world, has survived. The mood changes when you descend further into the Oise where the river of the same name takes

precedence, flowing with dignity, carrying its burden of barges. The real Picardy makes a brief reappearance in the *thelle* or plateau lands above Beaumont-sur-Oise but the character of the people has changed.

Chantilly, although so near to Paris, is situated in the Oise and therefore in one of the three departments of Picardy. It is famous for its château which contains one of the finest art galleries in France, and adjoining stables. As you feed the huge carp in the lake you may wish to recall Vatel, the leading chef of France who impaled himself in true Roman fashion on his sword in this château, dishonoured because the fish ordered for luncheon had failed to arrive and the guest of honour was Louis XIV.

Chantilly is elegant in a country way: tea-rooms and antiques shops can be found; the shops display English riding boots and Scottish cashmere. The horse-races there have known British Royal patronage. Lady Diana Cooper lived for many years in a lodge of the château, as a guest of the French Government. Chantilly, in fact, rather plays up its Englishness in the best French manner. The superb forest flowers in spring with wild anemones and they say you can still glimpse stag and boar.

Waterways meander through the marshy, low-lying stretches of Bray-sur-Somme, leaving little islands with houses and patches of intensely cultivated land.

Towns and Villages

Picardy is a region of small towns, rolling plains, forests, and the dunes and waterways of the Somme Bay. In Beauvais and Amiens it has two of the finest cathedrals in France. It is a region of ancient settlements: Cuiry-les-Chaudardes, a tiny village in the Aisne, contains houses dating back to the fourth millenium BC.

Industry developed early in the villages of Picardy, but by the mid-nineteenth century the region was far-outclassed by the nearby Nord. Picardy is very much a farming region, but like much of Eastern France, her soil has been furrowed more deeply by the sword than by the ploughshare, as time and again invading armies swept this way.

Processing industries have grown up since the last war around the main towns of the region: chemicals, mechanical and electrical engineering on the outskirts of Amiens; bicycles and cosmetics in the vicinity of Saint-Quentin. The largest concentration is around Creil, whose population has tripled since 1946. The outskirts of such towns have sprouted vast, American-style commercial centres, and ancient town centres have become surrounded by outgrowths of dreary apartment blocks. War had already successfully demolished certain town centres, such as Abbeville or Beauvais, and although not all the rebuild-

Left Elaborate costumes, such as this one with a magnificent plumed head-dress worn in Liévin, are a feature of northern festivals.

44 PICARDY

ing has been unrelievedly monotonous, planners do seem to have forgotten that man does not live by treeless streetscape alone. Where are the cafés, the corner grocery stores that were once the heart-beat of the French provinces?

Picardy lacks those bustling, flourishing metropolises that are such fun to stay in. Amiens, with its new university and its large civic centres, comes closest, as befits a regional capital. Its Maison de la Culture (a multi-purpose arts centre) is one of the largest in France. Other towns achieve distinction through their historical associations. Hugues Capet was crowned King of France in Senlis in 987. Senlis had been a royal city since the time of Clovis, and its medieval quarters, with many splendid old houses and churches, still retain a sense of ancient grandeur. Compiègne owes much of its attractiveness to the fact that it was once an aristocratic resort, and its château was a favourite with both Napoleon Bonaparte and Napoleon III. To the west lies Beauvais, whose unfinished Cathedral was to have been the biggest of all Gothic cathedrals: that was not to be, but her choir is still the loftiest. The people of Beauvais have long memories, for each year in June they commemorate Jeanne Hachette, who seized a standard from the Burgundian troops led by Charles the Bold, in 1472 during the siege.

But most of Picardy seems content to go about its business, making or growing, without much of a glance at the wider world. Many of the inhabitants of the Oise commute to Paris each day, leaving thousands upon thousands of cars parked along the country lanes around the mainline stations of Orry-la-Ville, for instance.

Along the coast, the villages from the Authie Bay to the Somme Estuary, such as Quend-Plage or Saint-Valéry-sur-Somme, attract a steady stream of visitors year-round. They come to explore the dunes of the Somme Bay; to hunt and fish; to sample the superb seafood; to take in the invigorating sea air as they stroll past the boarded-up summer houses in winter. Jules Verne spent five years in the attractive coastal village of Le Crotoy, and Joan of Arc was imprisoned in the château there before her removal to Rouen. Today, in the hotels of Le Crotoy at a Sunday lunch in November, you are more likely to meet an ex-socialist minister chatting with a writer, or local notables out with large families.

But for their commuter-belts and second homes, many villages in Picardy can hardly have changed since the 1900s or before. The tradition of setting a tall tree on fire and dancing round it at Easter, in the village of Chambly, must date from much earlier times. In Rollot, well-known for its soft-textured cheese, a town-crier still bicycles through the streets and surrounding countryside to keep inhabitants abreast of events. Or again, Crouy-en-Thelle has a horse-drawn hearse, driven by a peasant who plays the organ in church and writes poetry: an unusual combination.

Modernity, in these country villages, manifests itself in the youngsters' passion for mopeds: they strip them of their silencers and roar through villages shattering the peace of a Sunday afternoon, dreaming of larger, noisier, more powerful machines. They may be factory apprentices from Amiens or Saint-Quentin; farm-labourers from near Beauvais; or stable-lads from Lamorlaye.

Nearby Chantilly is one of the world's horse-breeding capitals. Each summer, a major meet brings the cream of European society to watch the Prix de Diane raced in the shadow of the vast former royal stables (which almost dwarf Condé's château in the background). Throughout the year, short, wiry jockeys and tweed-capped trainers school their horses along the long straight tracks that run through the forest of Chantilly, or trot in the morning mists across the main road from Paris to Amiens.

Above Picardy may be part of France's industrial north, but tranquil pockets still remain, where old mill wheels turn on quiet waterways.

Right Although most of the old city of Beauvais was destroyed in 1940, its magnificent cathedral, with the tallest choir ever built, still towers above the town.

Châteaux and Churches

One of the crucial steps in the evolution of the Gothic style took place in the twelfth century in the construction of a rib-vault roof over the Romanesque abbey church at Morienval, near Compiègne. During the subsequent centuries of spectacular architectural achievement, the surrounding province of Picardy was to be enriched with six major Gothic cathedrals, more than any other French region of comparable size. These superb churches – Amiens, Beauvais, Senlis, Noyon, Laon and Soissons – provide a unique insight into the style that became France's supreme contribution to world architecture.

The royal dynasty that commissioned or inspired so much of French art and architecture began at Senlis. It was there, in 987, that Hugues Capet, ancestor of all the succeeding monarchs, was elected king of France. The present cathedral, begun in 1153, stands in the midst of silent old streets and lanes – a charming medieval country town, surrounded by forests, yet not far from Paris. The cathedral's west end is Romanesque, with a main doorway intricately carved with scenes of the life of the Virgin Mary.

The present cathedral was completed in the thirteenth century, and is the perfect example of the transition between the Romanesque and the Gothic, combining the simple holiness of the earlier period with the soaring splendour of the new style.

One of the loveliest achievements of this first flowering of the Gothic is at Laon, an unspoilt hill town. The cathedral's seven towers rise above the roofs of old houses, overlooking the wide plain of Champagne. Stone effigies of oxen peep from upper windows – in honour of the beasts who made the construction possible by hauling blocks of stone up the hillside.

The greatest of all Gothic buildings, the incomparable Cathedral of Amiens, has none of the natural advantages, the graceful and appropriate surroundings, that enhance Senlis, Noyon and Laon. The miraculous survivor of two world wars, it stands in the midst of a modern city, and gains sublimity from the contrast. The west end, with its curious, unevenly-matched towers, its enormous rose-window and its host of finely-carved statues, is deeply impressive; but nothing can prepare the visitor for the awe-inspiring experience of the interior. The carvings in stone are innumerable, but perhaps the most famous is the serene figure of Christ over the main door, known as the Beau Dieu.

Top The open-traceried towers of Laon, one of the oldest Gothic cathedrals in France. The detail from the tympanum over the main doors (**right**) is a fine example of Early Gothic carving.

Above Grand formal gardens laid out by Le Nôtre surround the imposing Château of Chantilly, where Condé once entertained the populous court of Louis XIV.

In rivalry with one another, and in pursuit of their religious ideal, the Gothic architects of France champed at the physical limitations imposed by the nature of stone and the laws of gravity. At Beauvais, they finally over-reached themselves. The choir, 141 feet (43 metres) high, is the loftiest in the world. The builders then concentrated their efforts on an even higher central spire; it collapsed after only four years, and only a choir and transept remain.

The cathedrals at Amiens and Beauvais both survived twentieth-century battles that laid waste their surrounding cities. Soissons, the last of Picardy's six great cathedrals, was less fortunate. By the end of the World War I, it was almost a ruin, and the present cathedral is a superb work of restoration. The vast nave is one of the most delicate works of Gothic art. Amazingly, two fragile treasures escaped the war holocaust: the exquisite stained glass above the choir, and the great Rubens *Adoration of the Shepherds* in the North Transept.

Picardy has two secular buildings that must rank with its cathedrals: the royal Palace of Compiègne and the Château of Chantilly. Both are now rich museums.

Compiègne comes third in the hierarchy of French royal palaces (after Versailles and Fontainebleau). It was

the last before the deluge, completed almost on the eve of the Revolution. The magnificent State apartments, overlooking an enormous prospect of park and forest, contain fine furniture.

Chantilly, though never a royal possession, was the envy of many kings. It was the creation, successively, of two of the most powerful men in French history: the Baron de Montmorency, known as Le Grand Connétable, who was the power behind the throne in six reigns; and the oustanding seventeenth-century general, the Great Condé.

The romantic Renaissance château, with its steep slate roofs and domed corner turrets, rises directly from the waters of a formal lake. The surrounding gardens, with their lavish waterworks, were laid out by Le Nôtre in 1662, a forerunner and rival for his work at Versailles. The eighteenth-century stables were designed to accommodate 240 horses and 420 hounds.

Inside, the whole building is devoted to the Condé Museum, perhaps the finest collection of art, furnishings and jewellery to be found outside Paris. Among the priceless treasures are the fifteenth-century illuminated manuscript known as the *Très Riches Heures du Duc de Berry* and one of the world's most famous jewels, the Condé Rose Diamond.

Defying gravity, the builders of Beauvais Cathedral set out to create the highest possible structure in stone. The choir they built (**below**) is the loftiest in the world, but the soaring tower and spire collapsed, just four years after it was finished.

Left The quintessence of northern Gothic architecture, Amiens Cathedral is quite breathtaking with its wealth of carved details and huge rose window. Inside, 126 narrow pillars sweep the eyes upwards to the soaring roof of the nave.

Above The crowning of Louis XII at Amiens Cathedral in 1501, attractively depicted by a contemporary painter.

Cuisine

A vast, flat prairie of wheat, oats and sugar beet now covers the muddy battleground of Picardy, yet the memory of war lingers on – in the mass of plain, twentieth-century architecture of the village houses and the simple graveyards of the Somme. The market towns still have their cobbled squares, and nowadays the wealth of livestock, fish and poultry indicates that these are peaceful days, but there is a sadness in the air. Cafés abound, for they are the lifeblood of France, but the traditional cuisine has all but disappeared. For travellers hell-bent on the flesh-pots of Paris, Picardy is more likely to provide a roadside snack –

perhaps a toasted cheese sandwich (*croque-monsieur*), perhaps a slice of meat *pâté* and a glass of wine.

This is a shame for a few fine local dishes can be found. At the Au Royal in Amiens, boned duck is a speciality, roasted in herbs and wine (*ballotine de canard*) or chopped finely with a cream sauce and enclosed in pastry (*canard en croûte*). At the Petit Chef in Saint-Quentin there is also excellent veal, stewed in red wine and herbs (*matelote de veau*) and served with red cabbage, or a spicier veal dish flavoured with paprika (*veau au paprika*) accompanied by the famous Crécy carrots, drenched in butter and sprinkled

with chopped parsley. The local button mushrooms are also good: you will find them whole and raw with ham, cheese from the Haute-Savoie (page 187) and a lemon juice dressing in the Parisian salad (*salade parisienne*).

There are also a few traditional restaurants along the coastline, where the Somme estuary opens out to the sea. One is in the small, bright fishing village of Le Crotoy, where Madame Mado presides at the Hôtel de la Baie. Her supplies of lobster, crawfish, sole and monkfish, are delivered by the fishermen who caught them, and the restaurant decor of nets and oars pays tribute to their service. Her

CONF

menu includes fish soup (*côtriade*), prawns (*crevettes roses*) and monkfish in a white wine sauce (*lotte au vin*).

The long, straight, poplar-lined roads that lead to Paris are flanked by fields of cereal, which bring prosperity to the farmer and to the baker.

The cheeseboard is more likely to consist of cheeses from neighbouring regions, but there may be local offerings too. They are a mixed bag. Some, like Rollot, innocently white and pressed deceptively into heart-shaped moulds, are very sharp; others, like the mild, orange-covered Mimolettes, are easier on the newcomer's tastebuds and far more palatable.

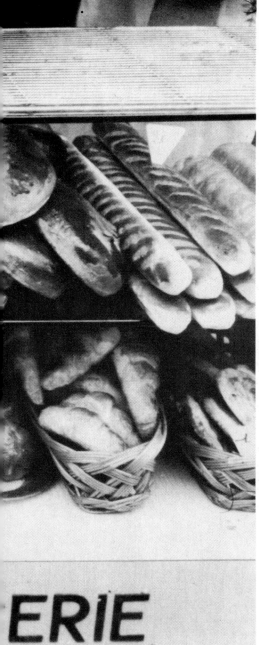

ERIE

Left In Picardy there is always an array of long loaves (*baguettes*), puff-pastry crescents (*croissants*) and egg-rich rolls (*brioches*) as well as the small tile-shaped oatmeal cakes (*tuiles*) and almond macaroons of Amiens (*macarons d'Amiens*).

Above Pâté, that ubiquitous delicacy, varies from region to region, with different ingredients and textures.

Wines and Spirits

In many regions of France, particularly in the Bordelais, roses are planted at the end of each row of vines. The reasons, one is told, are to attract the bees to pollinate the budding grapes, but more important at the time of horse-drawn ploughs, to force the horse to give a wide berth to the vine at the end by avoiding being pricked by the rose bush. There are many roses in Picardy but no vines, except a sprinkling of Champagne vines in the Aisne. Yet they drink a good deal of wine, along with cider from the neighbouring Normandy, and beer from the north and wine to go with their magnificent cuisine. It might be interesting to see how they buy this wine.

Wine is available everywhere food is sold. A more select choice is in the good *charcuteries*, accompanying their exquisite produce. A wider choice is in the supermarkets. The latter would not tend to have much of interest to the traveller, except a minor Bordeaux or Côtes du Rhône, but as consumption in France moves away from *vin ordinaire* to *vin d'appellation*, the choice will get better. Basically, the French drink wine as the English drink tea, with every meal and at all times, and the brand is not so important, but this is changing. Apart from buying from the local stores, if one is interested, the best bet is to buy direct from the vineyard. This means reading advertisements in the gourmet press for Châteaux and Domaines wishing to sell by mail-order, or merely taking the name off the label of a wine you have enjoyed and writing to the supplier. An extension of this are the mail-order wine clubs offering a full and interesting list of wines which can be purchased by filling in a form. Prices are usually better than retail and the choice very much more interesting. Then there are the local Town Fairs, generally with agricultural machinery but always with a few wine booths. These salesmen travel the country on a 'taste now and buy direct from the vineyards' basis, but the prices are not often competitive with the mail-order clubs and often one does not get the wine expected. Finally, the most enjoyable method of buying wine is an expedition by car to the vineyard country: visit the cellars and come away with a boot-load of wine and some happy memories. Failing that, visit one of the good wine merchants in Paris on your next trip. He will have done all the pre-selecting and risk-taking for you: his wine should be reliable.

Below In France wine is widely available and attractively displayed in shops and supermarkets, but the most enjoyable way of buying is an expedition to the vineyards.

Alsace-Lorraine

Distinctive as they are, Alsace and Lorraine are often mentioned in one breath. This is because they were transferred to Germany together in 1871, and back to France in 1918. Alsace, the more Germanic of the two, became part of France in 1648 by the Treaty of Westphalia, and Lorraine in 1766. They have, on occasions, made up a single territory. Both have strong Germanic elements, although Lorraine also produced Joan of Arc (and nobody could be more French than that) as well as the double-barred cross of Lorraine, symbol of France. Alsace, in spite of its Germanic appearance and dialect, is today totally Gallic in its sympathies and has a claim to the French national anthem. The *Marseillaise* was written in Strasbourg in 1792 by Rouget de Lisle, a young officer in the Army of the Rhine. Its debated nationality, its situation on the eastern border and Nazi attempts to annexe it, have nevertheless caused considerable suffering to Alsace and its people especially during World War II, when they found

Introduction

themselves in conflict with a race speaking their own language.

Today, Alsace is made up of two departments: Bas-Rhin and Haut-Rhin; Lorraine is composed of four: Meuse, Moselle, Meurthe-et-Moselle and Vosges. The Vosges mountains divide the two regions. Here the winters are colder than anywhere else in France. As ancient glaciers receded, they bared hills whose hollows captured the melting ice and retained it as a series of lakes. Firs grew to clothe the mountains. From a distance they etch a steel-blue undulation across the horizon. Autumn touches the brush and deciduous trees with flame and even the dark firs turn bronze as sap drops low. The poet Paul Verlaine, a child of the region, described these 'woods without number' and the wolves whose eyes still sometimes glimmer at night among the secretive boles of spruce and pine. There are ski resorts and two famous spas, Vittel and Contrexéville, with mineral water that is bottled for sale all over France.

The Vosges descend gently on the west towards the plateau of Lorraine. To the east they drop precipitously to the plain of Alsace. From the Grand Ballon, a summit of the southern Vosges easily accessible by car, on a fine day there are stunning panoramic views across the Black Forest, the Jura, the rest of the Vosges, and even the Alps when the light is very clear. The Rhine provides a natural national boundary between France and Germany.

The Lorraine plateau falls into two, low clay hills in the north and granite mountains to the south. The region officially has two capitals: Metz to the north, Nancy to the south. The area's iron ore deposits used to be among the richest in the world. A little coal is mined near the Saar border. Large quantities of salt are also produced. So are fine cherries, pears and apples and sweet *mirabelle* plums.

To a French art-lover the word 'Nancy' conjures up the natural forms and dusty colours of glassware by Emile Gallé and the brothers Daum and Müller. It also evokes the mastery which the eighteenth-century ironsmith, Jean Lamour, brought to his embellishment of the gates and railing of the Place Royale. This enclosed square has been renamed Place Stanislas after the Polish king, Stanislas Leczinski, to whom Louis XV presented the duchy with the stipulation that it return to France on his death. Not many fathers-in-law receive such a gift from their sons-in-law.

The cunning lines of Lamour's work were to inspire Gallé and his fellow-artists. Nancy and nearby Lunéville were important centres of the Art Nouveau style, which was to revolutionize the design of buildings, furniture, glass, ceramics and jewellery.

Most of all, though, Lorraine is remembered as the home of Joan of Arc whose birthplace, Domrémy, has extended its name to become Domrémy-la-Pucelle (Domrémy-the-Maid) in honour of the shepherd girl whose saintly voices commanded her to drive the English out of France. Her house is still standing and in the church, itself greatly restored, you can visit the font where Joan was baptized over 500 years ago.

Strasbourg, capital of Alsace and a city of international importance as the seat of the Council of Europe and a seat of the European Parliament, is the only French city on the Rhine, or more correctly, on the river Ill. This stream runs parallel to the Rhine and has provided the name for the area. *Elsass* in German is *Illsass* in the local dialect, and both mean 'the country of the Ill'. All French towns tend to be built back from the Rhine which floods along its western banks, whereas German towns advance towards it.

Like their German cousins across the way, the Alsatians are talented wood-carvers, sculptors and iron workers. Textiles and printing are traditional

crafts. It was while living here that Gutenberg thought out his revolutionary printing press. The houses look Teutonic, with half-timbered façades and wooden balconies, often bright with flowers. National costumes resemble those of the Black Forest. Alsatian is a Germanic language and France has in a sense imposed cultural hardship on the people by trying to stamp it out in schools. Yet the Alsatians are today such strong French patriots – having suffered so much from the Nazis – that they have not minded the post-1945 campaign to Frenchify them fully.

There are war memories here, as there are in Lorraine. This border has always been a sensitive point in France's armour. The gentle *route des vins* gives an opportunity for sampling fine wines, mostly white. Colmar, the birthplace of the sculptor Bartholdi who created New York's Statue of Liberty (a gift from France to the United States) has another claim to fame as the centre for an August wine fair. There are many charming little towns along the wine route which starts west of Strasbourg and ends at Thann in the south.

The celebrated storks whose ragged nests used to top chimneys and spires are being lured back to Alsace. An equally celebrated bird has never ceased to flourish: this is the Strasbourg goose, giving rise to *pâté de foie gras*. The Romans used to place the still-warm goose liver in milk to swell it. Today forced feeding can result in a liver one-tenth the weight of the bird. One would shudder at ever going near the resultant pink and creamy paste with its truffle flavouring, if it were not that one rather suspects the French do much the same thing to their own livers – and enjoy every moment of it.

Left Lovely towns such as Riquewihr, their flower-bedecked, gabled houses set amid vineyards growing on the eastern slopes of the Vosges, seem to exude the sense of well-being which their wines promote.

Above The river Meuse reflects the Alsatian countryside near Domrémy, where Joan of Arc was born.

Towns and Villages

Lorraine was long an industrial heartland of France: the great ironmasters of the nineteenth century established their foundries at Longwy, Thionville, Pont-à-Mousson (Meurthe-et-Moselle). The region is to some extent paying the price of early industrialization: the steel industry is in crisis, and the resultant closures and nationalization of plant is turning once-thriving places like Longwy into ghost towns. Luckily, new automobile factories are now arising. But Nancy, Lorraine's historic capital (today this role is shared with Metz), has a long tradition of education and its inhabitants are highly-skilled, with the kind of industrial experience behind them that is managing to attract new investors.

Hard work and a respect for education are characteristic of the people of Eastern France. Today, Alsatians and Lorrains often carry off the prizes in the national high school (Grandes Ecoles) graduation competitions, and their people fill many of the higher echelons of government. With its magnificent red sandstone cathedral, its delightful ancient houses in Petite-France, criss-crossed by canals, and its storks nesting on the chimney-tops, the image of pacific pride, private and civic, could mislead one into thinking the Strasbourgeois had never known war or misfortune. Nothing could be further from the truth: in the months of

Far left Kaysersberg is the birthplace of Albert Schweitzer, scientist, humanitarian and missionary, who won the Nobel Peace Prize in 1952.

Above The sixteenth-century charm of balconied houses in Petite-France, the old quarter of Strasbourg. Capital of Alsace, this rapidly growing town is now one of the largest in France.

Left This attractive half-timbered inn, the Auberge du Vieux Logis in Contrexéville, is typical of the buildings of this region.

August and September 1870 she was beseiged by Prussian troops, who lobbed 200,000 shells onto her town centre; for forty-seven years she was occupied by the Germans (1871 to 1918) and again from 1940 to 1945. Today, however, the wounds have been bound up and Strasbourg is a seat of the European Assembly, and has become a fully-fledged European metropolis. Her vast inland port, at the junction of the Marne-Rhine and Rhône-Rhine canals, her position astride the Ill River, close to the banks of the Rhine, have helped to bring her prosperity.

Colmar is the finest and most interesting city in Alsace after Strasbourg, and fittingly is the centre for trade in wines, *choucroute* and *eaux-de-vie*, spirits made from raspberries, pears, cherries, plums, or even bilberries. The people of Colmar revive their ancient traditions at the time of their Old Town festival, in the streets lined with countless ancient houses.

The waters of the Vosges mountains have been famous since Roman times. Bottles of spring waters bearing the labels of Contrexéville and Vittel are now exported all over the world. These, together with other spa towns such as Plombières (already popular with the Roman legionaries) and Bains-les-Bains, are situated in magnificent parks that merge gradually with the surrounding forests.

Historically, Lorraine has lain at the heart of France's ancient struggles with the Holy Roman Empire and its successors: Hapsburgs and Prussians. Strife has left its mark at Verdun, and in the shape of the Ossuary at Douaumont. Verdun was beseiged in 1792, again in 1870, while the French warfare on the hills to the north-east in 1916–17 was the bloodiest of World War I: some 400,000 French soldiers died.

Metz, Toul and Verdun were for centuries fortresses prized in war and traded in treaty negotiations. Today, Metz is a pleasant town at the confluence of the Moselle and Seilles rivers, built on several islets. It was occupied by the Germans from 1870 to 1918, and suffered both materially and humanly in World War II. It has traditionally rivalled Nancy, the historical capital of Lorraine, and its reward came in 1967 when it was named administrative capital of the region. Both cities hold carnivals halfway through Lent. Each Holy Thursday in the area, small pine boats bearing lighted candles are set to float downstream, to celebrate the festival of the *Champs-Golots*.

As well as heavy industry, certain towns in the region are noted for rather more unusual crafts. Mirecourt was long the centre of French violin-making, which was introduced to the town from Italy in the seventeenth century. A few years ago there were barely a couple of *luthiers* left, but efforts are now being made to revive the ancient craft.

Châteaux and Churches

In Nancy, capital of Lorraine, medieval quarters stand side by side with classical ones. The Place Stanislas, an excellent example of eighteenth-century town-planning, was meant to provide a magnificent setting for royal festivities, with its ornate railings covered with gold leaf, and its fountains and pools.

Nancy was the centre of a major school of Art Nouveau, the Ecole de Nancy, whose style was nicknamed *nouilles en délire* (delirious noodles). Here and at nearby Lunéville these disquieting curves proliferated as craftsmen such as Emile Gallé and Louis Majorelle, both natives of Nancy, applied new textures, shapes and colours to glass-making and furniture design. The Musée Historique Lorrain contains the work of two major local painters, Claude Lorrain and Georges de la Tour.

Metz is a town of many churches, and its basilica of Saint-Pierre-aux-Nonnais, is the oldest in France. The Gothic Cathedral of Saint-Etienne rises above the river with its lofty spires and proportions as harmonious as those of Beauvais and Amiens. Glorious stained-glass windows, some by Chagall and some from the sixteenth century, flood the interior with colour. Another landmark in Metz is the thirteenth-century château-fort of Porte des Allemands, a citadel perched high to guard the old road to Saarbrücken.

The unique character of this region is embodied in the old, half-timbered houses, ornately-carved, Germanic in flavour. One of the best examples is the Kammerzell House in Strasbourg, with its intricate façade. More work by the wood-carvers and craftsmen can be seen in the Oeuvre Notre-Dame Museum, itself a medieval building. Towering over the old quarter of Strasbourg, known as Petite-France, is the city's architectural triumph, the rose-pink cathedral built of sandstone from the Vosges, a marvel of perpendicular Gothic with one spire released skywards like an arrow. The cathedral's remarkable astronomical clock is also worth a visit. Always an artistic breeding ground, Strasbourg counts Gustave Doré among its sons.

In the vicinity of Strasbourg two of the most beautiful Romanesque churches in all of Alsace can be seen: Saint-Pierre-et-Saint-Paul church at Rosheim, pure and primitive with its yellow sandstone structure and octagonal tower, and Saint-Etienne church at Marmoutier, whose virtual lack of decoration is more than compensated for by the rare harmony of its construction and the warm hues of its pink and yellow local sandstone.

Among the regions of France, Alsace has been particularly successful in preserving its original character and architectural heritage, as can be observed in the many old townships which have survived almost unspoiled. Kaysersberg, Albert Schweitzer's birthplace,

Riquewihr, Barr and Obernai, for instance, with their half-timbered façades,
carved corner-posts, elaborately decorated doors and dominant tones of ochre,
faded pink and off-white, seem hardly to
have changed for centuries.

Further south is the picturesque old
town of Colmar, where gabled houses,
winding streets and ancient walls evoke
the past so powerfully. The Unterlinden
Museum, which is in fact a thirteenth-
century Dominican convent, houses one
of the finest examples of sixteenth-
century art, the celebrated Issenheim
altar-piece by Mattias Grünewald.

Alsace's troubled history has also left
less peaceful reminders of the past in the
form of brooding, virtually inaccessible
fortresses, such as the Château of Saint-
Ulrich near Ribeauvillé, which is placed
dramatically on a hill-top. The most
impressive of these impenetrable eyries is
Haut-Koenigsberg, with which many a
sombre legend is associated.

Above Charlemagne, king of France and
creator of the Holy Roman Empire, is
remembered in this beautiful stained-glass
window, one of several dating from the
twelfth and thirteenth centuries to be seen
in Strasbourg Cathedral.

Opposite The place de la Carrière,
Nancy, eighteenth-century town-planning
at its grandest. The scheme for Nancy was
conceived by Stanislas Leczinski, once king
of Poland, later father-in-law of Louis XV.

Above The fluid line of this sideboard by
Louis Majorelle is a good example of the
Nancy Art Nouveau style.

Top The Moselle flows gently by Saint-
Etienne Cathedral at Toul, with its twin
octagonal towers.

Cuisine

Here, in Alsace, the people are industrious and imaginative. Their traditional cuisine is unique, and plentifully served. Pork and goose fat give a characteristic flavour to many types of sausage and ham, as well as over forty types of *terrine* and *pâté*. But there is much more. The vegetables are excellent, often prepared with sweet-sour dressings, as in the sour cabbage (*choucroute* or *sauerkraut*), sometimes cooked in Champagne, as at the Terminus-Gruber in Strasbourg, sometimes served with pork and sausages (*choucroute garnie*). This, copiously served, is by far the most common dish in Alsace. Artichokes and asparagus tips may also be prepared sweet-sour, and occasionally fish, as in the jewish-style carp (*carpe à la juive*), cooked with raisins and vinegar.

Other river fish play an important part in Alsatian cuisine: perch, pike, roach and bream. They are usually cooked in a white wine *court-bouillon* and served with a white sauce, perhaps *hollandaise*, perhaps *au beurre blanc* (page 116); they also appear together in the local fish stew called *waterzoii* (found also in Belgium). At the restaurant Au Bec Fin in Metz, salmon are also served, wrapped in a light pastry and swamped with a delicate crayfish sauce (*saumon en brioche au coulis d'écrevisses*). Here you may also be offered jugged venison (*estouffade de cerf*) and other game from the Vosges, such as woodcock and partridge. In Alsace, chicken cooked in the local white riesling (*coq au riesling*) is a speciality, and so are the succulent snails (*escargots*).

Up on the rolling, green meadows of the Vosges, the restaurants are bright, cheerful and simple. At any time of day you can get a tasty snack of local sausage, bread and onions, or a hunk of Munster cheese, washed down with strong beer or Alsatian wine. Munster is said to have been invented by Irish monks who settled here in the seventeenth century: it is round, with an orange rind and a soft, yellow, tangy interior. A creamier cheese from this area, similar to Camembert, is the little square Carré de l'Est.

In Lorraine, the pig is an important animal, and pork dishes abound: pork in aspic (*porcelet en gelée*); pork chops (*côtes de porc*); pig's liver *terrine* (*terrine de foie de porc*); smoked fillets and loins of pork and the delicious smoked bacon, which is used in Lorraine's most famous dish – the *quiche* – a tart case filled with cheese, eggs, cream and bacon, baked in the oven till firm and golden-brown. At Le Gastrolâtre in Nancy, the *quiche lorraine* is individually baked for each customer.

From Nancy there also come *madeleines* – small, fragile, shell-shaped cakes – as well as excellent chocolate cake, but these take second place to the local fruit desserts: plum tart (*tarte aux mirabelles*), baked apricots with kirsch (*abricots au four*) and *vacherin*, a sumptuous confection of crystallized fruits, ice cream, whipped cream and meringue.

The Festivals of Metz and Ribeauvillé

Alsace, for centuries a pawn in the political affairs of France and Germany, celebrates her own traditional splendour at the annual *Fête de la Mirabelle* in Metz. During the first weeks of August, the old local costumes are pulled out of storage and cleaned, the traditional songs and dances rehearsed and performed, and the best local dishes are prepared in the kitchens of all true patriots. On the third Sunday of the month, everything comes out into the light of day. There is a splendid procession, rich in colour, which winds its way through crowded streets to the Place de la République. Much celebrating takes place at the annual feast day in Ribeauvillé, too, when giant cakes and other flower-bedecked floats are paraded around the town. The crisp white wines of the region – Rieslings, Muscats and Sylvaners – disappear down a thousand thirsty throats, adding an alcoholic sparkle to the day.

Above *Truite au riesling*, trout served with a cream and mushroom sauce, is attractively served with a fish-shaped pastry.

Left An enticing array of regional specialities at the Hôtel de Vosges, Obernai, including *quiche lorraine*; *kügelhopf* cakes, *pâte de foie en croûte* (pâté baked in pastry) and the ingredients for a hot-pot which include some of the excellent varieties of sausage.

Below left Gaily trimmed with little paper decorations, this *tarte aux cailles* (quail tart) is served with Alsatian wine in the traditional wine glass with a long green stem.

APPELLATION ALSACE CONTRÔLÉE

CIVA

Sylvaner

SÉLECTION DE LA CONFRÉRIE ST ÉTIENNE

COMITÉ INTERPROFESSIONNEL DU VIN D'ALSACE - COLMAR

Vin d'Alsace

Appellation Alsace Contrôlée

PRODUCE OF FRANCE

GEWURZTRAMINER

Cellier Interprofessionnel des Vins d'Alsace - Civa - Colmar

From the north-eastern corner of France comes the best beer, the wonderful fruity Alsatian white wines and the finest *eaux-de-vie blanches*. With the exception of the big breweries in the department of the Meuse, most of the alcoholic production is concentrated in the Bas and the Haut-Rhin, between the Vosges Mountains and the river Rhine. But before one crosses over the Vosges into Alsace, there are a few wines still being made in Lorraine. Wine from Lorraine was already famous in the sixth and seventh centuries, but, the vineyard has since been decimated and today is a tenth of its size in the 1860s. Two appellations remain, both V.D.Q.S.: the Vins de la Moselle (Moselle) and the Côtes-de-Toul (Meurthe-et-Moselle). The first are light, refreshing whites, mostly from the Riesling grape, the second pleasant, pale rosés from the Gamay and Pinot grapes, vinified as *vins gris*. Both are delightful on the spot but do not travel.

Having crossed the Vosges, one discovers the success story of French vineyards, the wines of Alsace. The vines run from Wasselonne, at the height of Strasbourg in the north, to Thann at the height of Mulhouse in the south, a continuous strip sixty miles (about ninety-six kilometres) long. They are planted on south or south-east facing slopes, sheltered from the north by the Vosges. For the tourist as much as for enthusiast, Alsace is the perfect wine region. There is a single *appellation*, Vins d'Alsace and the finer wines are known by the grape variety. The complete opposite of, say, white Burgundy, with one variety – Chardonnay – and many *appellations*. But the wine is as complex as the rules are simple. Each village has its microclimate, its special type of soil to suit the various grapes: the Sylvaner, light and thirst-quenching at its best at Barr in the north

and Rouffach in the south; the Pinot Blanc (Clevener, as it is known locally) and Pinot Gris (confusingly known as Tokay), fuller, headier whites, especially good at Pfaffenheim; the Riesling, the noblest wine, delicate and subtle, sinewy and suave all at once, perfect around Ribeauvillé and Riquewihr; the Muscat, deeply scented but bone dry, the perfect *apéritif*, excellent at Eguisheim; the Gewürztraminer (spicy Traminer), exuberantly aromatic, especially from Turckheim and Wintzenheim. And then there are the blends, Zwicker from the lesser varieties and Edelzwicker from the better, always dry, clean and fruity, generally served *en carafe*. There is even a little Pinot Noir, more usually seen as a full-coloured rosé than as a red wine.

The wine country of Alsace is the prettiest and most welcoming of France. Strasbourg is the most important city, but the wine trade is centred on Colmar. From this beautiful fifteenth-century town, the Comité Interprofessionel d'Alsace organizes day trips to the vineyards. Each wine village has its *weinstube* and most vintner's cellars are open for tastings. The wine town *par excellence* is Riquewihr, exquisitely beautiful, but a 'working' village dedicated to wine. The Alsatians are the only wine-growers to have their own bottle, the *flûte d'Alsace*, dark-green glass, slim and elegant. They also have their own style of glasses, as do most wine regions; the *ballon d'Alsace* has a smallish, clear crystal bowl, often decorated with vine leaves or grapes, on a long dark-green stem. As in Germany, wine is often drunk between meals as a *vin d'honneur* and beer is drunk with the meal: the style of wine is perfect for drinking without food when friends come by and the prettiness of the glasses adds to the pleasure.

There is seldom a bad year for wine in

Above Barrels of grapes are unloaded at the Eguisheim co-operative.

Right A vineyard in Alsace. The finer wines are known by the variety of grape; the labels (**left**) indicate the light, thirst-quenching Sylvaner and the aromatic Gewürztraminer.

Wines and Spirits

Alsace. The whites are naturally fruity and quite high in sugar, due to the special climatic conditions created by the Vosges mountains. Only a really cold, rainy year like 1972 will produce wines too acid to be enjoyable. While most are drunk within a couple of years of the vintage, the better wines, Riesling and Gewürztraminer, age marvellously. In great years, when a perfect summer gives a high natural sugar content and a long harvest season, some growers make a *vendange tardive* wine, late-picked to give a heady concentration of bouquet and flavour from superbly overripe grapes. These magnified and intensified wines are unforgettable.

While they are almost all white, the variety of Alsace wines accompanies superbly the brilliant cuisine. Sylvaner an *apéritif*, or Muscat, Riesling with the fish, particularly a *sandre du Rhin* (a kind of bass), Clevener or Tokay with the main course (often game in the winter and the cheese (Munster), and Gewürztraminer with the pudding.

No meal is complete in Alsace without a *digestif*, which means an *eau-de-vie blanche*. These are sometimes wrongly known as fruit liqueurs, but they are distilled in the Cognac manner, emerging colourless and spirited, the essence of the fruit being captured in the process. The best known are *Poire* (usually Williams Pear), *Framboise* (raspberry), *Mirabelle* (the small golden plum) whose planting replaced many of the Lorraine vineyards), *Quetsch* (blue plum and *Kirsch* (wild cherries). Then there are others, made from black cherries, mulberries, greengages, and even holly. *Marc* de Gewürztraminer is very popular and *Gratte-Cul* (literally 'scratch bottom') made from sweet briar has a bizarre enough name to get some takers. One should only drink the very best *alcool blanc* as some of the commercial blends are mostly synthetic flavours and neutral alcohol.

Beer rivals wine in Alsace as a national drink. It is very good the next day after too many *alcools blancs*. Kronenbourg and Kantebraü are leading brands. They are drinkable, but come nowhere near to rivalling the best beers of Belgium, Holland, Germany or Czechoslovakia. Try them all the same.

Above Wine barrels in a typical *cave* in Alsace.

Right This grape, the Gewürztraminer, or 'spicy' traminer produces one of Alsace's most delicious and particular-flavoured wines.

Champagne

The plateau of the Ardennes marks the dividing line between France and Belgium, most of it lying on the Belgian side of the border. Hunting is a way of life, for *sanglier* or wild boar and *marcassin*, young wild pigs. There was fierce fighting during the world wars. Much of the area was held behind the German lines in World War I and the Kaiser sometimes resided here. Charleville-Mézières, originally two independent towns lying within two loops of the river Meuse, form the capital of the French Ardennes.

Both Victor Hugo and George Sand described in rolling prose the Meuse valley which winds through mist and forest to the town of Monthermé. A rocky outcrop known as the Dames de Meuse offers a warning to unfaithful wives: these high-spirited matrons were supposed to have been petrified by divine wrath.

Today, this region consists of four departments: Ardennes, Aube, Marne and Haute-Marne. The old province of Champagne stretches from the Ardennes to Burgundy in the south. Most of it is chalky plain, with hills rolling towards the Jura. It owes its name to the Romans who called it *campania* or flat country from the Latin, *campus*, a field. Julius Caesar exercised his troops on this natural parade ground.

The area is subdivided into *Champagne pouilleuse* (poor Champagne) where sheep are raised and *Champagne humide* (damp Champagne) which has more fertile clay soil. The landscape of the Montagne de Reims lies between Reims and Epernay and it is on these hillsides that the vines grow. The wine produced was already sufficiently celebrated in AD 92 for the Emperor Domitian to order destruction of all the vineyards in an attempt to put France out of the contest with Italy.

Champagne finally attained French status when Philip the Fair ascended the throne in 1285.

The region is, of course, famous for the light-hearted, light-headed beverage it produces which the French call *le champagne* in contrast to the province itself which is *la champagne*. The wine, in spite of all its glamorous associations, is masculine; the landscape which nourishes it is feminine. It has supplied the setting for a good deal of French history. Clovis, King of the Franks, first King of France, was baptized at Reims by Saint Rémy in 496. The cathedral, rebuilt

Introduction

several times, was henceforth the traditional coronation place for the kings of France. Joan of Arc refused to consider Charles VII a true monarch until she had seen the crown of Charlemagne securely set on his head in Reims.

The church in more worldly mood was indirectly responsible for the most famous wine in the world. Champagne was not discovered until the seventeenth century when a monk, Dom Pérignon, chief cellarer to a Benedictine abbey in Hautvillers, first blended the already slightly sparkling vintages to make the variety we know today. Long before this, the still wines of the region had been appreciated by personalities as different as François I of France and Henry VIII of England – no mean connoisseurs – who, along with Henry IV and Pope Leo X, all had their private wine stores at Ay, not far from Hautvillers.

Nowadays the strictly controlled Région Délimitée de la Champagne Viticole is comprised of about 56,000 acres with vineyards belonging to about 16,000 *viticulteurs*. Most of it is in the Marne department and the area is crossed by the river of the same name.

Second, perhaps, only to the wine industry, is the de Gaulle industry in Colombey-les-Deux-Eglises. The General bought the house of La Boiserie in 1934 and died there in 1970. The grave is in the small churchyard. The village itself has become a place of pilgrimage and has accumulated all the kitsch trappings of a latter-day saint's shrine. The national memorial, a gigantic cross of Lorraine, symbol of the Free French Movement, stands on a hillside overlooking horizons which de Gaulle described as *vastes, frustes et tristes* – huge, blurred and mournful.

Reims, the capital of northern Champagne, suffered greatly through two world wars and yet Joan would still recognize its majestic cathedral. So beloved is this Gothic masterpiece that when French soldiers camped on the plains during World War I saw the town bombarded and the lead roof glaring molten red in the distance, they wept at the sight. In Paris strangers stopped each other in the streets with the heartbreaking news, 'Reims is burning.'

'*Clocher de Chartres, nef d'Amiens,*
Choeur de Beauvais, portail de Reims . . .'
go the old lines, ascribing particularities to some of France's most famous churches. For Reims, it is the West Front which is referred to, with its stone angel smiling a welcome at the door.

Epernay is the second wine capital of Champagne and glorifies the fact by having its main wine offices in the Avenue de Champagne, where there is also a museum of wine, local history and archaeology: well worth a visit.

Troyes, on the Seine, is the former capital of the area, so full of churches that the streets seem to be bordered with stone lace. In the old days they used to ask, 'What are they doing today in Troyes?' and the joking reply was, 'Ringing the bells, of course!' More prosaically, it is a centre for the hat and hosiery trades. Wooden-frame houses jostle in the narrow by-passes of the old town. In the little thirteenth-century church of Saint-Urbain you can pay homage to Notre-Dame-des-Raisins, a Virgin whose infant reaches with spontaneous delight towards a bunch of grapes: the wealth, pride and pleasure of Champagne.

Opposite Patterns of sunlit vineyards around Champillon promise another fine vintage at the end of the summer.

Left The Château of Montmort stands out from its forested surrounds with an air of pride – as well it might, for it is situated not far from Epernay, centre for France's most famous wine.

Towns and Villages

Above The elegant Place Ducale at the centre of Charleville-Mézières, where the poet Rimbaud was born in 1854. Today this composite town is an important centre for industry.

Right The Hôtel Vauluisant (now a history museum) is typical of the fine old buildings to be seen in Troyes, traditionally the centre of the French hosiery trade. Other industries such as tyres, locks and paper-making have grown up on the outskirts of the town.

The sparsely-populated Champagne-Ardennes region, none of whose departments comes near the national average in terms of population density, has suffered heavily from war throughout its history. In the last century-and-a-half, though, the chief drain on population has been the rural exodus, as peasants were pushed from the land by rising agricultural productivity, and were drawn by industry to the towns.

From the rip-tides of history, three important towns have emerged to form a compact triangle in the department of the Marne: Châlons-sur-Marne, Epernay and Reims. They revolve around the main road and rail links between Paris and the East, and between Lyon and the North. Châlons and Reims in particular are major crossroads, and present transport trends seem likely to accentuate the tendency.

In their contemporary rise to pre-eminence these three centres of Champagne have left the other potential poles of attraction, Troyes and Charleville-Mézières, out on a limb. This is particularly unfair on Troyes, once a brilli-ant centre of the arts and the ideal of courtly love, in the Middle Ages; but the motorways have passed her by.

Reims, the economic hub and administrative capital of the region, has played an important role in history ever since the Roman Empire. Clovis, King of the Franks was baptized here in AD 495; 1,350 years later, Eisenhower received the capitulation of the Third Reich.

Reims has been a major wool-spinning centre since the twelfth century, but today its industries include aircraft and automobile parts, food-processing and clothing. It is prosperous, complete with a new university; sedate and self-satisfied.

Epernay, the third city in the triangle, is of great importance: the major Champagne houses are based here. Their cellars burrow into the chalky hillside in a maze, offering visitors a full initiation into the art of Champagne-making.

What is so striking about the region, sparsely-populated as it is, is the depth and breadth of its historical associations. How can one resist pausing, as one gazes at the ancient quarters of Troyes, to grasp the full significance of Bishop Saint Loup's gesture, in 451, when he dissuaded Attila the Hun from attacking the city? Or, a thousand years later, the marriage of Henry V of England to Catherine of France, in 1420?

Scarcely a town or village in the region does not bear the scars of war. Perhaps most affected (although the competition is severe) were the villages to the northeast of Suippes which were devastated in World War I and never rebuilt, the area being used by the French army for gunnery practice ever since.

Charleville-Mézières, nudging the Belgian border, is an important industrial town, with engineering plants, foundries and a major railway junction. It was damaged in both world wars, but the people of this composite town (it was formed from the amalgamation of Charleville, Mézières and three smaller towns in 1966) have roots that burrow back through the centuries.

The Ardennes have seen some of the fiercest fighting in Western Europe over the last hundred years or so. Napoleon III was forced to surrender in the wool-weaving town of Sedan on 2 September 1870. Sedan was almost completely destroyed in 1940, and in rebuilding it, its architects have opted for a resolutely modern look. Many of the towns and villages of the Ardennes and the Haute-Marne were originally established as strongholds, and the hilly countryside, criss-crossed by rivers and valleys, provides many natural promontories and escarpments with commanding views.

The remarkable town of Langres is one such site. The Romans made it a major stronghold, and the ramparts are well worth exploring for their magnificent panorama. The plateau of Langres represents the hydrographical limit between the Channel and Mediterranean.

The almost desolate Haute-Marne contains a surprising number of sites with historic associations. The 'Wassy Massacre', a brawl that triggered the French Wars of Religion, occurred at Wassy-sur-Blaise, on 1 March 1562. The Château at Cirey-sur-Blaise played frequent host to Voltaire, who wrote his *Century of Louis XIV* here.

Left The Museum of Ancient Reims, housed in the Hôtel le Vergeur, traces the rise of this major city which has played an important role in French history for centuries.

Above Village houses nestle among Champagne's most famous feature: the vines producing grapes for Champagne.

Châteaux and Churches

Gothic architecture was at its peak in 1211 when the building of a new cathedral began at Reims. The original fifth-century cathedral had been gutted by fire, and its replacement was to provide a suitable setting for coronations. The result is one of the world's most famous buildings, and the quintessence of the Gothic style. Flanked by soaring twin towers, the west façade dazzles with the visual richness of its carving, its array of statues and sublime rose window.

Unity and harmony are the keynotes of this superb cathedral. The austerity of the interior heightens the impact of perfect proportions, and the bare stone is enhanced by the warm and glowing colours of the thirteenth-century stained-glass windows and modern ones by Chagall. Despite fire, revolution, and the ravages of two World Wars, Reims Cathedral stands today, lovingly restored, one of the most sublime buildings ever created.

Other buildings which survived the wartime battering of Reims include a third-century triumphal arch, the spectacular Porte de Mars: a reminder that Reims was once a major Roman town. The Basilica of Saint-Rémy is 200 years older than the cathedral, and is mainly Romanesque although the choir is Early

Above The splendid interior of Reims Cathedral was designed to allow space for great coronation ceremonies.

Right The west façade of Reims is one of the triumphs of Gothic architecture, with its numerous statues and huge rose window, 40 feet (12 metres) in diameter, above the central portal.

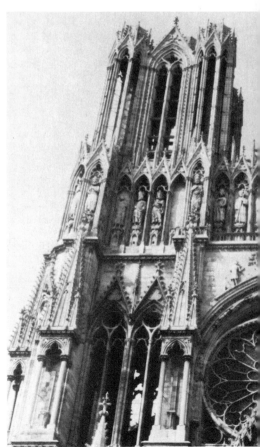

Gothic. The abbey nearby now houses an excellent museum of medieval art and architecture. The Musée Saint-Denis is one of the best Fine Arts museums in France, and is renowned for its collection of French paintings from the seventeenth century to the present day, from Le Nain to Matisse. Not far away is the modern Chapelle Foujita, designed by the Japanese painter of that name.

In Charleville-Mézières to the north, you can see a fine example of seventeenth-century town-planning: the handsome Place Ducale, reminiscent of the Place des Vosges in Paris. It is an imposing sight, with an arcade running all round the square and the soft red brick and ochre-coloured stone of the buildings with their sloping, slate roofs.

Châlons-sur-Marne, with its seventeenth and eighteenth-century townhouses and old bridges, is also the site of Saint-Etienne Cathedral renowned for its pure Gothic façade and stained-glass windows dating from the twelfth to the sixteenth century. The Church of Notre-Dame-en-Vaux, combining both Romanesque and Gothic elements, has a feature peculiar to the Champagne region: the elegant, isolated columns at the entrance to the chapels.

At Saint-Amand-sur-Fion, a village south of Vitry-le-François, one can see some well-preserved, half-timbered farmhouses, typical of the region; the twelfth-century church of Saint-Amand is an example of Champagne Gothic.

Langres, where Diderot was born, is perched on the edge of a high plateau. Encircled by five kilometres of ramparts topped by fourteenth and fifteenth-century towers, the whole town is something of a museum, with its charming old streets and Renaissance houses. Saint-Mammès Cathedral is a fine illustration of the transition between Romanesque and early Gothic, although its façade dates from the eighteenth century.

Troyes, once the capital of Champagne, offers a wonderful panorama of the past, with its network of winding streets and passages, its old and narrow-gabled houses, Renaissance buildings and amazing number of churches. Saint-Pierre-et-Saint-Paul Cathedral is a splendid Gothic edifice, known for its stained glass, including the rather macabre seventeenth-century window called the *Pressoir Mystique*, representing Christ and the Wine Press in which blood pours out of the wound in his side and into a wine chalice. The Fine Arts Museum has a well-known collection of fifteenth to twentieth-century paintings.

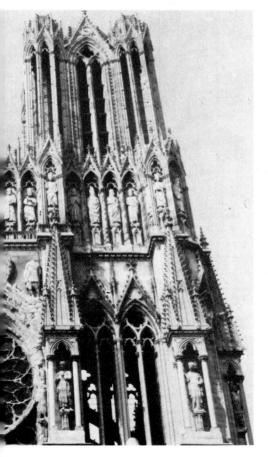

Top The Hôtel de Mauroy is a fine example of the many narrow-gabled, ancient houses to be seen in Troyes.

Above Sole reminder of the time when Reims was a major Roman city, the Porte de Mars is a third-century triumphal arch adorned with bas-relief carving.

Cuisine

Champagne, the very word evokes an effervescent tingle in the throat, a lightness in the eyes, a smile upon the lips. And yet this royal beverage, pressed from the vines of the Marne valley, is not alone enough: for it quickly stimulates the appetite, and then there must be food. Very well! If you are visiting the land of Champagne, you are also in the home of one of France's greatest cheeses – the nutsome-flavoured Brie.

For centuries, the kings of France held court in Reims, enjoying not only the wine and cheese, but also the best of royal game from the damp, eastern forests, the fattened pork from herds kept on the drier, northern plains and fish from the rivers – Seine, Yonne and Aube – that flow into the Paris basin. The region has been torn apart by intermittent war for centuries, and industry has taken over much of the land, but there is still a plethora of authentic traditional dishes.

One is the curiously delicious trotter of the pig, simmered at length in wine and flavoured vegetables (*court-bouillon*), then coated with breadcrumbs, rolled in seasoned butter and slowly grilled (*pieds de porc à la Sainte-Ménéhould*). At the Royal Champagne restaurant in Champillon,

pig's trotters are also used as an edible casing for a sausage stuffing, aromatically flavoured with herbs (*petits pieds farcis*), a stuffing whose contents are never quite revealed but whose flavour is also to be found in the famous sausages of Troyes (*andouillettes*). Other examples of the fine local charcuterie are the white pork pudding of the Rethel (*boudin blanc*) and the fat hams of Reims, sometimes covered with a light pastry (*jambon en croûte*).

Freshwater fish is the speciality of two local restaurants – Le Bourgogne in Troyes, where that otherwise dull and bony fish, the pike, emerges in a *soufflé*, served on a bed of spinach (*soufflé de brochet florentin*); and the restaurant Aux Armes de la Champagne at Epine, where the fish stew, flavoured with mushrooms (*matelote champenoise*) is excellent, and the crayfish mousse (*pain à la reine*) outstanding.

Game is less common but you may still find quail cooked in the embers of a charcoal fire (*caille sous les cendres*) or – as at Le Forum in Reims – cooked with cherries (*caille aux cerises*). Jugged hare (*civet de lièvre*) and roast partridge (*perdreau rôti au four*). Wild boar was once a

common enough dish but today its place is taken by the domestic chicken, gently fried in champagne (*poulet au champagne*) or in buttered mushrooms and garlic (*poulet aux champignons*) – such is life!

Local *pâtisseries* include a feather-light pastry served with ice cream and hot chocolate sauce (*profiteroles*) and a type of apple turnover (*rabotes*) served with whipped cream – both delicious.

Opposite Brillat-Savarin, on the terracotta plate, is a *triple-crème* cheese (minimum 75 per cent fat). Maroilles, in the foreground, is usually a plain cheese, but when misshapen it is mashed and mixed with herbs.

The King of Cheeses

Brie, the unctuous, delicately flavoured paste cheese from Champagne, is now one of the best known of all French cheeses. But it was not always so, for Brie became famous overnight. The scene was the Vienna Congress in 1814, when statesmen from all over Europe were laying the foundations for the post-Napoleonic period. Between negotiations, there were banquets, and at one a discussion arose as to which country produced the best cheese. Talleyrand, the French diplomat, proposed a competition and Brie de Meaux emerged as the most popular of the sixty or so entries: Brie was proclaimed king of cheeses.

Had a less well-ripened Brie been tasted at the Vienna competition, it might not even have found a place among the top three, for Brie – more than most cheeses – must be eaten at exactly the moment of its fullness. The timing depends on the variety – Brie de Montereau for example is different from that of Melun – but in none of them should consumption be later than the first slipping away of the creamy structure. Uniformly smooth, without a chalky interior, and before it begins to 'ooze', Brie is a dessert *par excellence*.

Wines and Spirits

Above The man who started it all: Dom Pérignon, the monk who invented *la méthode champenoise* in the seventeenth century, is immortalized in the Moët and Chandon wine museum.

Above right Unloading the grapes that herald the beginning of another Moët and Chandon vintage.

Right These racks of bottles are stored in *caves* hollowed out of the chalk subsoil.

Champagne, the wine and the country. It is impossible to be interested in the wine without knowing the region it comes from. Champagne is France's most northerly vineyard, on a latitude higher even than Alsace. Vines have been planted there since Roman times, and the wine, though not yet *le champagne*, was fine enough in the Middle Ages to rival that of Burgundy. The area covers four departments: the Marne, Haute-Marne, the Aube and the Aisne, the centre of which is the Marne. Here, the balance of climate, soil and vine plant is perfect. Despite its severe aspect and northern position, the climate of Champagne is milder than expected, more like southern England or a cooler version of the Loire, less variable than, say, the Côte d'Or. The soil is the limestone-clay mixture of the Bassin Parisien, the chalky top soil reflecting the sun to give extra heat and light to the vines. The grapes are the Pinot Noir and the Chardonnay, better known perhaps for their great red and white Burgundies, and in a minor key, the Pinot Meunier. Even with these perfect conditions, there is another element involved for *le Champagne* is a sparkling and above all a blended wine.

The heart of Champagne is divided into three main regions: la Montagne de Reims, la Vallée de la Marne and la Côte des Blancs. These three Champagne routes are clearly marked on the fold-out maps offered by the Comité Interprofessionnel de Champagne and the big Champagne houses, and the roads are well signposted. South of Reims, the capital of Champagne, (although the smaller Epernay is a more important wine centre), lie the vineyards planted in the Pinot Noir. For a vineyard so far north, the black grapes ripen well on the slopes of la Montagne and one small south-facing vineyard at Bouzy, as well known for its still red wines as for its Champagne, is even called the 'Frying Pan'. Wine made from these slopes forms the backbone of the great and sought-after Champagnes.

In the Vallée de la Marne, from the great vineyard of Ay, westwards through Epernay and towards Paris, vines are planted on both sides of the river, partly Pinot Noir but more commonly Pinot Meunier. The latter is a fine 'blender' grape, but weak on its own. South of Epernay lies la Côte des Blancs, planted almost exclusively in Chardonnay. These grapes, particularly from the villages of Avize and Cramant, bring the delicacy and finesse to Champagne. Some Champagnes, (essentially those made by the *vignerons* rather than the *Grandes Marques*), are wines of one single *commune* and carry the name of the village, but most great Champagnes are a blend from the three main regions. Elsewhere, the quality of the wine, due to the climate and soil, is less fine, especially from the vines grown in the Aube department.

Driving around, one has the impression that everyone is involved in the making of Champagne. It is, in fact, more of an industry than wine-making in other areas, as Champagne is a 'manipulated' wine. *La méthode champenoise* entails a strictly controlled system of wine-making. The basic rule is that only the best is good enough for good Champagne. Anything else is at the wine-maker's and wine-drinker's risk. After picking, the bunches are *épluché*, the damaged grapes being eliminated and then passed immediately to be pressed. Of the juice from the three pressings that follow, only the first should be used for Champagne, the second for the still wines, now known under the *appellation* Coteaux Champenois, and the third is for distillation. Fermentation is the same as for other still wines, the cold weather clarifying the new wine and a racking taking it off the lees. The difference happens in the very early spring: this wine from the chalky soil has a natural tendency to wake up and referment. At this point, great skill or technique is determinant in making the *cuvée*, often a blend of as many as fifty wines from different vineyards. Once selected, the wine is bottled with a booster of cane sugar and yeast to create the desired amount of sparkle. The bottles are then taken down to the cellars, stacked horizontally for the *prise de mousse*. Later, they are placed on racks for the *remuage*, removed and stacked upside-down, often for many years, prior to the bottling-line process of *dégorgement* or removal of the sediment caused by the secondary fermentation captured in the bottle. The *liqueur d'expédition* is then added to soften the wine for its various markets, before recorking and final dressing-up of the bottle. This long and expensive process is obligatory in Champagne and copied elsewhere in France and throughout the world for the best sparkling wine.

The traveller with even the faintest interest in Champagne must visit the cellars of one of the *Grandes Marques*, as the biggest firms are known. They are located in Reims and Epernay and a couple in Ay, and are open to the public five days a week. A tour through the endless galleries excavated from the chalky-limestone subsoil underlines the effort in experience, money and time that goes into making fine Champagne.

Above Sorting out Champagne corks. After the *dégorgement* process, which removes the sediment caused by second fermentation, the bottles are recorked.

Wines and Spirits

While the *Grandes Marques* are known all over the world, the *récoltant-manipulants* or growers make a speciality of selling direct from the cellars. Their wines are usually single-village-single-grape Champagnes. What you lose in complexity, you gain in individuality. Most Champagnes are non-vintage Brut, a blend of different years, different vineyards and very dry although still with a 0.5% to 1.5% 'dosage'. The really great harvests are 'vintaged' to highlight the character of the year. A little still white wine is made (or rather is *not* made into Champagne), fine and clean-cut, and a very little still red from the Pinot Noir, usually carrying the name of the village. The best is from Bouzy. The red wine is also used to add a dash of colour before bottling to the Champagne rosés, which look pretty and are fun to serve.

On the subject of rosés, the rarest in France is made at Les Riceys in the Aube. It is made from the Pinot Noir, deep coloured for a rosé, yet stylish and delicate. Since the grapes can be sold more profitably to make Champagne, the survival of the Rosé des Riceys is uncertain, which is a pity, as these rare and individual wines are most enjoyable.

Top right At the Heidsieck Champagne cellars, bottles are placed on wooden racks for the *remuage*, one of the processes essential to the making of good Champagne.

Right At the Château Saron, Epernay, a cheerful picker sorts out the good grapes from the bad. This process is called *épluchage*.

Ile-de-France

This is not, of course, an island, although roughly bordered by four rivers. It is, however, the heart of modern France. The vivacity of Paris spills over into the surrounding area, just as the Paris work force spills out each night from the main railway stations to apartment-block living in the near suburbs, to small *pavillons* or individual houses a little further away and even to substantial country dwellings.

The original nucleus of the French kingdom was the Pays de France. This area, decidedly untouristic today, lies north of Paris and reaches from the Saint-Denis plain to Luzarches, slightly north-east, and Dammartin-en-Goële, a few miles further east. Paris was not included. It was still called Lutetia, 'city of mud', named after the Gallic tribe which lived there. The Ile-de-France became a province only in the fifteenth century.

The region is growing more and more populated as Paris bursts its seams, with its ten million inhabitants, but it still retains its gentle aspect, old hunting forests where Parisians go to walk in the woods at weekends or gather lilies-of-the-valley in the spring, quiet river-banks for picnics and fishing and a scattering of great churches and royal châteaux with their attendant gardens, many of them laid out by the landscape

gardener, Le Nôtre, the French equivalent of England's Capability Brown. The light, diffused through a sky of pale blue or misty grey, caresses worn stone into life and brings a special, tender luminosity to areas of green.

The changing effect of this light on colours, river reflections, blossom, rock and the human form attracted painters to the Ile-de-France. In the nineteenth century Camille Corot, France's first true landscape artist, set up in the village of Barbizon, near Fontainebleau, much the same today as it was when he knew it. Until then landscape painting had mostly been a background to historical scenes or portraits. Corot concentrated on capturing the subtle hues of water and vegetation, the contrasts between dark forest thickets and new growth, the still depths and sparkling surfaces of springs and pools. He drew much of his inspiration from the nearby forest of Fontainebleau which covers over 57,000 acres with a mixture of oaks, pines, birch, chestnut and heath country. A whole school of painters followed him, led by Théodore Rousseau.

They were succeeded by the Impressionists who gave pre-eminence to the shifting effects of light with rapidly applied colours that travel and vibrate across

Introduction

the canvas, forming a whole only at a distance, in the eye of the beholder. Many of them lived and worked for some time in the Ile-de-France.

Van Gogh spent his last days in Auvers-sur-Oise and painted the church and the plains above the river. It was on this plateau that he shot himself in 1890 and died in the inn, now called 'Van Gogh' after him. You can still visit his room. His grave, planted with marigolds, is in the small Auvers cemetery above the church. His brother, Théo, lies alongside.

Not far away is the old, walled town of Pontoise where some of the medieval ramparts remain intact. Conflans-Sainte-Honorine, marking the junction of the Oise river with the Seine, is a barge town. There is even a barge chapel among the craft moored alongside the quay, as well as a museum of barge history on the hill overlooking the water.

Most of the kings of France are buried at Saint-Denis, a mere *métro* ride north of Paris but a long enough trek for the saint after whom it is named, especially as he is supposed to have undertaken it carrying his head under his arm after his execution at Montmartre (*le mont des martyrs*). Near here, Enghien-les-Bains is the only spa town in the Paris area, with the region's only casino.

So rich is the entire area in history and monuments that you could undertake a lifetime of excursions without seeing them all. Pride of place goes, of course, to the Château of Versailles where the Sun King, Louis XIV, ruled in splendour. It was inspired by the Château of Vaux-le-Vicomte, south-west of Paris, built by Fouquet, a Superintendent of Finance who was not above appropriating a few of the taxes for his own use. His interrogatory family motto was, 'Whither shall I not go?' Pride came before a fall. He made the elementary mistake of inviting Louis XIV to a banquet. Louis was temporarily embarrassed for funds through the cost of the Thirty Years' War, and also irritated that Fouquet could not only call on Molière and Lully for entertainment, but that he could also serve his eminent visitor off solid gold plate. Louis had been ignominiously forced to melt his own down. The king's thank-you letter consisted of telling him exactly where he could go – to prison – and claiming the services of his design team in order to transform Versailles. There he succeeded in outshining everybody's palace, everywhere, for ever. In his own estimation, at least: Fontainebleau, south-east of Paris, wins on charm. Napoleon, who loved it, called it *la vraie demeure des rois* (the true abode of kings); before leaving for Elba, he made a speech there.

Right The Queen's House, Versailles. This attractive building was created for Marie Antoinette, who found the immense palace of Versailles too overwhelming . Here she built a 'hamlet', where she and her companions led a make-belief rural life.

Towns and Villages

Over ten million people, one-fifth of the French population, live in the tiny region of the Ile-de-France, only a fiftieth of the country's total area. Of this population, two million live in the capital itself, and many of the remainder are crowded into suburbs and dormitory towns, recently developed.

In the early 1960s, new towns such as Sarcelles grew up around Paris, creating windswept canyons of apartment and office blocks: soulless environments to live in. However, twenty years later, Sarcelles has now discovered its soul, and although it is still no beauty, it is an animated and reasonably pleasant place. The newer 'new' towns, such as Cergy-Pontoise, are attractively designed, with many English-style, individual houses and plenty of provision for cultural life.

Inevitably, much of this densely-populated region is covered by motorways, airports and industrial estates. But there can be few places in the world where so many people live so close to beautiful countryside and superb works of architecture.

This, of course, is the royal heart of France. Its great buildings – cathedrals and chapels, as well as castles and palaces – arose from the inspiration and ambition of a dynasty that included both Saint Louis, builder of the church of the Sainte-Chapelle at Saint-Germain, and Louis XIV, the creator of Versailles. But the Ile-de-France is also surprisingly, a land of secret wooded valleys and unspoiled villages and market towns. Their survival so close to a thriving twentieth-century capital city also owes much to a royal legacy: many of them are sheltered by the great deer forests, formerly sacrosanct as the private hunting grounds of kings, today carefully protected.

The vast wooded parks of many châteaux have also provided a barrier to the city's expansion – and a refreshing refuge from its turbulence. Among the loveliest of these man-made landscapes is the park created by Le Nôtre at Sceaux,

only twelve kilometres south of Paris. The Château contains a museum devoted to the Ile-de-France, providing marvellous glimpses of vanished towns and villages now swallowed by the advancing city.

Even the ancient settlements that remain so near and yet so far from the modern city and its suburbs, have an atmosphere of gentle poignancy, resulting from their long and gradual decay. Provins, a beautiful hilltop town that once ranked next to Paris and Rouen as the third greatest city in France, has been in a state of gradual decline since the end of the thirteenth century. Its octagonal keep, known as the *Tour de César*, was heavily fortified by the English during the Hundred Years War. The town is also renowned for a particular red rose that grows here. It is said that this rose was brought back from one of the Crusades.

The plain of Beauce, one of Europe's richest grain-growing areas, opens up south of Fontainebleau, and Étampes, with its ancient streets and fine twelfth-century churches, seems as golden, in late summer, as the fields of wheat ripening all around it.

Another beautiful village in the shadow of the Fontainebleau forest is Milly-la-Forêt, famous for the cultivation of medicinal herbs, or *simples*. It has one of the finest covered markets in

The little village of Barbizon lent its name to the school of painting developed by Corot, Millet and Rousseau, who often frequented the Auberge Ganne (**above**).

Right Joinville stands beside the river Marne, which flows right through the Champagne district and joins the Seine just north of Paris.

France, a magnificent timber-framed building dating from 1479. The ancient Chapel of Saint-Blaise-des-Simples was decorated by Jean Cocteau who made his home in an old gatehouse in the town and was buried here in 1963. Another modern resident was the fashion designer, Christian Dior.

From the earliest times, these secluded towns and villages of the Ile-de-France have provided cherished homes for princes, courtiers, courtesans, artists and writers, as well as more commonplace citizens, who have tired of the bustle of city life. Nowadays, many wealthy people have built their spacious villas amid forest land near Saint-Germain. North of Versailles, at Parly Deux, there is a fascinating up-market garden estate where the *nouveaux riches* lead a possibly idyllic Californian life-style, with their sun-terraces, built-in barbecues and swimming pools.

The stone village of Montfort-l'Amaury in the charming Valley of the Chevreuse was the chosen refuge of Victor Hugo, and also of Ravel, who composed much of his music there. The house where he lived is now a museum. The village church has richly colourful stained glass, illustrating the life of Christ in scenes that would have been familiar to every inhabitant of the Ile-de-France in the fifteenth century.

Numerous dormitory towns, such as Evry (**above**), have sprung up in the Ile-de-France, the most densely-populated region. Planners of later developments have tried to avoid the mistakes that led to the soulless estates of the early 1960s.

Top Fortifications partly encircle the town of Provins, one of the oldest in the Ile-de-France, and once the third greatest city in the country, after Paris and Rouen.

Châteaux and Churches

Top One of the many châteaux of the Ile-de-France, Rambouillet is surrounded by what was once a royal hunting forest. The château combines elements of several periods, and is the official summer residence of the French President.

Above A detail from Fontainebleau. This beautiful palace, less overpowering than Versailles, is a model of Renaissance classicism. Sumptuous interiors were designed by Italian artists, such as Primaticcio; gardens, lakes and terraces were the work of André Le Nôtre.

Hidden away in one of Paris's busiest industrial suburbs to the north, stands the Cathedral of Saint-Denis: a solemn island surrounded by modern buildings. Here, for twelve centuries, most of the French kings were buried, from Dagobert in the seventh century to Louis XVIII in the nineteenth. The present church was built in the twelfth century by the abbot Suger, friend and advisor to Louis VI. One of the earliest Gothic churches, it helped to launch the style that was to transform medieval architecture. Innovations such as the rose window and ogive (or pointed arch) vaulting rapidly spread to the other great sees of France.

At Fontainebleau, to the south of Paris, stands the most appealing of French royal palaces. Originally a hunting lodge, it was transformed into a chief residence by François I during the sixteenth century, who brought artists and craftsmen from Renaissance Italy to work on it. Succeeding monarchs all left their imprint on it, as did Napoleon.

At nearby Barbizon, the memories of such nineteenth-century painters as Théodore Rousseau, Millet and Courbet are kept alive in the Musée de l'Auberge Ganne, a humble inn where these forerunners of the Impressionists used to gather for meals. Several of their cottages

have been preserved in their original state. On the other side of Fontainebleau is the picturesque riverside village of Moret-sur-Loing, with its twelfth-century town gates and old houses.

Near Melun, stands the lavish Château of Vaux-le-Vicomte with its spacious gardens by Le Nôtre. It was built in the seventeenth century by Nicolas Fouquet, Louis XIV's minister of finance, who was subsequently imprisoned for his ostentation.

North of Paris, not far from Chantilly, are the majestic remains of the Cistercian Abbey of Royeaumont built in the thirteenth century by the pious Louis IX, later canonized as Saint Louis. Over the centuries Royeaumont was richly endowed by his royal successors and remained an important cultural centre until the French Revolution, when the buildings were badly damaged. Now partially restored, the magnificent cloister and surrounding ruins provide a unique glimpse of medieval communal living. The buildings are now used for conferences and music festivals.

To the south-west is the town of Pontoise, where Cézanne and Pissarro painted in the 1870s. Their contemporaries, Monet and Renoir, enjoyed the carefree life of Bougival, a pretty village.

Further south is Saint-Germain-en-

The splendour of Versailles: the mirror of a king. This aerial view (**right**) gives some impression of the sheer scale of a palace that could accommodate 5,000 people.

Below Broad vistas of avenues, overlooking parks and carefully-placed trees, characterize the formal gardens at Versailles. Designed by Le Nôtre, these gardens were among the finest creations of the age.

Below right *L'architecture ogivale*, or the Gothic style, originated in the Ile-de-France. Characteristic slender pillars rise up to pointed arches; external buttresses allow the use of much stained glass.

Laye, for five hundred years the summer residence of the kings of France. Mary Stuart spent ten years of her childhood here and reigned briefly as Queen of France until the death of her husband, François II. The gardens laid out by Le Nôtre include a Grande Terrasse, just over a mile in length providing a spectacular view towards Paris. Much of this celebrated *château de plaisance* was demolished after the departure of Louis XIV's court for Versailles. What remains is a sixteenth-century castle, incorporating a chapel built by Saint Louis in 1235 and an impressive keep.

The most famous secular building of the Ile-de-France is, of course, Versailles, perhaps the world's most impressive and ostentatious palace. Originally a brick-and-stone hunting lodge maintained by Louis XIII, it was enlarged in the seventeenth century by his son, the Sun King, who commissioned the foremost craftsmen of his time including the architects Le Vau and Jules-Hardouin Mansart, to make it into the greatest work of art in Europe. The palace was designed as the seat of royal government, providing a residence for the Royal Family, together with one thousand nobles and four thousand servants. Versailles is one of the greatest architectural and artistic treasures of French history.

Cuisine, Wines and Spirits

Paris is girdled by thick forests and rich farm lands. Here the Parisian spends his weekend afternoons, exploring the châteaux of the Seine, wandering through stately cathedral towns or enjoying the races at Chantilly. The restaurants, though less cosmopolitan than those of the metropolis, serve food of many different kinds.

Local resources provide a range of vegetables that find their way onto most menus: asparagus from Argenteuil, green peas from Clamart, cauliflower from Arpajon and white beans from Soissons. At the famous Hostellerie du Coq Hardi at Bougival, they garnish lobster and sole from Brittany, Poitou beef and Normandy poultry, prepared in the culinary style of every part of France: the *coq au vin de Bourgogne*, *gratin de homard normand* and *croûte landaise gratinée* are outstanding. Some cheese is produced in the region, a few *pâtés*, and an excellent cider, but the basic spirit of the place is eclectic: it draws on the best France has to offer, presenting a splendid choice.

There is not a speciality of France that is not imported to the Ile-de-France. After centuries of being alcoholically independent, producing its own beer, wines and *eaux-de-vie*, now only a hint of the industry remains. At Argenteuil and at Suresnes, a tiny amount of white and rosé wine is produced for consumption in the local restaurants. At Issy-les-Moulineaux, on the edge of Paris, there is a bus stop called Le Chemin des Vignes, but the vines this spot was named after have been replaced by blocks of flats. The inhabitants of the Ile-de-France have thus escaped the chauvinism of wine-producing areas where they drink only their own produce. If there is any pattern to what one drinks here, it is fashion plus the classics. Beaujolais Nouveau and Sancerre – now almost classics themselves – and then Chablis, Côte de Nuits, Côtes de Beaune, Saint-Emilion, Graves and Médoc. There is still more emphasis on light and elegant wines from the northern vineyards then the more robust wines from the south, with Champagne perhaps appreciated most of all, as it is in many other places.

Above Artichokes are among the many vegetables which make their way from the provinces to the menus of numerous restaurants throughout the Ile-de-France. Others include *champignons*, and *petits pois*: fresh, green and one of the delights of French cuisine (**right**).

Paris

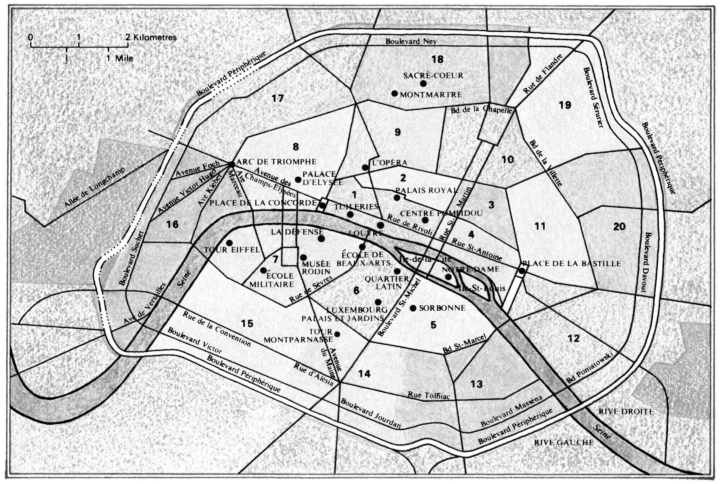

Paris has for centuries cast a spell over its visitors. Its splendour provides only part of its success as a city, which can attract ten million visitors each year and has proved so seductive to European and American artists. The other attraction of Paris is its earthiness. People live here. It is the humdrum vitality of the small-town 'unplanned' parts of the city, contrasting with the stately magnificence of its wide boulevards and vast monuments, that gives Paris its distinctive personality.

The city takes its name from the Parisii, a tribe who occupied the Ile-de-la-Cité until around 53BC when the Romans began a 500-year occupation. By the early Middle Ages the marshy right bank of the Seine had been drained and the city began to spread into the surrounding countryside. By the mid-nineteenth century it had rolled out over six different city walls, swallowing up outlying villages, called *faubourgs*. The *faubourg* came to symbolize the separation not only of city from suburb but of bourgeois Paris from working-class Paris. Victor Hugo wrote: 'It is above all in the *faubourgs* that the Parisian race is found; that is where their blood is purest; there the people work and suffer and suffering and work are the two faces of mankind.'

In the 1860s the intense organic growth of Paris fell under the hand of Baron Haussmann, master planner to Napoleon III. Haussmann is variously felt to have made and to have ruined Paris. To him the city owes not only its broad, elegant boulevards and spacious aspects, but also the loss of the Marché des Innocents, the Convent of the Jacobins, the old church of Saint-Benoît, and many of its tortuous little alleys and streets which gave it such character.

Introduction

Paris has been an artistic centre since medieval times, when many Italian and Flemish painters worked there. At the end of the last century and the beginning of the twentieth, the Parisian vogue was elevated almost to a mania. Young writers and artists from almost every country flooded to the *ville lumière*: Eugene Ionesco from Romania, Samuel Beckett and James Joyce from Ireland, Picasso, Miró, Juan Gris from Spain, Nikos Kazantzakis from Greece, George Orwell from England, Henry Miller and Hemingway from America, to name but a few.

Variety and contrast provide part of the magnetic appeal. Medieval Paris exists side by side with Roman ruins. The Gallo-Roman baths in the Hôtel Cluny off the Rue de Cluny were part of a third-century complex including a theatre, now the Lycée Saint-Louis, and an arena.

The world-famous Latin Quarter owes its name to the Middle Ages when Pope Innocent III authorized the creation of the University of France in 1215. The quarter is named after the language in which all subjects were taught. Vestiges of this medieval past adorn the streets, from the tiny church of Saint-Julien-le-Pauvre, which served as a church to the university during the Middle Ages, to the little passageway behind it leading to the *oubliettes*, lugubrious underground prisons where enemies of the king were conveniently forgotten. And across from Notre-Dame, itself begun in 1163, is a stairway leading up to a tiny house on the Quai de Montebello where in the twelfth century the two famous lovers, Abélard and Héloïse, used to meet.

A stroll through the Luxembourg Palace and gardens built in 1612 by Marie de Médicis, or through the Tuileries gardens with its many fountains and ornamental basins, is a stroll through aristocratic Paris, a reminder of the splendour in which Paris's aristocracy lived when the mass of its inhabitants lived in squalor. And if one looks hard enough, in a corner of the Tuileries, Le Nôtre's beautiful example of a French-style garden, an incongruous flower patch, lies hidden.

Stones in the pavement at the Place de la Bastille still mark the spot where the once-formidable prison was stormed on 14 July, 1789, and the Mur des Fédérés at Père Lachaise cemetery where Thiers and the Versaillais troops executed 147 survivors of the Commune of Paris in 1871, is covered in flowers every spring to commemorate one of the most important moments in French history.

Those who come in search of student Paris will find their counterparts struggling over musty manuscripts in the Bibliothèque Saint-Geneviève, that venerable institution built in 1844 by the architect Labrouste, or wandering through the streets around the Panthéon and the Law School, and the Sorbonne itself, just off the Boulevard Saint-Michel (known to students as the 'Boul Mich.'). With its thirteen universities spread throughout the city proper and in the suburbs of Vincennes and Nanterre, Paris has enough institutes of higher learning to occupy innumerable 'eternal students'. The visitor, if he wishes, can join them at their lectures: French university education is completely open to the public.

The lights in the Place de la Concorde blaze, affirming Paris's nickname, and the Eiffel Tower – that strange and ugly monument to the age of electricity – remains ever after a symbol of the city.

Left Haussmann's *grands boulevards* radically changed the face of Paris, replacing idiosyncratic, medieval old quarters with sweeping vistas like this view along the Champs-Elysées to the Arc de Triomphe.

Opposite This figure sits in silent contemplation of the Eiffel Tower, that strange monument of iron lace which remains the most enduring symbol of the city.

Quartiers

Right A controversial vision of the new France: these clusters of skyscrapers form part of La Défense, an ambitious urban renewal scheme.

Below *Loterie* kiosks, a common sight.

Opposite right A blaze of neon marks Le Moulin Rouge, that symbol of Paris nightlife in the 'Gay Nineties', immortalized so vividly by Toulouse-Lautrec.

Opposite Left Enthralled by the Gothic splendour of Notre-Dame, the ubiquitous artist works at his easel on the bank of the Seine.

Baron Haussmann, with French precision, divided Paris into twenty *arrondissements*. These are artificial creations, but some of them have their own distinctive character, from the clamorous, close-knit streets of Montmartre to the aristocratic seclusion of the Faubourg Saint-Germain; from the bustling internationalism of the Marais to the commercialized grandeur of the Champs-Elysées. The most familiar division of Paris, however, remains that of the 'left' and 'right' banks; while the Left is traditionally the artistic area, the Right is concerned with business and commerce. The terms *Rive Gauche* and *Rive Droite* have an almost philosophical significance for Parisians.

The Latin Quarter (the fifth and sixth *arrondissements*) is one of the oldest parts of the city which, while touristy, still retains its flavour. A maze of small streets wend their way up from the Seine to the Panthéon on the hill. Parallel to the river, perhaps *the* picturesque Paris street, is the Rue de la Huchette, where George Orwell lived out some of the experiences which he describes in *Down and Out in Paris and London*. In the same street, amid cafés and clubs, is a theatre which has been showing the same Ionesco double-bill for some thirty years. And towering above all the polyglot restaurants, university colleges and Tunisian shops piled high with their exotic pink and green pastries, is the colossal dome of the Panthéon, burial place of the famous.

The western part of the Latin Quar-

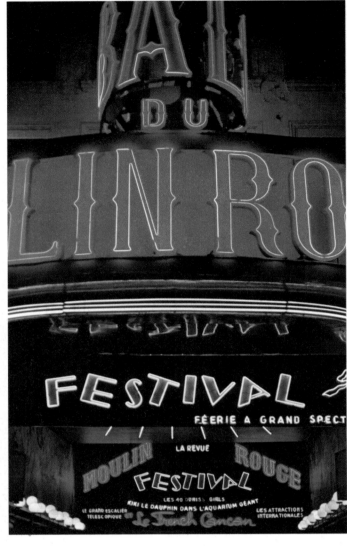

ter, the Saint-Germain-des-Prés/Odéon area, has undergone a more profound change over the years. Little remains of the illustrious Benedictine abbey built by Clovis in 542 in the middle of the wheat fields. Nevertheless the Church of Saint-Germain-des-Prés is, despite its numerous restorations and transformations, one of the loveliest examples of Romanesque architecture. The church is not the only witness to the passage of time. In pre-war days an inexpensive neighbourhood known for its quaint cafés, cheap restaurants and quiet, winding streets, the area has become a commercial paradise inhabited by rich bohemians, and wealthy widows, thronged with tourists and bourgeois intellectuals. Dress shops abound, as do pizza parlours, Greek and Chinese restaurants and expensive bistros where couples dine by candle-light on red-and-white chequered table cloths. So the quarter has its exciting modern side but has not entirely lost its old charm. Street artists still abound.

The Montparnasse area, to the south-west, has always been a centre for entertainment, second only to Montmartre; Régine, queen of Paris nightlife, holds court here. Before and after World War I it was the cradle of the modern movement in art and in the 1920s its cafés became a centre for American literati. The area is not quite what it was in the days of Picasso or Hemingway, but where are the Picassos and Hemingways of today? The Maine-Montparnasse tower, the highest skyscraper in Paris, now dominates the area, but is fortunately not too visible from café level.

The seventh *arrondissement* is a middle-class residential area, stretching to the other side of the Eiffel Tower, mainly of interest for its diplomatic connections. The palatial old houses of the Faubourg Saint-Germain, once the homes of aristocrats, now house embassies, government ministries and, in the Rue de Varenne, the residence of the Prime Minister himself. The area is dominated by the Hôtel des Invalides, the enormous mausoleum containing Napoleon's tomb, and around here there is a great sense of space, contrasting with the intense congestion of some parts of the city.

Over the Seine on the Right Bank lies the heartland of the bourgeoisie, the sixteenth *arrondissement*. Here success is supreme. The top end of the *arrondissement* is the most exclusive, with the Avenue Foche the Parisian equivalent of Millionaire's Row. This area is contained by the Boulevard Périphérique, the motorway which circles the twenty *arrondissements* and firmly separates them from the suburbs, in which four out of five of Paris's ten million population live.

Running between the Arc de Triomphe and the Place de la Concorde is the Champs-Elysées, perhaps the most famous avenue in the world and one of Paris's greatest tourist magnets. Times have changed and the gracious old boulevard has come down a bit in the world. The smart restaurants – such as

Quartiers

Fouquet's – are still there, but many more have given way to the worst sort of fast-food chains.

Hanging mirage-like at the end of the Champs-Elysées is a controversial vision of the new France, the Manhattan-style towers of La Défense, planned twenty years ago as an overspill area for Paris. Many people consider it an eyesore, blocking what used to be an unobstructed view from the Place de la Concorde through the Arc de Triomphe to clear sky beyond. But in fact the grouped nature of the skyscrapers (eighteen of a projected thirty have so far been completed) makes a pleasant impression.

In Montmartre, the high white dome and cupolas of the Sacré-Coeur Basilica rise righteously over the sleazy night clubs and brothels of Pigalle at the foot of the hill. Visitors old and young struggle at varying speed up the long, steep steps to the famous church, which may be said to owe much of its attraction to its position, and many stagger still further to the top of the building where a view second only to that from the Eiffel Tower may be had. All round lie the narrow, tourist-crammed streets of the old village of Montmartre, which somehow retains its charm despite the onslaught. The Place du Tertre, with its many restaurants, is a pleasant place to sit and watch the camera-clicking world go by. Hawkers, buskers, and artists keen to paint a portrait prey on the milling crowds.

The triangle formed by the Opéra, the Louvre and the Place de la Concorde contains the plushest Parisian establishments: first-rate hotels like the Ritz, top shops like Cartiers and famous restaurants like Maxim's (also the best English bookshops in Paris). The grandiose bulk of the Opéra houses a company recently elevated into the international top rank of opera houses. This is part of a general revival, almost a boom, in music in France. In the Louvre, the *Mona Lisa* smiles indulgently down at the constant column of visitors.

Until a few decades ago, the Marais was considered by many a squalid and even dangerous area. Beautiful *hôtels particuliers* had fallen into ruin, buildings needed painting. Even the Place des Vosges with its charming square and picturesque arcades, originally called the Place Royale when it was built in 1612, was showing signs of neglect.

Then in 1962 the Marais was declared a sector of historic interest and plans were undertaken to restore it. Today most of its sixteenth, seventeenth and eighteenth-century private hotels have been renovated; antique shops and art galleries have replaced garment workshops and furriers. Property speculation is rampant: tiny studio flats with exposed beams are fetching huge rents. During June and July the Festival of the Marais animates the usually quiet neighbourhood. Plays, concerts, dance performances, take place in the Hôtel de Sully or the Hôtel de Sens, while clowns, mimes and street musicians enliven the tiny Place du Marché Sainte-Catherine.

The only area of the Marais which has remained relatively untouched is the old Jewish quarter around Rue des Rosiers and Rue Ferdinand Duval, once called the Rue des Juifs, for this was a medieval ghetto. Many Jews immigrated here in the past. The latest wave of immigrants, young intellectuals from the Left Bank, seem a bit out of place among the bearded old men and behatted youngsters. On Sunday morning Rue des Ecouffes resembles a former Jewish village in Algeria: barrels of olives and exotic vegetables spill out on to the street. The odour of mint permeates the air. Old women sit outdoors talking in a mixture of Arabic and French while the men gather on street corners to discuss the state of the world. This *quartier* includes Les Halles, site of the former great food market, still a chic eating area.

The romantic heart of Paris lies in its oldest areas, the twin islands of Ile-Saint-Louis and Ile-de-la-Cité, where lovers still stroll hand in hand along the old quais, and the ancient buildings in the shadow of Notre-Dame exude the calm gravitas of old age. Open-air bookstalls still trade on the banks of the Seine.

Opposite Perhaps the most famous *quartier* of all, Montmartre spreads out around Sacré-Coeur, its streets still the centre of 'risqué' nightlife.

Above left Much of the city's fascination comes from its contrasts of old and new. High-rise developments look to the future, sprouting crops of Manhattan-style skyscrapers, but elsewhere Paris retains its old charm (**top**).

Above right *Le Monde* is France's most prestigious daily paper, read mainly for its authoritative political and social commentary.

Châteaux and Churches

Paris is an architectural and artistic cornucopia. Although few examples of Roman architecture remain, the city was the cradle of Gothic art. One of the finest examples of the development Gothic is Notre-Dame Cathedral, the impressive simplicity of its Early Gothic interior contrasting with the later, ornate exterior details. The east end of the cathedral, with its flying buttresses, is a masterpiece of High Gothic, as are the superb stained-glass windows and stone lacework of the Sainte-Chapelle. The ambulatory of the Eglise Saint-Séverin, and the Tour Saint-Jacques at Place du Châtelet are fine examples of the fifteenth-century Flamboyant style. Saint-Etienne-du-Mont shows the transition from Gothic to Renaissance, with elements of both styles.

Paris's many monuments show the evolution of architectural styles and taste, from the solid simplicity of the Pont Neuf, built in 1578 and now the oldest bridge in Paris, to the grandeur of seventeenth and eighteenth-century Classicism with its use of columns and great domes: the Hôtel des Invalides (where Napoleon lies buried) and Soufflot's great edifice, the Panthéon.

The nineteenth century contributed the Madeleine, with its great colonnade of columns 60 feet high (20 metres); the huge Arc de Triomphe commemorating Napoleon's victories; and Garnier's Opéra, with its ornate façade, white marble staircase and ceiling by Chagall. The huge iron-and-glass structures of the Grand and Petit Palais date from the turn of the century, as do the Art Nouveau swirls of Guimard's designs for the *Métro*.

Paris has always been the centre of French art, and the first years of the twentieth century especially saw the blossoming of movements which were to change the whole history of art. Modernism flourished on the grassy slopes of Montmartre. Song-writers and poets such as Francis Carco, Pierre MacOrlan and Aristide Bruant gathered at the cabaret Lapin Agile, while another group of artists including Max Jacob, Kees Van Dongen, Maurice Utrillo and Pablo Picasso, met together at the Bateau Lavoir. This motley group of poverty-stricken painters revolutionized our whole way of seeing and gave birth to Cubism and its offspring, Dadaism, Surrealism and Abstract Art.

By 1913 the tourist invasion had already begun to chase the artists south. 'The truth is that Montparnasse has replaced Montmartre,' wrote the Symbolist poet Guillaume Apollinaire, 'that old Montmartre of artists, entertainers, windmills and cabarets, not to mention hashishovores and the first opiomaines.'

When the Picasso group abandoned Montmartre, the Left Bank was already inhabited by artists and writers: Matisse lived on Quai Saint-Michel, Apollinaire on the Boulevard Saint-Germain while Gertrude Stein held court every Saturday at Rue de Fleurus. Suddenly, in the heart of Montparnasse, a colony of young artists from all over the world sprang up: Chaim Soutine and Marc Chagall from Russia, Foujita from

Above The flowing lines of the *Métro* entrances are typically Art Nouveau in style, the work of a major designer, the architect Hector Guimard.

Above right Although Paris has a legacy of superb churches, the most prominent of all is one of the less distinguished. Sacré-Coeur, begun in 1876, is an uneasy blend of Romanesque and Byzantine styles.

Opposite top This detail of François Rude's sculpture *La Marseillaise* on one side of the Arc de Triomphe, captures the mood of national pride and the grand gesture, which prevailed at the time.

Japan, Man Ray from the United States, Juan Gris from Spain. They all used to meet in the local cafés, the Dôme or the Rotonde. Today, both cafés are still frequented by artists, and the nearby Coupole is still a *brasserie* in vogue with intellectuals. But the neighbourhood is now overshadowed by the 59-storey Maine-Montparnasse tower with its surround of glassy boutiques and ultramodern shopping centre.

Reminders of Paris's great artistic history are preserved in more than ninety museums throughout the city, from the Louvre, biggest museum and largest palace in the world, to the Jeu de Paume, home of the Impressionist collection, the Musée des Arts Décoratifs, and the National Museum of Modern Art at the Pompidou Centre.

The Pompidou Centre

The Georges-Pompidou Centre, commonly called the Beaubourg, has taken the city by storm since it was opened in 1977 and now attracts more visitors than any other Paris monument. Designed by the architects Richard Rogers, from Britain, and Renzo Piano, from Italy, in the most avant of avant-garde styles, the centre comprises a huge public library, language laboratory, *cinémathèque*, a musical research centre run by Pierre Boulez and the National Museum of Modern Art, where famous canvasses are effectively displayed.

The area around the Beaubourg used to be filled with grocery stores and markets, but has been taken over by art galleries and antique stores. Hippies selling incense, clowns doing cartwheels, fireaters, itinerant artists and ambulant musicians gather on the gently sloping square outside the centre to ply their various trades. It is lively and intriguing. The Beaubourg is an outstanding success, and one of the few justifiable doubts must be over its ability, with its colourful exposed metal piping, to withstand the ravages of weather without extensive and costly care.

Cuisine, Wines and Spirits

The Paris Café Waiters' Race

For fast service, no one can beat the annual Paris Café Waiters' Race. Each spring waiters from all over France gather at the capital to run four miles through the streets of Montmartre, wearing freshly-starched aprons and carrying a tray weighing 12 pounds on one arm. The trays are loaded with bottles of beer, spirits and Coke. The beer is real and bottles are uncapped to prevent unsportsmenlike waiters from cheating by slipping them into their pockets. Capped or uncapped that is no easy feat – and it's uphill most of the way.

The race and its prizes are organized by the hotel industry. In 1977 a precedent was broken and women ran in the race for the first time. Frenchmen and foreigners alike line the streets for the occasion and after the race is over, a celebration takes place at the Place du Tertre to the music of the Montmartre Firemen's Brass Band.

Above A restaurant in the Place du Tertre, at the centre of Montmartre. Once the lively hub of bohemian nightlife and a meeting place for artists, Montmartre today is besieged by tourists.

Opposite A familiar sight in every *quartier*: the delivery of wine.

Above Paris cafés have had both culinary and cultural importance, as meeting-places for artists and writers such as Hemingway.

Although it has no regional dish of its own for which it is famous, no spices grown uniquely on the Ile-de-France, nor vineyard from which a *grand cru* is made, Paris is the world capital of gastronomy. Before the invention of restaurants in 1767 by a Parisian named Boulanger, meals were eaten in cabarets, taverns, inns or at *tables d'hôtes*, forerunners of the restaurant, consisting of a long table at which customers sat according to a hierarchical seating arrangement, nobles and important people at the head of the table, latecomers and simple folk at the bottom.

Today, Paris has more than 8,000 restaurants and every country and dish is represented: Vietnamese and Chinese in the Latin Quarter and off Rue de Gravilliers, Greek on Rue de la Huchette, Algerian specialities in Belleville, Japanese at Palais-Royal and Opéra, Jewish delicatessens off Rue des Rosiers and gourmet French cuisine at famous and historic restaurants such as the Tour d'Argent, Lasserre, the Grand Vefour and Maxim's, known for the many celebrities who go there to see and be seen. Some of the best and most fashionable restaurants specialize in the *nouvelle cuisine* now so much in vogue, promoted by the famous chef Paul Bocuse and others.

The institution for which Paris is most famous is the café. At the turn of the century when apartments were small, dimly-lit and poorly heated, cafés were warm, bright meeting places for all classes and categories of people. It is said that the French Revolution was planned at the tables of the Café Procope, oldest café in Paris, while during the late 1940s Sartre and Simone de Beauvoir preached existentialism at the Café Deux Magots in Saint-Germain-des-Prés. Twenty year earlier Henry Miller had his mail sent to him c/o La Coupole, largest café in Paris, and Chaim Soutine and Foujita spent hours over a cup of expresso at Le Dôme or La Rotonde. All these cafés still serve good-to-excellent fare and are well worth a visit.

Les Halles, the great food market

Cuisine, Wines and Spirits

known as the 'belly of Paris' (removed in 1969 to a more practical site near Orly Airport) also became a popular eating centre. Restaurants like the Pied de Cochon and Vattier sprang up where *les forts*, the porters of Les Halles, and the butchers would go after an early morning's work to drink a glass of wine and down a sandwich of liver pâté. The restaurants remain, and tourists and Parisians still go there late at night to have a bowl of onion soup or a plate of pig's trotters, even if the market is no longer there to amuse them.

Today, the need to supply the thronging tourists with quickly prepared food has led to a certain devaluation of Parisian cuisine. 'Le Wimpy' and worse have become the stock-in-trade of many cafés in the more crowded areas. It is possible to get a very bad meal in Paris. But a discerning visitor can still find the very best food at more moderate prices than those of most other cities. Lesser known establishments like La Petite Chaise (Rue de Grenelle) and the Polidor (Rue Monsieur le Prince) offer good, cheap, traditional meals; the Au Beaujolais in Rue de Lourmel, one of the last authentic bistros in the city, is still relatively inexpensive, and there are a whole host of old restaurants whose standards have changed little over the years. The old, honest Paris cuisine survives in its family restaurants, where the roots go deep, but the conscientious diner must seek these out.

Above An ice-cream seller near Sacré-Coeur. Besides its wide range of international restaurants, Paris provides many an opportunity for a delicious snack.

Left Ornate, old-fashioned scales are used for weighing vegetables on this market stall.

Loire Valley

The river Loire is the longest in France. It begins at the foot of Mont Gerbier-de-Jonc in the Massif Central and glides through Nevers, Blois, Tours and Saumur all the way to the sea at Nantes. It is wide and changeable, sometimes a mere string of related waterways, sometimes charging and full-bodied, with shifting beds of shingle that render navigation difficult and have prevented it from ever becoming one of the great water highways of France.

Spring comes early to the Loire Valley. Medlars and magnolias grow in the soft climate. Skies are a delicate blue, as fragile as old porcelain. Spring flowers thrive in this delicate and civilized air. Hyacinths trouble the gardens with their bitter-sweet scent. Narcissi nod in a breeze born in the Atlantic.

What the river lacked in reliability it made up for in surges of generosity. Spring and autumn floods deposited a fertile soil called *limon*. As a result, the

Introduction

area around Tours is referred to as 'the garden of France'. As well as the queen river itself, there are the tributaries of the Loire, the Cher, the deep, reedy Indre and the Vienne, silky green, the colour of old satin, mirroring the city of Chinon, with its splendid ruined fortress.

Yet all is not turreted palaces and ripening fruit. The Sologne, with its lakes and trees, is the best game country in France but it is infertile. The forest of Orléans, rather less forest than sketchy woodland, is a continuation of the Sologne, characterized by sandy soil. The plain of the Beauce, around Chartres, celebrated as the setting for Zola's novel, *La Terre*, produces much of France's wheat and is flat and monotonous.

The castles dominate the landscape. Here you can name-drop from morning to night and never run out of names. Many kings of France built along the Loire. The Court resided at Chinon in the first half of the fifteenth century, when Henry IV of England was ensconced as King of Paris and Charles VII had to be content with the sarcastic nickname, *Roi de Bourges* – King of Bourges.

It was in the Château du Milieu in 1429 that eighteen-year-old Joan of Arc made her way to him through the crowd of courtiers to where he hid, disguised in someone else's robes. To her this uncrowned king was still only a prince, her *dauphin*. She claimed him as 'the Lieutenant of the King of Heaven who is the King of France', destined to be annointed and crowned in Reims.

The memory of Agnès Sorel, Charles's favourite and *la dame de beauté*, lingers at Chinon even though she left it for Loches after the king's son had publicly slapped her face. Agnès wished to be buried in the castle church at Loches but in spite of the gifts she lavished on the chapter the canons considered her too scarlet a sinner. It was Charles's son, Louis XII who, in an act of magnanimous repentance insisted that if her remains were removed the gifts would go with them; the church, sourly and hard-headedly, gave in.

Louis XI built the Château of Langeais at the junction of the Loire and the Roumer rivers. There, in 1491 Charles VIII married Anne of Brittany. Blois

is associated with Louis XII who moved the Court here on the death of Charles VIII. His successor, François I added a wing. Immense Chambord grew under the demanding eye of François I who built it originally as a hunting lodge with Henri II adding a great deal to what his father had begun. Louis XIV often stayed there complaining, however, that he felt cramped in a château comprised of a mere 440 rooms and fifty staircases.

Other names ring through the soft air. Rabelais was born in Chinon. Balzac was a native of Tours and often stayed at the Château de Saché where his study is kept as nearly as possible as he left it. Jean Fouquet was born in Tours and rendered Agnès Sorel yet more celebrated for posterity by giving her pale skin and fragile features to his painting of the Virgin. Leonardo da Vinci was invited to Amboise by François I. He stayed at the Manoir du Clos Lucé until he died and was buried in the castle church. His remains are now in the Chapelle Saint-Hubert. Descartes was born in the Loire.

Pierre de Ronsard, France's great sixteenth-century poet, was born, lived, loved and died in the region and it was at Talcy he met Cassandre Salviati and addressed her with the passionate lyrics of his youth.

The old well in the courtyard at Talcy has a rosebush planted beside it in memory of one of the loveliest poems in the French language: '*Mignonne, allons voir si la rose . . .*' and a road edged with rose-trees connects Talcy to the village of Mer.

Away on the edge of the Loire Valley stands Chartres, with its Cathedral of Notre-Dame. Chartres is the brilliant introduction or the sublime climax to a trip through the region. The town lies on the left of the Eure river and the cathedral can be seen from miles away across the grain-laden plains of the Beauce.

This was a holy spot long before Christianity claimed it. The Gallo-Roman well in the crypt marks the place where druidical ritual sanctified the spring on which Chartres is built long before Agnès Sorel or Jean Fouquet or Pierre de Ronsard were ever thought of. 'The strongest stem that ever burst upward', the poet Charles Péguy called it, in a surge of ecstasy equalled only by the cathedral's own.

A lasting image of the Loire region is that of Chartres Cathedral, its towers soaring skyward above the wide Beauce plains.

Towns and Villages

Above Tall, medieval houses cluster at the centre of Bourges, capital of the former province of Berry. The Cathedral of Saint-Étienne is one of the finest in France.

The present-day Loire Valley region (its official name is 'Centre') begins in the north near Paris, in the Beauce plain, where outer dormitory suburbs merge into fields of waving corn. Suddenly, as one travels south-westwards, a tiny dot emerges from the rolling countryside; one quickly distinguishes two spires to which is soon added a swelling nave. The Cathedral of Chartres dominates its surrounding countryside as it has dominated the spiritual imagination of a multitude of Europeans, Catholic or otherwise, for centuries. Charles Péguy, late nineteenth-century poet and thinker, was so enthralled by Chartres that he inaugurated a pilgrimage to the cathedral, still made annually by hundreds of Catholic students, setting out on foot, in spring. The picturesque old town of Chartres huddles protectively about the cathedral, while almost equally ancient lace-makers busily juggle their multitude of cotton bobbins, seated on rickety wicker chairs facing the Western Front: their intricate patterns seem to echo the elaborately carved portals. South-west of Chartres, the little town of Illiers was the birthplace of Marcel Proust, and is the 'Combray' of his great novel. Today it is a centre of literary pilgrimage, and the house of Proust's aunt, where he lived, is a museum.

Orléans has been fought over throughout history. Joan of Arc's heroic relief of the besieged city in May 1429 has given rise to a cult devoted to the heroine, with a grand festival being celebrated in the city each year on 7–8 May. In December 1870 the French themselves were defeated outside the city, this time by the Prussians. In 1940 the town centre was destroyed by bombing; this has since been tastefully rebuilt, and new quarters and endless suburbs have sprung up all around as new industries, such as perfume and electronics factories, have arrived from Paris.

Above Music festivals are prevalent in the Loire Valley region, from international organ competitions held at Chartres, to folkmusic at Montoire-sur-le-Loir. Here, a musician plays the *cornemuse* (bagpipes) in Lignières.

Right Houses in the little town of Chinon line the bank of the river Vienne, overlooked by remains of three châteaux, built on a rocky outcrop. The writer Rabelais lived here for a time during the sixteenth century.

Tours lies between the right bank of the Loire and the left bank of the Cher. This spacious town is traversed by broad boulevards along the river banks. In 1974 its mayor achieved national prominence in a bid for French presidency on a platform of opposition to pornography and large supermarkets.

As the first large city on the road from Paris to the south-west, Tours has twice, in less than a hundred years, served as headquarters to a French government in retreat – in 1870 and 1940. Its reward has been bombardment on both occasions. In 1940 part of the city was razed by aerial bombing. It still abounds with ancient monuments, old streets and houses; but its recent growth, like that of all the cities along the Paris-Bordeaux road, is the result of an influx of the most modern industries and the decentralization of numerous administrative services jobs: tall office towers fill the new quarters of Tours and Orléans.

Julius Caesar, when he came to Bourges to do battle with Vercingétorix (in 52 BC), called it one of the most beautiful cities in Gaul. So it remains to this day, with its many fine buildings, and especially Jacques Coeur's palace, the most splendid residence to be built by a commoner in the fifteenth century.

Besides being almost at the exact centre of France, Bourges is the capital of historic Berry and is still a major centre for trade in sheep, cattle, cereals and wine. The town has acquired a new stratum of inhabitants with the arrival of the aircraft factory in the 1960s. It is no doubt for the benefit of its well-educated technicians and engineers that the Maison de la Culture (Cultural Centre), just outside Bourges, runs a full time experimental music group and an annual festival of contemporary music, where the latest in computerized music and synthesizers can be heard.

It was at Nohant, in the Berry, that George Sand was brought up (under her real name, Aurore Dupin), and where she later played hostess to Lizst and Chopin, as well as to many of the leading poets, writers and painters of the nineteenth century. Her own rustic novels (such as *Valentine*) admirably portray the life of peasants in the Berry countryside while advocating the idea of free association between men and women. Nohant itself is a small, quiet country village, its chief attraction being George Sand's home, now a museum.

To the north of the Berry lies a region of drained marshes, lakes and forests, known as the Sologne. This is a favourite hunting and fishing ground for wealthy Parisians, covering most of the eastern part of the Loir-et-Cher. The half-timbered and brick buildings often remind one of those in Normandy. The novelist Alain Fournier was born and brought up in the Sologne, and here he set his haunting romance of adolescence, *Le Grand Meaulnes*. The book vividly evokes the Sologne countryside.

The crowning glory of the Loire Valley, though, are its châteaux, impressive monuments to the continued presence of the great and mighty in this region. Now many are tourist attractions. Some, though, are still in private hands (Chenonceaux, for instance), while the grandest of all, Chambord, is still used by the French president as a hunting lodge to impress his guests. Yet others stand in the middle of busy towns, as in the case of Amboise or Blois.

Above This cobbled street winds through the Halles quarter of Tours, which is rapidly expanding today, with the increase in industry and the decentralizing of many administrative jobs.

Châteaux and Churches

Above Curving upwards like the spiral in a seashell, the François I staircase at Blois is one of the great achievements of French Renaissance architecture.

Right Villandry is most notable for its series of extraordinary gardens laid out by Italian landscape gardeners. These have been restored to their original sixteenth-century design; the clipped box hedges bordering the beds form allegorical symbols.

Right This monumental structure, the Château of Chambord, is perhaps the most memorable, and certainly the largest, of the Loire Valley châteaux.

Left The effigy of Jean Duc de Berry, great patron of the arts, in the crypt of Bourges Cathedral.

The legendary châteaux of the Loire Valley offer a panorama of French architecture through seven centuries. From sombre fastness to decorative *château de plaisance*, no two are the same; each holds its own secrets and offers its own delights; famous names linked with them fill the pages of French history.

Anet, on the very northern edge of the Eure-et-Loire region is said to be the first Renaissance building where French and Italian styles were integrated. The elegant Renaissance entrance gate of pale stone and black marble bears a copy of Benvenuto Cellini's *Diane couchée*, alleged to be a likeness of the fascinating Diane de Poitiers, beloved mistress of Henri II, twenty years her junior. Not far away is the deceptively austere Château of Maintenon that Louis XIV gave his mistress, whom he later married in a secret ceremony at Versailles.

Looming above the river, the forbidding exterior of the fifteenth-century Château of Châteaudun belies its graceful Renaissance courtyard and lovely Flamboyant Gothic chapel. Blois, to the south, was a royal residence for centuries; the François I wing, with its famous Renaissance winding staircase, is reminiscent of Italian palaces, but the styles of four centuries can be traced.

The surrounding area is studded with myriad châteaux great and small. Northeast of Blois is the somewhat severe Talcy, home of Cassandre Salviati, for whom the poet Ronsard wrote many sonnets. Her daughter was to be the ancestor of another great poet, Alfred de Musset.

From afar the turrets and cupolas of Chambord rise above the treetops like a mirage. This harmonious building, the largest of the Loire châteaux, was built at the height of the Renaissance. The remarkable terrace and particular details such as the mosaic patterns of slate along the chimneys were inspired by the Italian Quattrocento. Perhaps its most famous feature is the double spiral staircase, where those going up never meet those going down (some people think this may have been the brainchild of Leonardo).

Cheverny, described by one seventeenth-century visitor as an 'enchanted palace', is a serene, harmonious building dating from the reign of Louis XIV, unusual in that it has retained intact its superb seventeenth-century furnishings.

Amboise, a medieval fortress enlarged and decorated in the fifteenth century by Italian artists brought to France by Charles VIII, Leonardo da Vinci among them. A royal residence throughout most of the sixteenth century, it was turned into a prison after the horrible mass executions of Protestants that occurred here in 1560 under the very eyes of François II and his queen, Mary Stuart. Leonardo da Vinci, who died here in 1519, lies buried in the Chapelle-Saint-Hubert, an exquisitely decorated Flamboyant Gothic building. The château itself is early Renaissance in style.

Another château with a dark history is Loches, a medieval stronghold whose dungeon, formerly the French State prison, had earned it an evil reputation before it was transformed into a royal residence. Since then, its very name has conjured up that of Agnès Sorel, the

Chenonceaux

Romantically straddling the river Cher, Chenonceaux is one of the finest examples of French Renaissance architecture, set in beautiful parklands. Originally a fortified manor house flanked by a watermill, it was acquired in 1513 by Thomas Bohier, who removed everything but the fifteenth-century keep which now stands alone at the right of the entrance. The mill was converted to an elegant country-house built over the water. When Bohier died, the property was taken over by the crown. When François I's son Henri II became king in 1547, he gave it to his mistress Diane de Poitiers, the legendary beauty. It was she who built the five-arched covered bridge across the river, and the fine gardens.

When Henri II was killed in a jousting accident in 1559, his widow Catherine de Médicis seized the opportunity to evict Diane de Poitiers, who retired to her château at Anet until her death seven years later. Catherine, who had coveted Chenonceaux for some time, further enlarged and embellished it, adding a two-storied gallery to the bridge.

In the eighteenth century, Chenonceaux was acquired by Claude Dupin, *Fermier-Général* under Louis XV, and the château became the setting for brilliant literary *salons*, held by Madame Dupin. Jean-Jacques Rousseau was engaged as a tutor, and composed his treatise on education *Emile* for her son. Madame Dupin was so beloved by the villagers that the château was spared during the French Revolution.

Châteaux and Churches

beautiful mistress of Charles VII. Her remains are buried here underneath a recumbent figure believed to be her likeness, near the tower known as the 'Tour de la Belle Agnès'.

Further west stands Azay-le-Rideau, whose foundations are rooted in the riverbed and whose elegant silhouette hovers above the water. Balzac described it as a 'multifaceted diamond set in the river Indre'. A marvel of grace and harmony, it is considered to be the purest among the Loire châteaux, and now houses a Renaissance museum.

The Italian influence can again be seen at the nearby Château of Villandry, with its astonishing terraced gardens: the top terrace consists of a water garden covering about a hectare, beneath it is a formal garden in which close-cropped box-hedges form allegorical symbols, and below this is the extraordinary vegetable garden set out in geometric designs.

The once-formidable Plantagenet fortress of Chinon still looks awe-inspiring, even though today it is no more than a skeleton, stretching for some distance above the little town with its picturesque streets, the birthplace of Rabelais. Langeais, to the west, a fifteenth-century feudal fortress built of grey stone, has been left virtually intact and so sheds some light on the daily life within fortified walls in those days. It contrasts strongly with nearby Ussé, which with its white walls and host of white turrets is said to be the model for the castle in Perrault's story *The Sleeping Beauty*.

Near Le Blanc, in the Berry region to the east, stands the Benedictine abbey-church of Fontgombault, a magnificent Romanesque edifice partly restored in the nineteenth century. To the north of it is the little town of Châtillon-sur-Indre with its delightful old winding streets and an eleventh-century Romanesque church whose wonderful capitals are alive with extraordinary carved animals.

The pride of the Loire Valley's religious buildings is, however, the Cathedral at Chartres, described by Rodin as the 'Acropolis of France', and considered by many to be the most sublime example of Gothic architecture anywhere. Its splendid thirteenth-century stained-glass windows with their shimmering reds and famous *bleu de Chartres*, and the majestic, finely-carved statues on the portals are unforgettable.

The Cistercian abbey of Noirlac, a sober and harmonious edifice, is exceptionally well-preserved, while to the south stands the medieval Château of Culan, whose pretty round towers boast the highly unusual feature of wooden corbelled galleries known as *hourds*, a unique sight since by the twelfth century most of these had been replaced by stone parapets.

Bourges is the site of two renowned landmarks of French architecture: Saint-Etienne Cathedral, celebrated for its five magnificent portals flanked by two asymmetrical towers, and for its remarkable stained-glass windows dating from the twelfth to the seventeenth century; and the Palais Jacques Coeur, a superb example of Gothic domestic building.

At Mehun-sur-Yèvre, to the north, stand the remains of a fourteenth-century château built by the Duc Jean de Berry, the great patron of the arts who commissioned the famous illuminated manuscript *Les Très Riches Heures du Duc de Berry*, now at the Condé Museum.

This mellow valley region with its staggering array of châteaux encapsulates both the richness of France's architecture heritage and the splendour of its rich and beautiful countryside.

Above In contrast to the great, Renaissance châteaux of the Loire Valley, the Tours de Larzay in the Indre department, are medieval in appearance, with machicolated towers and pepper pot roofs.

Left White stone walls and clusters of turrets give a poetic appearance to the Château of Ussé, said to be the setting for Perrault's *Sleeping Beauty*.

Top left Pillars in the gallery of the Louis XII wing at Blois. Dating from the early sixteenth century, the rich decorations shown here mark the beginnings of the Italian style in France.

Above A superb legacy of thirteenth-century Gothic stained glass can be seen at both Chartres and Bourges.

Cuisine

From the sparkling springs of the Massif Central, the rivers of the Loire tumble down into one of the most serene and beautiful areas of all France: in the east, the game-rich marshes and forests of Sologne; and in the west, the broad, sweet plain of Touraine. Here in the plain, in the so-called 'garden of France', with its mild climate and rich soils, a vast array of nut and fruit trees grow, a source of pleasure and prosperity for the French aristocracy for 500 years.

The sweet dishes of Touraine have travelled to every part of France. From the soft-fruit centre of Saumur come the fresh cream cheeses called *crémets*, made of whipped cream and egg white and served with seasonal fruits – raspberries, strawberries or blackberries, and in the winter quince or raspberry jelly – and sweetened, unwhipped cream. In the almond town of Pithiviers they make an almond-and-rum pastry called *pithiviers*, about which Robert Courtine of *Le Monde* has written: 'It is the quintessence of Sunday in Touraine, a cake one buys at the famous pastry shop after Mass.' The rum is still imported from the West Indies, and is used in another local dessert – *savarin* a rich bread, baked in a circular *savarin* mould, which is impregnated with rum syrup and served with crystallized fruit.

Walnuts and plum are specialities of Tours, the capital of Touraine. The plums are stuffed with almond paste (*prunes fourrées*), made into a creamy pudding (*pâte de prunes*) and cooked with pork (*noisettes de porc aux pruneaux*). Walnuts appear in salads and savoury stuffings, and you may also find them pickled in sour grape juice (*cerneaux de verjus*). At the grand and famous restaurant of Charles Barrier, the most imaginative and delightful salads are dressed with walnut oil and red wine vinegar.

Perhaps the most famous of the Loire's sweet dishes is not from Touraine but Sologne: the *tarte tatin*, which the irrepressible French gastronome Curnonsky described as 'pure, noble and simple, like the light from the skies above.' The Hôtel Tatin at Lamotte-Beuvron, where this rich, toffee-flavoured apple tart was first made by the daughters of the house, still stands, and the original recipe is still respectfully observed.

This small village is also a hunting centre, and local game is a regular feature of the menu. Two specialities are pheasant casserole (*faisan en barbouille*), flavoured with local vegetables and brandy, and venison cutlets (*côtelettes de chevreuil*), fried in butter and served with either a wine vinegar sauce (*sauce poivrade*) or a black cherry sauce (*sauce aux cerises*). Wild duck, hare, partridge and lark are all served at the splendid old Auberge Saint-Jacques at Orléans, as well as two delicious quail dishes: a pie (*pâté de cailles*) and a quail spread (*cotignac*).

The river brings a variety of fish: trout, salmon, pike, barbel and many smaller varieties. At the Hôtel Budan in Saumur, the smaller fish are often fried together (*friture de la Loire*) or pressed into a paste (*terrine de poissons*). Other interesting fish dishes here are fried ablette and salmon grilled over a wood fire. Pike are common, but must be very fresh: they are made into stews, boiled in white wine or wrapped in vine leaves and cooked on a spit. Their dryness is balanced by serving them with a creamy shallot sauce (*brochet au beurre blanc*).

Left Restaurants of the Loire Valley offer comprehensive menus, having at their disposal plentiful supplies of fish, game and poultry, besides the famed fruits of the region.

Above Many types of game are hunted here, from venison and pheasant, to partridge and hare. Regional dishes include such delicacies as venison cutlets (*côtelettes de chevreuil*) served with a black cherry sauce (*sauce aux cerises*) and quail spread (*cotignac*).

Top Touraine. Goats provide milk for several good cheeses in this region, including Sainte-Maure, Selles-sur-Cher, Valençay and Crottin de Chavignol.

Above The final stages in the production of Crottin de Chavignol cheeses.

Wines and Spirits

The Loire, the longest river in France, is not content with the royal magnificence of its châteaux: the wines grown along its banks from over 500,000 acres of vines are amazingly varied. Climate, soil and grape variety change all the time, but the meandering luminous aspect of the river seems to give the wines a family resemblance, one of elegance, grace and charm.

The most northern point of the Loire is in the department of the Loiret. The capital, Orléans, used to be the main wine centre for Paris. Now only a few acres of vines remain, mostly the Gris Meunier, from which a rosé or light red is made for drinking young. They are delightful when drunk on the spot, especially the marvellously named Clos de l'Enfer. Orléans is more famous for its vinegar industry, based at first on the

Above Harvesting the grapes in the Cher department, where Sancerre and Pouilly wines are made from the Sauvignon grape.

Right The name of this restaurant in the valley bears witness to the excellent wines of Touraine, where a near-perfect climate produces whites, reds and rosés of great complexity.

Above right Wines of the Loire Valley region.

Opposite Pouilly-sur-Loire. Grapes are pressed in a hydraulic basket with slatted sides to allow the juice to run out. The skins (*marc*) are then distilled to make brandy, or used as fertilizer.

countless hogsheads of wine from Burgundy and further south which were left already *piqué* from the slow journey to Paris. Further inland along the river there is some pleasant wine made at Gien: light dry Sauvignon white and slightly acid Gamay reds.

In the department of the Cher, the river runs into Burgundy. Not surprisingly therefore, the most famous vineyard of the area, Sancerre, used to be planted with the Pinot Noir from Burgundy. The greater success of the Pinot in Burgundy caused the rather rough Sancerre red to fall from favour, and the scourge of phylloxera put paid to it. Now Sancerre is famous for the white wine made from the Sauvignon grape, perhaps the most perfect expression of this *vin sauvage*. There are two types of Sancerre, one grown on the chalky soil around the pretty village of Chavignol, very grapey and with some bite, and that grown on the clay soil around Bué, fruitier and fuller. Both the *vignerons* of Chavignol and Bué, and other villages of Amigny and Verdigny, are convinced that their particular style is the right one, and they are all keen to prove it, offering free tastings to prospective buyers. Sancerre is an interesting wine, not too serious, and is best drunk the year after the vintage, especially with river fish, chicken and the local goat's cheese. Apart from the marvellous white, there is a little pink rosé and slightly rustic red, both made from the Pinot Noir. The popularity of Sancerre has brought to light some other good Sauvignon whites: Menetou-Salon on the way to Bourges, and Quincy and Reuilly just below Vierzon, almost as good as Sancerre if not so striking. Forty miles south of Bourges, half in the Indre and half in the Cher, are the vineyards of Châteaumeillant, an attractive, fruity V.D.Q.S. (medium quality) red made from the Gamay with a touch of Pinot Noir and a refreshing rosé, vinified as a *vin gris*.

The two main grape varieties for white wines in the Loire are the Sauvignon, originally from the Bordeaux area, and the Chenin Blanc (or Pineau de la Loire), the river's own variety. The château country of the Loir-et-Cher sees the change-over from Sauvignon to Chenin, and once we are in the Indre-et-Loire (really the Touraine), the Chenin is exclusively used for finer wines. There are some lovely wines made around

Wines and Spirits

Blois, Cheverney and Chambord: Sauvignon and Chenin for the whites, the former being the better, Gamay for the reds and Pineau d'Aunis for the rosés. They used to be known as 'Coteaux de Blésois', with no real *appellation*, and now justifiably have the V.D.Q.S. *appellations* of Chambord and Cheverny. The whites travel better than the reds, and they are all perfect picnic wines.

Moving west, we come to Touraine. The near-perfect climate and the local *terroir*, made up of chalk, gravel and limestone, produce wines of great complexity and harmony. The Coteaux de Touraine reds are delicate and scented, the rosés light and fruity and the whites may be bone dry, fully sweet or even sparkling. These wines are low in alcohol and lose their charm and *goût de terroir* if drunk much outside the region. Certainly the best known wines both locally and all over the world come from Vouvray and its little brother Montlouis. Here the *appellation* is exclusively white wine from the Chenin, but there are many styles of Vouvray: sometimes light and dry, less obvious and firmer than the Sancerre; sometimes semi-sweet with a lingering bouquet of honeysuckle; in great years a full, rich, golden wine capable of outlasting any wine in France; finally and perhaps best known as an elegant sparkler. The cellars, dug into the hillside or hewn out of the rock under the vines, are all open to visitors to appreciate that Vouvray is best *à la température de la cave*. One leaves determined to drink Vouvray more often.

The other great wines of the region, also east of Tours, are the reds from Chinon and Bourgueil. Both are grown from the Cabernet Franc, known locally as the Cabernet Breton. As in Sancerre, two different types of soil give different wines, lighter and more perfumed from the gravel, bigger and longer-lasting from the clayey limestone. Most Bourgueil and Chinon come from small holdings offering very much a hand-made wine for the enthusiast who may distinguish between the bouquet of raspberries on the former and violets on the latter. Tasted with the *vigneron* or drunk in the local restaurants, one cannot imagine a better wine. There is also a little rosé for summer drinking.

Below In the fertile Loire Valley region, the vineyards produce wines as varied as the châteaux they surround, from the delicate Coteaux de Touraine reds, to dry Vouvray whites and Sancerre.

Western Loire

The Loire river becomes wide and majestic in its valley heartland, as it makes its slow way by Tours, Saumur and Angers. By the time it reaches Nantes and is preparing to meet the sea, it carries a heavy load of shipping, and industrial buildings are installed along both its banks.

The region known as the Pays de la Loire is made up of many oddly-contrasting areas. Administratively, it is composed of the Maine-et-Loire, the Sarthe, the Mayenne, the Loire-Atlantique and the Vendée. The landscape varies from hills to swamp, the buildings from châteaux to Renault factories and the cuisine ranges from the jellied ox-tongue celebrated around the town of Cholet to the baby eels called *civelles* netted in thousands near the mouth of the river.

Beauty spots include the turreted castle in Saumur which René the Good, poet duke of Anjou, called 'the castle of love'. It still appears fairly much as it did in a fifteenth-century miniature preserved in the *Très Riches Heures du Duc de Berry* (now in the Condé Museum, Chantilly). But they also include the pastel sands of Atlantic beaches, the salt-marshes of Guérande and the pewter-coloured waters of the Brière marshes, each with their own attractions.

Introduction

Personalities who have left their imprint are as different as the Duchess Anne, Henri IV, Le Douanier Rousseau (the primitive painter who was born and is buried in Laval), and Gilles de Rais, the French 'Bluebeard', who attempted to carry out a pact with the devil at Tiffauges.

Le Mans is the capital of the Sarthe. Charlemagne was impressed by it when he stopped off on his way to Spain and would be even more impressed now if he happened to strike the Le Mans circuit during the motor-racing season and get caught up in the annual 24-hour race. There was once a huge and beautiful forest called after the city. What remains of it is known as the Forêt de Bercé. It rolls up hill and down dale and attains timeless magnificence in the Futaie des Clos where ancient oak trees, some of them hundreds of years old, spread their huge limbs in a living silence that Tolkien would have appreciated.

The pretty little Ervé river runs below the village of Saulges, where there are stalactite caves, inhabited in the Stone Age. Not far away a dour-looking building in neo-Gothic style is the Abbey of Solesmes, famous as the place where the Benedictine Order was re-established in France in 1833. Farnborough and Quarr in England are two of its offspring. It holds a particular place in European Catholicism and many great Frenchmen and women have chosen to spend a period in retreat here, among them the airman-writer Saint-Exupéry, author of one of France's best-loved books, *Le Petit Prince*.

Due south is a religious building with more bizarre associations. The Abbey of Fontevrault is the burial place of England's early Plantagenet kings. Henry II, his wife, Eleanor of Aquitaine and their son, Richard Lionheart, are all here. It has also been a religious community of mixed sexes, resulting in tales of bawdy misdoings that would have sent Chaucer wild with delight. Among the communities was one for repentant prostitutes. The founder upset the authorities by sleeping with an unclad girl novice on either side of him – but put it right by explaining that he was doing it to chastize the flesh by pushing himself to the very limits of temptation. They believed him, but drew the line at canonizing him.

Above Bicycles are everywhere in France, home of the marathon cycle race, the gruelling Tour de France.

Right The changing moods and colours of the Loire: the Château of Saumur looms above the town.

The building has spent part of its life as a prison. Jean Genêt, the avant-garde French writer, was a gardener there and used it as background material for his book, *Le Miracle de la Rose*.

Angers is on the Maine river. The landscape is still pleasant and green, a continuation of the Touraine countryside, but the nearby Loire is swelling with an abundance of tributaries, already spreading in anticipation of the sea. It can no longer devote itself entirely to the luxury of reflecting royal turrets and ancient spires but bends its back to a busy load of water traffic. Finally, it arrives at Nantes where there is thriving industry.

Officially, Nantes is the capital of the Pays de la Loire region but some local people still think of it as a Breton town, as it was until the French Revolution.

Nantes, a big, busy city of 400,000 people, has other claims to fame. It was here in 1598 that Henri IV signed the edict which gave freedom of worship to French Protestants. Jules Verne was born here. Gilles de Rais was hanged here. This brilliant soldier, ex-comrade of Joan of Arc, made a pact with the devil which involved the daily sacrifice of small boys. He had two châteaux in the area and it is said that the skeletons of his young victims are still sometimes unearthed, 500 years later. 'A phantom castle, mute, deserted and accursed, full of unspeakable memories', is how Flaubert described it.

One of the many fine beaches along the Atlantic coast is at La Baule, with a sheltering backdrop of pines mastering the unruly sand-dunes. South of the river mouth lies Les Sables d'Olonne, a long expanse of sand and a famous fish market. Near here is a *bocage* area of small fields and hedges, where the local peasants, known as the Chouans, joined forces with the nobility and fought a long guerilla warfare against the Republican Army of the Revolution.

North of La Baule is the Grande Brière, a region of waterbirds and marsh-dwellers who farm islets of arable land and in the summer turn peat-cutters. This area, once a lagoon, is largely flooded in winter. The people travel in flat-bottomed boats known as *blains*. Little island cottages rise almost out of the water, thatched with rushes cut from the swamps.

Above Further downstream, where the river widens, a summer sunset stains the water gold.

Towns and Villages

The Western Loire is clearly, as a glance at a map will show, a limb amputated from Brittany, with an admixture of Normandy and the Loire Valley thrown in just to confuse. It is also the geographical prolongation of the Loire Valley itself, the great river gathering speed and breadth as it flows through Saumur, Angers and Nantes, before soaking the marshes of the Grande Brière on the northern shore of the estuary, in the hinterland of Saint-Nazaire.

Le Mans is the first big town of the region as one arrives from the east. The city straddles a major crossroads between Normandy, Paris, Brittany and the Loire Valley. Like many French towns, the remains of 2000 years of history are ever-present, in the shape of the Gallo-Roman wall surrounding the old town. When

Above Farrier shoeing a horse, Western Loire. Horses are celebrated in this region in a special Musée du Cheval, housed in the Château of Saumur. The town also has a renowned cavalry school.

Above Old towns line the banks of the river Loire.

Right Nantes, former capital of Brittany, became part of the Western Loire region after the Revolution. Its prosperity came from overseas trading through its seaport, which is still important today.

Charlemagne passed through in AD 778, it was already one of the busiest cities in France. That description holds true to this day, with a large Renault car plant, paper mills, and factories churning out the chief gastronomic speciality of the Sarthe department *rillettes*, a pâté made from pork and fat. The *Circuit de la Sarthe* comes alive once a year as crowds pour in from all over the world to watch the gruelling 24-hour Grand Prix, probably the most famous of all car races.

La Flèche, on the Loir (a tributary of the Loire), and on the western edge of the Sarthe, contains a Jesuit college founded by Henri IV of France, the Prytanée or Royal College, where the French philosopher Descartes was a pupil from 1604 to 1614.

Angers, with its impressive, sooty-walled château, is traditionally an administrative city, as the seat of the former Dukes of Anjou. Since the last war it has diversified considerably, and industrial workers are now almost as numerous as white-collar ones.

The thickly-wooded region south of the Loire and west of Layon, the *bocage* of Les Mauges, with its valleys and its damp air, is a secretive, self-contained little world, and has been so for centuries.

The department of Mayenne is still predominantly rural. Its population is well below its nineteenth century peak due to the rural exodus, and only three of its towns have more than 10,000 inhabitants. Laval is one of the few industrial towns in the department, specializing in electronics, telephone equipment, and food-processing. Château-Gontier, an old town terraced up both banks of the Mayenne River and dominated by a Romanesque church, stands in contrast to Laval. Its cattle market is one of the biggest in France, and its traditional poultry and rabbit market will appeal to lovers of traditional French life.

Although it stands some thirty miles upstream from the sea, before the Loire splays out into its estuary, Nantes is nevertheless a major seaport and industrial town. Railway and subway carriages made here are in service all over the world. Food-processing and ship-building industries are based here, and there is also a big university.

The other important town in the Nantes area is Saint-Nazaire, scene of one of the most daring feats of arms of the World War II: on the night of 27–28 March 1942, British commandos sailed in and briefly held the port, leading the Germans to expend disproportionate efforts on securing it from further attack. The town was reduced to rubble by bombing in 1943, and after the war it was rebuilt on a spacious open plan. It is the chief centre of French shipbuilding, although today this has been hit by the slump in the industry.

Just a little further down the coast from Le Croisic, Le Pouliguen is both a popular holiday resort and a picturesque fishing port. Close by is its more fashionable neighbour, La Baule, surpassed only by Royan and Biarritz along the Atlantic Coast. La Baule possesses five miles of fine sand beach, a superb sea dike fringed with an unbroken succession of hotels and luxury villas.

Above Gathering camomile flowers, grown for herbal remedies. The mild climate here is ideal for horticulture, and there are numerous tree nurseries and fruit and vegetable gardens.

Châteaux and Churches

Angers is the historic capital of Anjou, an ancient province and centre of a medieval empire. Churches, abbeys and fortresses were legion, and despite the terrible ravages wrought by warfare and wilful destruction, a splendid legacy of architecture has survived.

The magnificent thirteenth-century pentagonal château at Angers, with its seventeen towers of granite ringed with schist, houses the world-famous fourteenth-century Apocalypse Tapestry, over 550 feet (168 metres) long, a superb and colourful work of art vividly depicting Saint John's vision of the end of the world. Among many other treasures at Angers, the fifteenth-century Maison d'Adam is a picturesque town house with its half-timbering and sculptures decorating its façade. Nearby, the Château de

Brissac, a five-storey seventeenth-century edifice built on an earlier fortress and a fine illustration of the transition between Renaissance and Classical architecture, contains some superb seventeenth-century furniture.

Beside its famous cavalry school, Saumur has many a treasure to offer, from its fourteenth-century château whose interior houses two good museums, the Musée des Arts Décoratifs and the fascinating Musée du Cheval (tracing the horse through the ages), to the remarkable sixteenth-century tapestries in Notre-Dame-de-Nantilly church. The town contains many delightful fifteenth-century houses, while nearby are two memorable châteaux – Montsoreau to the south, and Boumois.

Fontevrault, one of the area's main

curiosities, is an eleventh-century abbey, once a mixed community. The Plantagenets showered the abbey with gifts and chose to be buried there, and the handsome Romanesque abbey-church has a domed roof characteristic of the Plantagenet or Angevin style of architecture. One of the abbey's most fascinating features, however, is the twelfth-century kitchen, an octagonal pyramid surrounded by a cluster of turrets whose roofs are topped by twenty pepperpot chimneys.

All that remains of the once-prosperous Benedictine priory at Cunault is a twelfth-century church, famous for its beautiful sculptures, especially on its 223 pillar-capitals. The vaulting in the nave is typical of the Angevin style.

The little town of Le Lude is the site of a fifteenth-century château, square with

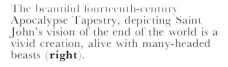

Above Seemingly impenetrable, the Fortress of Angers, with its seventeen towers, looms above a formal garden laid out in the old dry moat.

Above right The Château de Brissac, begun in 1614, contains a fine collection of seventeenth-century furniture.

The beautiful fourteenth-century Apocalypse Tapestry, depicting Saint John's vision of the end of the world is a vivid creation, alive with many-headed beasts (**right**).

round towers at each corner, that has been modified so often over the centuries that it has become a showcase for the evolution of architectural and decorative styles, from Louis XII through Henri IV to Louis XVI. The eighteenth-century wing has a superb oval room.

To the north-west stands the charming village of Asnières-sur-Vègre, whose thirteenth-century church is famous for its painted murals. More remarkable frescoes can be seen at the Notre-Dame-du-Rocher chapel at Lassay, near the Norman border.

Laval is the birthplace of the primitive painter Le Douanier Rousseau and of Alfred Jarry, author of *Ubu Roi*. Besides its beautiful old houses and Renaissance château, Laval has an unusual little church, Notre-Dame-de-Pritz, an eleventh-century edifice where chains of bricks outline the ruins of an earlier structure, and where not long ago some very interesting eleventh-century frescoes were discovered.

As the most important French port in the sixteenth and seventeenth centuries, Nantes was a prosperous town and the site of many splendid town houses, a prestigious ducal palace with lovely late Flamboyant ornamentation, and a Gothic cathedral that is none the worse for having been completed at the end of the nineteenth century. Its lofty interior is of white stone rather than the granite traditionally used in the area, and contains the remains of François II and his queen Anne de Bretagne. Their magnificent tombs are outstanding examples of Renaissance art at its height.

Renaissance carving at its height can be seen in the tomb of François II, Duke of Brittany, in Nantes (**above**).

Top Saumur stands, as splendid today as the contemporary illustration of it in *Les Très Riches Heures du Duc de Berry*, circa 1416.

Cuisine

There are two great vine-growing areas on the west coast of France and each one has a distinctive cuisine. Around Bordeaux, at the mouth of the Garonne, the wines are mostly red and the cooking rich with meat and pungent sauces; around Nantes, at the mouth of the Loire, the wines are mainly white and the food is light, with emphasis on fish, poultry and vegetables.

The region's most famous sauce is appropriately white (*beurre blanc*), delicately flavoured with shallots, white wine vinegar and butter. Elizabeth David, in her charming book *French Provincial Cooking*, writes that '*beurre blanc* started off as a sauce to counteract the dryness of freshwater fish such as shad and pike (but) it became so popular that now any excuse is good enough to eat it.' Both are commonly served *au beurre blanc*, but shad is also stuffed (*aloses farcies*) and grilled with sorrel (*alose à l'oseille*) while pike finds its way into the traditional freshwater fish stew (*pochouse*), where it is cooked in the company of perch, tench

and eel, well flavoured with garlic and wine, so abundant in this region.

Eels may be fished from the river but most are caught off shore. In cooking you will find them stewed in white wine (*bouilliture*) or baked into a mousse (*terrine d'anguilles*). Other sea-fish like bass may be boiled in a wine-flavoured *court-bouillon* and served with *beurre blanc*, or fried, or grilled – as sole is Chez Biret in Nantes – with tarragon (*sole à l'estragon*).

Second to fish as the main food of Nantes is the Nantais poultry, especially the small, tender ducklings. At Le Coq Hardi, they are roasted in their own juices and served with tiny green peas and young turnips. From the northern part of the region there are also chickens and ducks, which have the reputation of being equal to those of Bresse (page 186). La Flèche is a poultry centre and the philosopher Descartes, who once studied at the military academy here, presumably enjoyed the local *poule au pot*, *poulet à l'estragon* and *poulet rôti*. At the Restaurant Calandre, they are served with the

leeks of Touraine in a *béchamel* sauce (one of the basic French sauces).

Normandy is close and its influence is felt in the use of apples, cider and Calvados. Duck breast in cider (*aiguillettes de canard au cidre*) and rabbit in cider (*lapin au cidre*) are specialities of Le Mans. The Norman monastic tradition of cheese-making has also spilled over into the north of this region. At Entrammes, the monks have been making small, cylindrical cow's milk cheeses called Port-du-Salut for over 700 years. So popular are they, that little ever leaves the region, but a similar product, Port Salut is made in the dairy factories and is available throughout France. The authentic version is far superior. Another cheese derives from the windswept coastal area of Vendée, south of Nantes: it is the Fromage du Curé, named after the anonymous priest who is said to have first made it. This little square cheese, with its pleasant mild flavour, is also to be found in Brittany, where it is called Petit Breton, where it accompanies the cider.

Top The influence of Normandy can be seen in the use of Calvados, cider and apples in cooking. Rabbit in cider (*lapin au cidre*) is a speciality of Le Mans.

Above left Tender Nantais ducklings and succulent chickens rival those of Bresse for pride of place as the best French poultry. Market stall, La Flèche.

Above A trap is prepared for catching eels, a great speciality of the Nantes region: they are often served in white wine, or made into a *mousse*.

Wines and Spirits

The Western Loire comprises the departments of the Sarthe and the Mayenne to the north, the Maine-et-Loire and the Loire-Atlantique in the middle, and the Vendée to the south. Quite logically, the Loire departments are the main wine areas, although there is a little wine from the Sarthe: the Coteaux du Loir. Mostly white from the Chenin Blanc, they resemble the wines from Touraine. At Lhomme, the historically famous Jasnières, very like a Vouvray, is produced in ever diminishing quantities. With the exception of Champagne and Alsace, these northern vineyards of France are steadily disappearing. Drink Jasnières with the local *rillettes* or *lapereau à la crème* and you will agree it is a pity.

To the south-west, the first vineyards in the Maine-et-Loire around Saumur are really the extension of the Touraine even though they are classified as Anjou. The best red in all Anjou is Saumur Champigny, already celebrated in the Middle Ages, a rather more robust version of Bourgeuil or Chinon. The whites, planted in Chenin Blanc (also known as Pineau de la Loire) on both sides of the river, are always dry, light, but with a firm backbone. These remarkable, long-lasting wines have been overlooked in favour of easier tastes like Sancerre and Mâcon and on their own ground by Saumur *mousseux*. In the deep chalk cellars, these light wines take on their sparkle in the same way as Champagne, and no Saumurois can imagine a party without them. Perhaps more seductive is

the delightful Rosé de Cabernet (Franc) with just a blush of colour.

The river takes us to the ancient province of Anjou, where the softness of the climate is reflected in the wines. The greatest wines of this area are the sweet whites made along the Layon River, one of the many tributaries of the Loire. The Coteaux du Layon grapes are picked late in the autumn, often after the *pourriture noble* has attacked them, and make wine that is soft and unctuous, delicate but richly scented. The best areas are Bonnezeaux and Quarts de Chaume, the less fine being sold off simply as Anjou. A Quarts de Chaume from a fine year with its explosion of honeyed fruit, yet never over-ripe, is an unforgettable experience. Apart from these great and rare wines, sweet wines have fallen from popularity. Anjou is famous for its rosé, Cabernet (Franc) d'Anjou, but legally this must be semi-sweet; the current taste is for Rosé de la Loire, clean and dry. The Anjou red, with no grand *appellations*, is fruity and appealing, but cannot compare with the Touraine reds.

Just below Angers is the little village of Savennières, with its own *appellation*. The wines, all white and all from the Chenin grape, are dry, wonderfully elegant with great depth of flavour. The most famous vineyard is La Coulée de Serrant, covering a mere four-and-a-half acres, very much sought after. Savennières in general is much underrated, despite its reflection of the most notable characteristic of the Loire: harmony.

Left A vineyard in the Anjou area near Beaulieu-sur-Layon. The main grape type here is Chenin Blanc, sometimes called Pineau de la Loire. Anjou is also known for its rosés.

Above A lasting image of France is her fine old buildings surrounded by ripening grape-vines.

Right Western Loire wine labels.

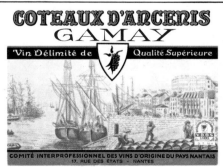

Wines and Spirits

As one leaves Anjou and heads towards the sea, the wines become less splendid, less complex. Mostly it is Muscadet country, but around the town of Ancenis, there is some soft fruity red made from the Cabernet Franc and the Gamay (at its best in the Beaujolais), attractive rosés and pleasant whites, a little less tart than those from the Pays Nantais. But most people drink Muscadet. This dry white is made from a grape which was originally known as Le Melon de Bourgogne, became quickly called Le Breton by the *vignerons*, and has ended up being known as Le Muscadet. It does have a slightly musky bouquet, but the main quality is the freshness, the soft fruitiness with a bite in the aftertaste. There are three *appellations*: Muscadet Coteaux de Loire, from around Ancenis. Muscadet de Sèvre-et-Maine, south-east of Nantes and Muscadet to the south-west. The Sèvre-et-Maine Muscadets, especially those from around Vallet have the best reputation, and the very best come from the *propriétaires-viticulteurs* who bottle their own production. Whether they are small local farmers or grand landowners of royal ancestry, like the Marquis de Goulaisne, it is the soil and climate which give the quality. With this advantage, some growers make a Muscadet *sur lie*, bottling the wine off its lees to keep the youthful freshness and a hint of sparkle. Muscadet is good with everything, except red meats, but the real enthusiasts of shellfish often prefer the Gros-Plant du Pays Nantais, a light, almost tart white wine of little finesse but great honesty. It tastes best within view of the sea. Many Nantais – and others – think it better than Muscadet.

Below The caves storing wines from around Saumur. The best red from this area is the robust Saumur Champigny, but the sparkling (*mousseux*) whites are the most well known.

Bottom The delicious sparkling wines of Saumur are made by the Champagne method (*la méthode champenoise*). Here, the wine-grower uses a 'thief' to fill the tasting glass.

Burgundy

Burgundy is a varied region, with forests and undulating terrains; harmonious, with a tapestried landscape of green, rolling country, serried vineyards and mellow towns.

It is named after the Baltic tribe which seized it in the fifth century. They intermarried with the Gauls and with Romans who had settled in the area. Their chief, Clovis, was baptized into Christianity by Saint Rémy. In the fifteenth-century *les grands ducs d'Occident*, the mighty Dukes of Burgundy, ruled lands that extended between the Loire and the Jura mountains, took in Lorraine, Luxembourg, Flanders, Artois, Picardy and a great deal of Belgium and the Netherlands. Their House was justly described as *de plus en plus princière et envahissante* and they were more than a match for the French crown.

Modern Burgundy is composed of the departments of the Yonne, the Nièvre, the Saône-et-Loire and the Côte-d'Or. Three rivers unite to form the river Yonne in the north-west, while the Loire forms the south-western boundary of the region.

Wine and fine food to go with it, architecture,

Introduction

landscape and the hearty goodwill of its inhabitants are more than enough to make any area attractive. Twenty centuries of tradition have gone into Burgundy's wines. The Romans planted them, the monasteries improved them, the Burgundian Dukes appreciated, encouraged and publicized them and the world acknowledges the results.

The most famous wine area lies on the slope of *La Côte d'Or*, a narrow strip which starts six miles (ten kilometres) south of Dijon and finishes thirty-one miles (fifty kilometres) further south at Santenay. Here, wine is a passion, an art, an income and a way of life.

The domain of the Clos de Vougeot (near Nuits-Saint-Georges) was acquired at the beginning of the twelfth-century by the Cistercians, whose strict poverty and self-denial provoked many generous donations. In the fourteenth century they enclosed it with the high walls that add the word *clos* to its name. The Renaissance château is sixteenth-century and in 1944 the building (but not the surrounding vineyards which are the property of about fifty *viticulteurs*) was bought by the Confrérie des Chevaliers du Tastevin.

The Feast of Saint Vincent is held each year in a different town. Saint Vincent is the patron of wine-growers and after mass is paraded with a nice blend of gaiety and respect through the chosen town, preceded by the Chevaliers. The event is held on the Saturday closest to 22 January.

For it, the wise men of wine wear their best bib and tucker, scarlet robes, with the *tastevin* (pronounced 'tâtevin'), the silver cup which is the symbol of their art, strung around their necks. The *tastevin* is a simple tool of the trade to any Burgundian wine-grower or connoisseur. Ornamental though it appears, it is designed for practicality not looks. It is flattish and wide to permit appreciation of the wine's bouquet, and decorated inside with raised surfaces for visual assessment of the colour.

The region lost one of the most beautiful churches in Christendom when the abbey-church of Cluny was broken up after the Revolution. It was the largest in the world until Saint Peter's in Rome took the title.

Cluny was the chief monastery of the fairly relaxed Benedictine order whereas Cîteaux, of which even less remains, was the future Saint Bernard's home for four years until he left to found Clairvaux on the border of Burgundy, in the Champagne region. From Cîteaux comes the word 'Cistercian' to describe Saint Bernard's strict ideals of austerity. The monks could eat nothing but vegetables seasoned with oil or salt and dark bread and they drank no wine –

Above The *tastevin*: an important utensil for the professional wine taster. This little silver cup is designed to allow a full assessment of the wine – bouquet and colour, as well as taste.

Right Summer in the countryside near Brancion. This is the Mâconnais, source of the red and white Mâcon wines.

painful preparations for the next life in a Rabelaisian setting like Burgundy.

Sens, well to the north and in the modern department of the Yonne, was one of the major religious centres of the Middle Ages. The motto of its cathedral, 'Campont', stands for the initial letters of the bishoprics of Chartres, Auxerre, Meaux, Paris, Orléans, Nevers and Troyes, over all of which Sens took precedence. Thomas à Becket lived there during his exile. The late twelfth-century Becket window shows Henry Plantagenet and Thomas together.

In the centre of Burgundy is the Morvan, a land of forest and water where thousands of wild flowers embroider the springtime banks of the Yonne valley.

This is the birthplace of many of the Christmas trees sold every year throughout the country. Acres of natural forest remain intact. Planting continues.

In the Middle Ages, Paris depended on the area for firewood and made use of two practical rivers, the Yonne and the Seine, to transport logs to the city. To begin with, they were carried in *margotats*, flat-bottomed boats, but a little thought produced the better, cheaper method of floating them to their destination by taming springs along the way and then releasing the water to speed the lumber. When coal replaced wood as fuel the trade stopped, but nowadays two charcoal factories supply the demands of the relatively new French craze for barbecues.

Towns and Villages

Some of Christendom's most celebrated abbeys are concentrated within the relatively narrow confines of Burgundy. The Benedictine abbey of Cluny, Cistercian abbeys of Cîteaux, Vézelay and Fontenay, all testify to the region's importance as a spiritual centre. But for centuries it has also been a major focus of cultural and political life.

When at the height of their power, in the fifteenth century, the Dukes of Burgundy made Dijon one of the most brilliant capitals of Europe. Poets and musicians such as Guillaume Dufay or the Englishman John Dunstable thronged the Ducal court, and to this day the city's many fine Gothic, Renaissance and Classical edifices lend to it something of the atmosphere of a small capital city. The Burgundians remained independent-spirited well after their incorporation into the kingdom of France.

Certain sites in the Côte d'Or are less imposing for what human artistry and taste, or centuries of careful vine-

Top An old Burgundian farmhouse.

Above Place François Rude, Dijon. Long associated with wine, fine fare and condiments (Dijon mustard is world famous), Dijon holds an annual food fair: a major rendezvous for gourmets.

tending, have laid before our eyes than for their historical resonance. Flavigny is a superb village on the plateau surmounting Mount Auxois. A few miles away is the hilltop site of what was the Gaulish oppidum of Alésia, where Vercingétorix, the last major leader resisting complete conquest of Gaul surrendered to Caesar, in 52 BC.

The attractive town of Montbard, not far from the Abbey of Fontenay, sits on the banks of the glassy Canal de Bourgogne. This was the birthplace of the Comte de Buffon (1707-1788), who was not a clown but a renowned naturalist, who played a major part, as Keeper of the King's Garden, in the development of botanical studies in the eighteenth-century. The Parc Buffon, with its shaded walks and rare plant specimens, stands as a memorial to his work.

Mâcon, another centre of the wine trade, was also the birthplace of the French poet Lamartine, one of the key figures in the nineteenth-century Rom-

antic movement, and briefly a leading personality in the provisional government after the Revolution of 1848. The town stands at a point where the Saône broadens out, making a fine stretch of water for rowing regattas.

Nevers stands at the confluence of the Loire and the Nièvre. Like many old provincial towns the impact of modern industry, springing up on the periphery, is being felt in the town centre too: the ancient palace of the Dukes of Nevers is now almost obscured by parked cars and traffic signals. When in the sixteenth-century Nevers was acquired by the Gonzaga family of Mantua, the new owners introduced the manufacture of ceramics, and for several centuries the city enjoyed fame as the home of Nevers faïence or tin-glazed earthenware. Italians also introduced the manufacture of glass figures, historical, mythological or allegorical, fashioned from glass rods and tubes, which were very popular in the sixteenth and seventeenth centuries.

Two earthenware factories still exist (there were eleven in the mid-eighteenth century), but not surprisingly their importance is now overshadowed by factories manufacturing railway carriages, rubber goods and otherwise engaged in mechanical engineering.

The principal industrial centre of Burgundy, Le Creusot, is one of the main steel-making towns in France. It was here, in the eighteenth century, that coal was first used in place of wood to smelt iron. The Schneiders founded their steel mills here in 1836, laying the basis for one of Europe's largest industrial dynasties.

The most northerly department of the region, the Yonne, possesses yet more celebrated vineyards around Chablis, on the river Serein, a tributary of the Seine. The town of Joigny, not far from the vineyards, contains some very attractive sixteenth-century houses around the Place du Pilori, whose original purpose is indicated by its name; it is hard to repress a thought for victims long past.

Left The Flamboyant Gothic tower at Clamecy. Close to the Morvan forest, this was a major lumber-exporting port.

Far left The ancient, mellow towns of Burgundy combine find old buildings with a sense of good living, in this region of excellent food and wine.

Châteaux and Churches

A cultural crossroads since Gallo-Roman times, Burgundy has an abundance of architectural and artistic riches. Here the Romanesque style flourished and took many forms; great and powerful abbeys such as Cluny and Fontenay were centres of religious and cultural life, and innumerable fine châteaux were built, many of which still stand today.

One of the earliest and best-preserved examples of Romanesque art in the whole of France, the abbey-church of Saint-Philibert in the old town of Tournus, dates from the tenth century. The slightly later, majestic Cluny style influenced the design of many churches. Not much remains of Cluny itself, once the most powerful abbey of the Middle Ages, whose church was the longest in the world until Saint Peter's in Rome was built. Characteristic of this style is the use of elegant, decorative sculpture on buildings. The church at Paray-le-Monial is a smaller copy of the one at Cluny.

The Cistercian order introduced a more austere form of art, the most impressive example of this being the abbey of Fontenay with its beautiful cloister and arcaded gallery. The earliest true Gothic cathedral in France is found at Sens, where the overwhelmingly spacious interior is accentuated by alternating pairs and clusters of slender pillars. Among the cathedral's 'Treasure', the second richest in France, are numerous precious items such as ivories, tapestries and ecclesiastical vestments. At Auxerre, the crypt of the Gothic abbey is in fact a Carolingian church where frescoes dating from 850 have been found. There are several other Carolingian crypts preserved in Burgundy, including those at Saint-Bénigne-de-Dijon.

Formerly a major cultural centre, Dijon is a veritable museum with an inexhaustable array of treasures, such as the fourteenth-century Chartreuse-de-Champmol built as a ducal mausoleum by Duke Philippe-le-Hardi. Although most of it was destroyed during the French Revolution, one can still admire the remarkable statuary around the calvary attributed to Flemish sculptor Claus Sluter. The elegant seventeenth-century houses of the former Place Royale designed by Hardouin-Mansart face another splendid building, the Palais Ducal.

Autun's importance as a major Gallo-Roman capital is recalled in two imposing arched Roman gates with upper galleries, as well as the remains of what may have been the largest theatre in Gaul. Saint-Lazare Cathedral, famous for its sculpture, in particular the *Last Judgement* tympanum signed by the sculptor Gislebert in 1135, was built on the model of Cluny. The Musée Rolin contains the celebrated *Nativity* by the fifteenth-century 'Master of Moulins'.

The great châteaux of Burgundy span many periods and take many forms, from fortresses to Italianate country-houses. The imposing thirteenth-century Château of La Rochepot (renovated in the fifteenth-century), has the gaily patterned roofs of varnished tiles that are so typical of Burgundy.

Burgundian Renaissance art is seen at its height in the beautiful Château of Ancy-le-Franc, with its fine frescoes.

Les Hospices de Beaune (The Hôtel-Dieu)

This spectacular building with its gaily patterned roofs is probably the world's most curious hospital. Founded in 1450 by Nicolas Rolin, Chancellor of Burgundy, as a charitable hospital for the poor, it has continued to operate as such ever since. Here the nurses still wear the hooded medieval costumes worn in the fifteenth century. The Hôtel-Dieu is one of the most beautiful of Gothic secular buildings: old timber galleries line a courtyard that was planned for open-air treatment; the gabled roofs with their little dormer windows are a mosaic of coloured, varnished tiles. In the Grande Salle des Pôvres, hospital beds are set in the original Gothic cubicles with their floor-length scarlet curtains. The hospital has a fascinating museum, and its treasured possession is Rogier van der Weyden's magnificent *Last Judgement* polyptych, commissioned by the founder.

Left The Renaissance Château of Tanlay, with its imposing entrance porch and domed towers overlooking the moat.

Top left The quiet serenity of Saint-Philibert, in Tournus, one of the earliest Romanesque churches in France.

Above This beautiful stained-glass window dating from the fifteenth century can be seen in Semur-en-Auxois. Called the 'Weaver's Window', it shows a craftsman cutting cloth.

Cuisine

Opposite Simple yet superb: crayfish lightly simmered in a *court-bouillon* (*écrevisses à la nage*).

Above The special pancake of Vonnas (*galette vonnassienne*).

Above Goat's milk is used for Burgundy's major cheese: the creamy Epoisses, which are made from a mixture of chilled evening milk, and milk collected early in the morning.

'Better a good meal than fine clothes' runs the local proverb, and though the good burghers of Burgundy do not lack for funds to clothe themselves, it is the stomach that dominates the scene. The best of beef, plump poultry, pork and lamb – simply prepared with wine-dark sauces and served on massive heavy plates – are the customary fare, washed down with glass upon glass of the splendid local wines. Enjoy your meal, of course, but follow the example of the burgher, who pays homage to his golden goose by selecting the wine first.

Then let the meal begin: indulge yourself, for who knows when next you will be offered such a treat? To tone your taste buds, take the parsleyed ham (*jambon persillé*), baked in white wine then marinated in a pot of parsleyed vinegar, or – if the evening is cool – a bowl of warming leek and potato soup, subtly flavoured with salted pork (*potée de Bourgogne*).

Now an hors d'oeuvre, a side-dish to stimulate without filling. Perhaps it should be snails, those famous snails of Burgundy, drenched in parsley and garlic butter (*escargots à la bourguignonne*) or a sunnier mixture of orange, spices, tomatoes and herbs (*escargots à la suçarelle*). But there are sometimes reservations about eating these tasty 'slugs in spiral shells' as the Romans called them. Never mind – there is always an alternative in this gastronomic fairground: per-

haps a slice of crisp leek tart (*flamiche*) or a poached egg dressed in Burgundy sauce, the rich yolk just merging with the sauce as the waiter hurries the dish to your table.

Yet this is only the beginning. Perhaps the first bottle of wine is running low? Very well, order another: this is no time for petty meanness. There are trout and carp in the kitchen and – if you are lucky – crayfish, all too rare these days, as any Frenchman knows. Simply simmered in a white wine *court-bouillon* (*écrevisses à la nage*), or baked in a rich cheese sauce (*écrevisses gratinées*), they are delicious. Sample them, as you might the sunset over the vineyards or your morning *croissant*, but do not become attached, for the secret of good eating is in the delight of the moment.

Now you will be ready for the meat, and what better than the deep red, marbled Charolais beef, prized throughout France but abundant only in Burgundy, its homeland? Perhaps tonight the chef has grilled steak, still pink and raw in the middle but well-toasted on the outside, served in a wine and madeira sauce (*entrecôte grillée Charolaise marchand de vin*), or with a thicker shallot and mushroom sauce (*entrecôte à l'échalote*); perhaps a well-stewed pot of boiled beef, veal and oxtail (*pot-au-feu bourguignon*), pleasantly flavoured with vegetables and a mixture of local herbs.

Cuisine

Boiled beef? Then this is the time for Dijon mustard. A traditional, rather silly jingle expressed horror at the idea of the one without the other:

De trois choses Dieu nous garde:
De boeuf salé sans moutarde,
D'un valet qui se regarde,
D'une femme qui se farde.

(God preserve us from three things: salted beef without mustard, a valet who admires himself, a woman who makes herself up.) Times have changed: servants are few and women not only use make-up but even run their own restaurants. Nevertheless Dijon mustard retains a place in the gastronomic heart. Since the fourteenth century, local vinegar-makers have used the recipe of Palladius son of Exuperantius, Prefect of the Gauls, to make what is now called *moutarde à l'ancienne*, which is coarse and piquant. Whenever a dish is called *à la dijonnaise* expect a sauce made with this type of mustard. A more modern variety is also available, milder and flavoured with wine and verjuice – made from un-ripened grapes – as well as vinegar.

Perhaps this is not your first Burgundian meal but the third or fourth? Then stick to the poultry, those plump young birds from Bresse, stewed to perfection in red wine (*poule-au-pot à la bourguignonne*) or fried in butter and lightly cooked in white wine and chicken stock (*fricassée de poulet au Chablis*).

For those in need of the gamier taste of wild meat, consider the saddle of hare (*lièvre à la Piron*), marinated in shallots and *eau-de-vie*, a clear liqueur, or baked venison cutlets (*côtelettes de chevreuil à l'ardennaise*). There is more chance of venison, and even wild boar (*marcassin*), at one of the better restaurants of the Côte d'Or than anywhere else in France.

And where are these restaurants? Shall one be singled out – like Les Trois Faisans in Dijon, with its succulent snails, braised ham with wild mushrooms and veal in mustard sauce? – and if not one, then why not many more? The successful restaurateur of Burgundy commands as much respect as the lawyer or surgeon, and probably more. Visit, if you can, the Rôtisserie du Chambertin in Gevrey-Chambertin, where the *patronne* – Madame Menneveau – is rated by some as the most skilful woman in the business; or one of the splendid tables of Beaune, where the annual wine auction in November draws discerning diners from all over the world: the Hôtel de la Poste, le Restaurant du Marché, l'Hostellerie du Vieux Moulin and many more. Follow your nose, consult the *patronne* on your choice, and you cannot go wrong, the Lameloise at Chagny,

the Hôtel de la Poste at Avallon, and the Espérance just outside Vézelay (specializing in the *nouvelle cuisine*) are probably the three best restaurants in Burgundy, all expensive.

So the main dishes are past, and your belly is distended, but the flush in your cheeks is a sure sign that things are going well. Now comes the cheese. Perhaps fortunately, this is not an important cheese region: only the rich, soft Epoisses will match up to the rest of your meal. You will, however, be excused the cheeseboard altogether if you can manage a dessert.

Here is a raspberry pudding (*pudding de framboises*), the like of which you have never seen, light with puff-pastry but rich with whipped cream. Or is it the redcurrant tart that catches your eye? Or the pears poached in a syrup of butter and sugar (*poires pochées au sirop*)? Burgundy is well endowed with fruit: it is a regular feature of the table and has given the honest burgher his favourite liqueur – blackcurrant *cassis*. Mixed with white wine, it serves as an *apéritif* called *kir*, named after Canon Kir, former mayor of Dijon, whose favourite drink it was. But after your meal, take it as a pleasant medicine: like all such potions, it aids digestion.

Left Goat cheeses maturing in a farmyard safe. Although not a great cheese-producing area, Burgundy Epoisses are well worth sampling.

Above *Gâteaux de foie blond* (literally 'cakes of pale liver') are made from the chickens of Bresse, which develop yellow livers from their diet of corn. A speciality of the Rhône region, it is also eaten in Burgundy.

Far left *Jambon persillé* (parsleyed ham) is baked in white wine, then marinated for a time in parsleyed vinegar: the perfect beginning to a Burgundian feast.

Wines and Spirits

Left The old château in the Clos de Vougeot, Côte de Nuits. *Grand cru* red wines are produced here, and the château is the headquarters of the Confrérie des Chevaliers du Tastevin.

Below Whatever the wine, the taster must inhale deeply, for this will tell him most about the wine: the taste in the mouth will confirm the information.

Burgundy is France at its most French. Where wine is concerned, it could claim to have the best that France has to offer, equal to Bordeaux. The vineyards start in the north in the region of Chablis in the Yonne department, then there is quite a gap until one reaches Dijon and the Côte de Nuits, Beaune and the Côtes de Beaune. Then farther south the vineyards run through the Côtes Chalonnaises into the Mâconnais region and finally the Beaujolais, which geographically belongs outside the Burgundy region. The immense variety of *appellations* and types of wine both great and small made in Burgundy is belied by the strictly-controlled grape varieties: Chardonnay for the whites and Pinot Noir for the reds; Aligoté for the minor whites and Gamay for the minor reds. Thus the richness of Burgundy lies in its ever-changing climate and the soil, and also more than anywhere else in France, in the hands of the man making the wines.

Chablis is the most northern vineyard in Burgundy and the soil is much the same as in Champagne, limestone-chalk. Here the soil gives the Chardonnay a toughness, even a mineral hardness which is quite unlike the fuller wines from the Côte de Beaune, Meursault, for example. At the best time, Chablis, particularly a *grand cru* or a *premier cru*, is at its best only after three to five years in the bottle. The seven *grand crus* are: Blanchots, Bougros, Preuses, Clos, Valmur, Vaudésir and Grenouilles, to which is sometimes added La Moutonne. These, along with perhaps Monts de Milieu, Montée-de-Tonnerre and La Fourchaume from the *premiers crus*, are the very best Chablis has to offer. They are the perfect accompaniment to shell-fish or light white meat dishes, especially *jambon au Chablis*. While the *appellation* Petit Chablis is not worth looking out for, except in the local restaurants, just plain Chablis from a good supplier can be very fine. It does not have the greatness of the *grand cru* but it does have the austere flintiness which is typical, and should be drunk within three years. Chablis is the vineyard the most exposed to frost in France. In 1957, the whole area was destroyed and in most years there is a risk up to the beginning of May. This limits the production and helps to explain the high price of its fine wine.

From the same region, a little to the west, come the reds and rosés of Irancy. Usually sold as Bourgogne-Irancy, the reds are made mainly from the Pinot Noir and tend to be a little harsh when young. Often the wine is simply vinified into rosé to keep the fruit. Next door to Irancy is a tiny village called Saint-Bris where the Sauvignon is planted (not too far from the Loire) which makes a delightfully fruity *vin d'apéritif*. Finally, throughout this area and even around Chablis, the Aligoté grape makes a pleasant, dry, white wine always sold under the name Bourgogne-Aligoté.

To the south-east for 100 miles (160 kilometres) there are no vines of importance until one comes to Dijon, the capital of the Côte d'Or. Here, the Burgundy wine country begins in earnest. For some wine-lovers, the only true Burgundy is from the twin Côtes, the Côte de Nuits and the Côte de Beaune. Certainly, Chablis apart, everything that is great in Burgundy is here.

The Côte de Nuits runs from Fixin,

Above Burgundy's ever-changing climate and different types of soil make for a wide variety of wines, with about one hundred *appellations contrôlées*.

Right Wines of the region.

Wines and Spirits

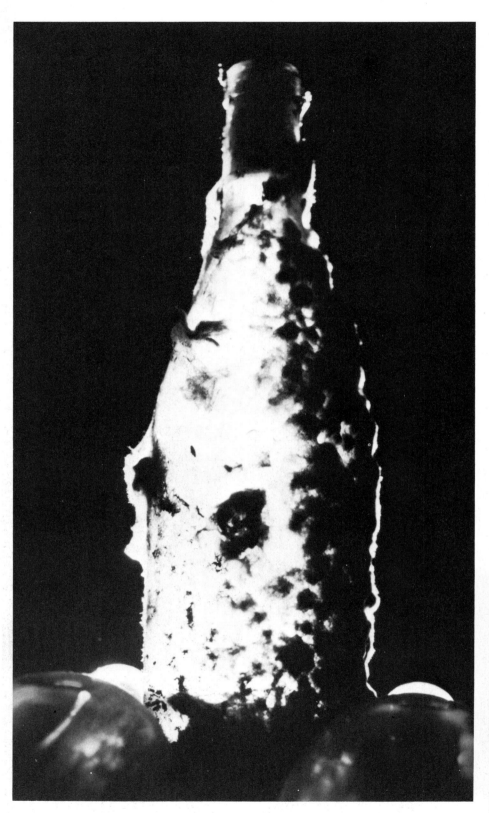

just south of Dijon, to Prémeux just south of Nuits-Saint-Georges. Descending the Route Nationale 74 is like descending a battle order of great names in wine. Gevrey-Chambertin, Le Chambertin, Morey-Saint-Denis, Chambolle-Musigny and Le Musigny, Clos de Vougeot, Vosne-Romanée-Conti, and Nuits-Saint-Georges. The habit has been for the bigger villages to tack onto their names the name of their most famous vineyard, hence the addition of Romanée, Chambertin, Musigny and Saint Georges. Here, virtually no white wine is made, the red being full-bodied and sinewy. Each *commune*, as the villages are known, has its own character. The wines from Musigny, Chambertin, Bonnes-Mares and the Romanée-Conti vineyards rival the best in the world. All Burgundy is expensive and great Burgundy very expensive, but there is no explaining the intensity of flavour and depth of subtlety which these wines can attain.

The Côte de Beaune starts at Aloxe-Corton, runs up to Savigny-lès-Beaune, descends through Beaune and follows the road up through Pommard, Volnay,

Above A fine bottle of white wine in the Caves Calvet, one of several good wine merchants based in Beaune, the wine capital of Burgundy.

Right From Bordeaux to Burgundy, Champagne to Chablis, the vineyards of France produce a greater variety of wines than any other country in the world.

Monthélie and Auxey-Duresses to the right and Meursault to the left. Then, following the Route Nationale 74, one leaves Meursault for Puligny-Montrachet, Chassagne-Montrachet and finally Santenay. The part north of Beaune is more famous for its reds. The wines from Aloxe-Corton and the *grand cru* Corton vineyards are the longest lasting in the Côte de Beaune, magnificent Burgundies, beautifully structured. The white wine from the Corton-Charlemagne vineyard has a leanness and a nuttiness which sets it apart from the richer, more stylish wines from Meursault. Savigny-les-Beaune makes elegant, pretty wines with more finesse than body, while the Beaune *appellation* is famous for its reds (95%) of distinction, grace and harmony. Pommard is probably the best known name on the Côte and produces well-made, sturdy wines of which the very best are from the *climat* Les Rugiens, while Volnay, the opposite in style, produces subtle wines of a rare distinction, for many the finest wines of the Côte.

While one can imagine replacing a red Burgundy with, say, a Pomerol from Bordeaux or a Hermitage from the Rhône, there is no wine which can substitute for the white Burgundies grown in the *communes* of Meursault, Puligny and Chassagne-Montrachet. The soil and micro-climates produce the wonderful, rich, almost overpoweringly full Meursaults, fully yellow in colour with a hazel-nut after-taste, the elegant and racy Puligny-Montrachets and the slightly firmer Chassagnes. Then come the *premiers crus* and *grands crus*: Les Pucelles, Les Caillerets, Bâtard-Montrachet, Chevalier-Montrachet, each with its particular facet of finesse or grandeur, and finally Le Montrachet, dry but sumptuous, powerful yet with a perfect distinction: the greatest dry white wine.

Going south, we leave the Côte d'Or and come to the department of the Saône-et-Loire. Here Burgundy continues in the Côte Chalonnaise. The reds merit comparison with the Côte-de-Beaune-Villages and are sometimes, as in the case of Mercurey, even on a par with the better wines. The whites of Rully, often like a Meursault, and Montagny are particularly good. The other reds

from Rully and Givry are a little light. A lot of Gamay is grown here to make a Bourgogne-Passetoutgrains (minimum $\frac{1}{3}$ Pinot Noir to $\frac{2}{3}$ Gamay) which is a pleasant Burgundy.

At the tip of the Saône-et-Loire we come to the Mâconnais, where the red wines are not of much interest, the Gamay being better in the Beaujolais and the Pinot Noir better in Burgundy, but where the great star is Pouilly-Fuissé. Here, on a chalky limestone soil, the Chardonnay produces a wine of no great depth, but of immense style and panache, sometimes with a tinge of green in the colour, an exquisite bouquet and great charm. The basic wine here is Mâcon Blanc, also from the Chardonnay but a minor wine compared to the Pouilly family, the other good villages around Fuissé being Loché, Solutré and Vinzelles. White wines from the Mâconnais are best drunk young.

Thus, while the white Burgundies run from the austere Chablis in the north to the racy Pouillys in the south, the red Burgundies tend to find themselves in the middle around Beaune and Nuits-Saint-

Above Jovial members of Burgundy's exclusive wine fraternity, the Confrérie des Chevaliers du Tastevin, enjoying a banquet in the Clos de Vougeot.

Wines and Spirits

Georges. The Burgundy-lover has a myriad of wines to choose from, since Burgundy, with only the Chardonnay and Pinot Noir as grape varieties, harbours more than sixty *appellations controlées*. Add to this the twenty to fifty *climats* (rather like a Château in Bordeaux), in each *appellation*, and you can see the complication. And add further that there may be six or seven *propriétaires* in each *climat*, who may bottle their own wine or may sell it to a *négociant*.

The most famous institution in Burgundy is the Hospices de Beaune, began with an endowment of vineyards and since then, wealthy landowners have bequeathed their vines to the Hospices, the produce of which is sold by auction on the third Sunday of November. The proceeds of this auction now makes the Hospices de Beaune the largest charity in the world. The sale at the Hôtel-Dieu, or Hospices, always coincides with the famous Trois Glorieuses of Burgundy, a weekend of feasting second to none. Anyone who has sat through the Chevaliers du Tastevin dinner at the Clos de Vougeot on the Saturday night, a large luncheon and then the Dîner aux Chandelles in the Cathedral in Beaune on Sunday night, and then the riotous Paulée de Meursault, a lunch for the *vignerons* where everybody brings his own wine and more, will understand the meaning of a *crise de foie* happily attained. Between them, the Hospices de Beaune and the Chevalier du Tastevin play an inestimable role in the fortunes of Burgundy. To be made a member of the order of Chevaliers, and to attend their banquets is a great honour.

Above right
Expressions of pleasure and anticipation as the tasters prepare to sample some Monthélie wine. This *commune* produces very good red and white wines some of which are sold at the annual Hospices de Beaune auction in November.

Right The vineyards of Burgundy can claim to produce the best wines France can offer, equal to Bordeaux.

Franche-Comté

This high region is the border territory of France which butts up against northern Switzerland. The Jura massif forms a dividing line, rising abruptly on the Swiss side, descending like a wooded staircase on the French side. A local saying goes:

'There is wind and snow for ten months of the year. The rest of the time the weather is superb'.

Many French holiday-makers know the region well, but not so many foreign tourists come here: they are put off by the distance and the climate. Winter holds the mountains trapped in silence. Melting snows break it with myriad streams and cascades. Later, crocuses shoot yellow and purple jets from the earth and gentians spread in a golden host as memorable as Wordsworth's daffodils and a great deal more practical, since they go to make a bitter-sweet gentian *apéritif*.

Those visitors who come this far find a prime sporting and skiing area. There is game in the forests and plenty of fish in the waterways, from crayfish (which are growing fewer) to carp, pike, trout and salmon trout. Mushrooms are gathered in the woods and the creamy cows patched with russet which graze on the high pastures, their bells tinkling by mountain streams, give milk for the Comté cheese, a type of Gruyère.

'*Comtois, tête de bois*' is another French saying about the region. The 'lumber-headed' quality referred to is the population's reputed stubbornness but it could equally well describe their dependence on the timber trade. The forests which, from the air, look like a well-combed pelt covering crests and slopes, are the area's traditional resource. Felling is controlled according to the speed of regrowth. Everything seems to be green – the rivers, the lakes, the forests and pastures – with a flicker of blue licking from the depths like the flame in a good emerald.

The importance of wood has influenced building styles. Wide-roofed, chalet-like houses are common in all snowy mountain areas but the excessively extended eaves in some villages here result from the

Introduction

fact that wood supplies were allotted in accordance with roof area. In other villages it was the number of householders or number of fireplaces which decided the matter and there the eaves are less exaggerated. La Joux forest contains superb pines known as 'the Spaniards', since they are supposed to have been saplings 400 years ago when Spain occupied this territory. The *Route des Sapins* (Fir Route) leads to a tree known as *le Président*, chosen to rule for life over lesser forest species. The present holder of the title is over 200 years old but cannot claim the grave distinction of 400.

It seems absurd that Spain should ever have administered this verdant slice of French countryside but it did. It became a Spanish possession through the marriage of Marie of Burgundy. Louis XIV finally reclaimed it in lieu of Queen Marie-Thérèse's dowry. Now it is divided into the modern departments of the Haute-Saône, the Jura, the Territoire de Belfort and the Doubs (pronounced 'doo').

The Doubs is also a river. (Most French departments are named after rivers.) It received its name from the Latin *dubius*, meaning 'doubtful', since it twists and doubles back so often on its way to the Saône that one doubts whether it will ever reach it. Most of the streams around here have minds of their own. One of their eccentricities is the habit of retreating underground every so often and then reappearing where they are least expected. In the thaw they thunder and somersault down waterfalls like the Saut du Doubs and the Hérisson. They also nourish great hydro-electric lakes.

Salt, so decisive a factor in human history, lies in deposits. Once this whole region was under the sea. The Romans used to flood the salt pans then boil away the water to obtain a saline deposit, using the handy supply of firewood. The Romans also enjoyed the spas, like those at Lons-le-Saunier and Salins-les-Bains. Arc-et-Senans was planned as a salt town in the eighteenth century but was never finished.

If you enter the Franche-Comté from Basel, you pass through the Belfort Gap, the usual route for old-time invaders. Beneath the Vauban fortifications, themselves founded on the ruins of a Roman temple of Jupiter, is the Lion of Belfort, forefeet outstretched, not roaring but presumably rumbling with achievement. He was carved by Bartholdi to honour the town's courage in defending itself in 1870 for 140 days against 40,000 Germans with a garrison of only 15,000 men. The Place Denfert-Rochereau in Paris contains a tame replica of this vast beast.

Besançon is the capital of the old province. The original part of the town is gathered into a picturesque knot by the Doubs river. Victor Hugo was born here, more by accident than good management since his father, who was in the army, was temporarily stationed in the city. The brothers, Louis and Auguste Lumière, pioneers of the cinema, were also born in Besançon in the 1860s.

The cathedral has an astronomical clock, fittingly symbolic, because this is the centre of French clockmaking. Besançon produces artifical fibres, too. The process was perfected here and the first factory in the world set up in 1890.

The pretty town of Dole, also on the Doubs, is where Louis Pasteur was born in 1822. His father was a tanner and his birthplace has been turned into a fascinating museum.

Artois, on the Cuisance river, is where he grew up and experimented on wine before turning his attention to milk. The region's vineyards lie south and yield white wines and yellow.

When the Romans were in power, wines from Sequania, as the area was called, were sometimes doctored with pinecones to give them a taste like Greek retsina. A regional beverage is made from soaking pine boughs. There is still a pine liqueur. Old people swear by it as protection against *la grippe*.

Above The famous pines of Franche-Comté encircle Lake Chaillexon, in the Doubs department. The major resource of the region, these pines have shaped the architecture and even flavoured a liqueur.

Opposite Baume-les-Messieurs, site of an ancient abbey, enjoys a respite from the long, hard winter.

Towns and Villages

Houses in Lods (**top**) and Ornans (**above**) line the very banks of the river in the Loue Valley. The painter Courbet was born in Ornans, and the surrounding countryside is celebrated in many of his works.

Besançon, Montbéliard, Sochaux and Belfort are sizeable industrial towns. Their prosperity fluctuates with modern conditions – some industries are declining, while others are taking their place. Villages in the Jura are taking a fresh lease of life as holiday resorts. True, watchmaking, diamond-cutting or ivory-carving, the kind of skills that grew up in the high valleys in the long winter nights, are being driven out of business by technological change. But pipe-making, as at Saint-Claude, flourishes today perhaps more than ever; the solitary artisans of 200, and even fifty, years ago, have been corralled in factories, and the brand names on these pipes, made from the renowned briars of France, are sold all over the world.

Besançon has been capital of Franche-Comté since 1676, after the capture of Dole, the former capital, by Louis XIV two years previously. Besançon is an important centre of cultural life in France. Its annual music festival attracts the world's finest musicians.

In the eighteenth and nineteenth centuries, the whole of the Jura area, both French and Swiss, was a region of skilled craftsmen, and the Swiss in particular developed watch and clockmaking to a fine art; this they brought to Besançon in the eighteenth century, and for 200 years the men and women who machined and assembled watches, ground lenses, built sophisticated mechanisms, formed the élite of Europe's industrial working class. They were among the earliest organizers of trade unions and of the International Working Men's Association, among whose leaders were Karl Marx and Bakunin. Even recently their strikes and factory occupations have been innovative, as when the workers at the famous LIP watch-factory at Besançon took it over and ran it themselves.

Besançon's earlier technological edge has, arguably, been taken over by Belfort, where computers and big electrical turbines are made. The city gained renown in 1871, when it heroically resisted the Prussians; in its honour Auguste Bartholdi sculpted the Lion of Belfort, a giant 72 feet (22 metres) long.

Just next door to Belfort, Montbéliard is the home of two big French industrial dynasties, the Peugeots and the Japys. This is a town of cotton-weavers and spinners, machine-tool makers, engineering plants, and, like Sochaux, soccer. Sochaux, a suburb of Montbéliard, was the birthplace of the Peugeot car firm and contains its largest car-making plant, one of the biggest factories in the

French provinces.

Nearby Salins-les-Bains was an ancient stronghold and spa town, like Luxeuil-les-Bains, where Roman legionaries came to bind up their wounds. These spa towns have none of the glamour and glitter of Vichy or Evian: they have an almost business-like air about them, people coming here strictly for the salt waters or the Jura air.

The Central Jura contains some of the highest peaks in the range. This is also the most frequented part of the Jura. Large villages stand at the entrance to valleys known as *reculées*, which penetrate the steep, western slopes of the massif. The attractive town of Poligny, where Comté Gruyère cheese is made, stands at the entrance to one such valley; Château Chalon, famed for its wine, lies at the entrance to another which culminates in the impressive mountain amphitheatre, the Cirque de Ladoye.

The former capital of Franche-Comté was Dole, whose beautiful town centre has remained substantially unchanged over the centuries. The powerful fortifications built by the Emperor Charles V in the first half of the sixteenth century withstood the French in 1636; but when Louis XIV came in person in 1674 the defences succumbed.

Above One traditional craft of this mountainous region has seen a new lease of life. Pipe-makers, once working as solitary artisans, now work in factories to produce pipes that are sold all over the world.

Left Five villages make up the winter sports centre of Métabief, where holiday-makers gather to ski and skate.

Châteaux and Churches

Due to its geographical position, set high in the Jura mountains, and with a long history of wars and invasions since Gallo-Roman times, Franche-Comté has traditionally needed most of its energies to survive and rebuild, so that the arts never flourished here to the extent they did elsewhere. Despite this, however, the region has its share of riches.

A major landmark of twentieth-century architecture is Le Corbusier's Notre-Dame-du-Haut Chapel built on a hill with a backdrop of trees and rocks at Ronchamp near Lure. A building whose requirements are no longer bound by the technical limitations of earlier ages, it stands as a free-form sculpture. The interior, made dramatic by the architect's use of space and light, is pierced by mellow shafts of light from deep-set windows. The roof sweeps up to form a huge canopy.

The remains of Vauban's great fortifications, which once protected the vulnerable town of Belfort, include the seventeenth-century Porte Brisach bearing the arms of the Sun King. Close by is Bartholdi's monumental statue of a lion.

South-east of Besançon stands the twelfth-century Abbey of Montbenoît, whose cloister is a mixture of Romanesque and Gothic architecture, and whose church is renowned for the magnificent sixteenth-century carvings on its pews.

Further north is the picturesque town of Ornans, birthplace of Courbet, who drew much of his inspiration from the area. The house in which he lived, a handsome eighteenth-century building, is now a museum which contains several of his works, while the town also retains many sixteenth-century corbelled timber houses, reflected in the waters of the river Loue.

Besançon's architectural and artistic legacy goes back as far as Roman times, as can be seen from the ancient Porte Noire, so called because of its age-old, blackened patina. Among the many Renaissance buildings and town houses, the sixteenth-century Granvelle Palace stands out. Traces of the long Spanish occupation can be noted in some architectural details. The twelfth-century Saint-Jean Cathedral harbours a remarkable Fra Bartolomeo of the *Virgin with the Saints*, painted on wood. The

Musée des Beaux Arts contains an excellent collection of Dutch, French, Italian and other paintings, and a fine collection of drawings including works by Tiepolo and Géricault.

To the north stands the elegant, late eighteenth-century Château of Moncley, designed by a pupil of Claude-Nicholas Ledoux, that remarkable architect and man of vision who was responsible for the startlingly modern Saline Royale (or saltworks) at Arc-et-Senans, south-west of Besançon. Although the project was never completed, it is an unusual example of early industrial town-planning and Ledoux is considered a forerunner of modern architecture.

At Lons-le-Saunier, one may be tempted to stroll along its picturesque sixteenth-century arcaded Rue du Commerce before taking a look at the eleventh-century Saint-Désiré church, one of the oldest in the area. The local museum houses some Gallo-Roman and Merovingian objects of interest, as well as paintings by Breughel and Courbet.

The substantial remains of the thirteenth-century fortified castle of Le Pin, a rugged but good-natured looking place, with a rustic timber gallery under the rafters of the courtyard; the solid, square keep with its *chemin de ronde* are pointed reminders of troubled times.

Saint-Claude Cathedral in the town of the same name is a fourteenth to eighteenth-century edifice, renowned for its magnificent fifteenth-century carved pews of superlative craftsmanship.

Left Designed by Le Corbusier, one of the most influential architects of the twentieth century, the Chapel of Notre-Dame-en-Haut stands at Ronchamp like a giant sculpture.

Top The belfry of the Abbey at Baume-les-Messieurs, founded in the sixth century by an Irish monk. Monks from this abbey were founders of Cluny, the major religious and cultural centre of the Middle Ages.

Above Modern stained-glass by Jean Bazaine in the baptistry of Sacré-Coeur at Audincourt, near Belfort.

Cuisine

Gruyère: one of the great French cheeses and the pride of Franche-Comté cuisine. It is made from cows' milk, enriched by the lush mountain pasturelands (**above**).

Most versatile of cheeses, Gruyère (**right**) is firm enough for grating, yet ideal to melt smoothly in sauces and *fondues*.

Below The process of making Comté cheese in a local village *co-opérative*.

France meets north-west Switzerland on the peaks of the Jura, the forested mountain range that runs from the Rhône Valley near Lyon to Basel on the Rhine. Among its slabbed peaks there run a thousand ice-cold streams, which gather into rivers flowing west: they irrigate the vineyards of Arbois, the broad green pastures inhabited by dairy cows and – dropping to the plain – they irrigate the cereals and vegetables that grow in the plain.

Here, not far from Besançon, is Dole, where the father of microbiology, Louis Pasteur, was born. His discoveries led to the process of pasteurizing milk, thus preventing it from souring so quickly. But alas, the heat treatment tends to spoil the flavour of the milk. Raw milk, and cheeses made from it, still hold the smell and taste of the pastures, and this is true of the region's greatest cheese – the Comté Gruyère.

Few cheeses are more adaptable to cookery than this: it is firm enough to grate into omelettes, soufflés and cheese sauces (*sauces au gratin*), yet soft enough to melt quickly and smoothly. This makes Comté ideal for a melted cheese pot (*fondue*), for the local cheese tarts (*tartes au fromage*) and cheese fritters (*palets Prinsky*). Comté is a high-pasture cheese, made by groups of herdsmen in their

mountain huts called *fruitières*, and ripened for six months in the valley warehouses. Other local cheeses are the blue-veined ones from Gex and Septmoncel, some pleasant goat cheeses (*chèvres*), and an unripened curd cheese (*cancoillotte*) which is sometimes blended with butter and garlic before serving: a rich but delicious combination.

The second great food of the Jura is fish, which abound in the local rivers: pike is the humblest, best when stuffed with herbs and pork or chicken mince (*brochet farci*); trout has more flavour and requires only simple frying (*truite meunière*) or a light cream sauce (*truite à la crème*) to bring the best out of it; but the finest of all, without a doubt, is the rose-pink salmon trout, baked in its own juices (*truite saumonée au four*) and served with a thick sauce – perhaps a green herb and butter sauce (*sauce verte*), perhaps the local walnut and horseradish sauce (*sauce raifort aux noix*) which so impressed the culinary encyclopaedist Escoffier when he visited the region over a century ago.

Among the vineyards on the lower mountain slopes there are numerous hares, and you will find them cooked in many ways, at the Hôtel de Paris in Arbois stewed in local wine (*chaudronné de lièvre au vin d'Arbois*); marinated in wine then roasted and served with a shallot sauce (*lièvre rôti en sauce de la Vieille Charlotte*); or packed into pâté (*pâté de lièvre*). Poultry is also popular: the *coq au vin* and *poularde à la crème* are both excellent.

Local vegetables are served with every meal, either as a soup or with the main course, simply garnished with a light dressing or a heavier cheese sauce. Most of the soups are thick, and two in particular bear investigation: cherry soup (*soupe aux cerises*) and nut soup (*potage aux noisettes*). Of the vegetable dishes, try the mushrooms stewed in white wine and tarragon with fried bacon (*fricassée de champignons*), potatoes slowly baked with ham (*pommes boulangères*) and stuffed cabbage (*fechuns*).

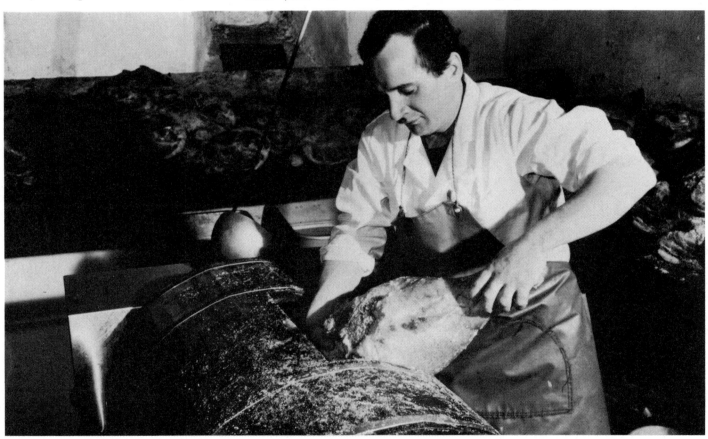

Left This special chicken dish, served in Arbois, would not be found outside the region. Called *coq au vin jaune aux morilles*, it is made with the rare, golden-coloured *vin jaune*, produced here and nowhere else.

Above Plump legs of ham in Franche-Comté are dried, then smoked in this special smoking-box, and eaten thinly sliced.

Wines and Spirits

The ancient province of the Franche-Comté covers the departments of the Haute-Saône, the Doubs and the Jura, the last being the only producer of wine. Centred on Arbois, one of the prettiest wine towns in France, the vines grow on well-exposed slopes parallel to the Côte d'Or in Burgundy, the next-door province. Phylloxera and the disinclination of the *vignerons* to continue working the near-impossible slopes have severely reduced the production, but the range remains considerable: whites, reds, rosés, sparkling wines and the very rare *vin jaune* and *vin de paille*, to say nothing of a better than usual *marc*.

The best known *appellations* are Côtes du Jura and Arbois, the latter being better and more expensive. For the whites, the Chardonnay makes a lighter less typical wine than the Savagnin (seen as the Traminer in Alsace) which is fuller and has a nutty character. For the reds, the Poulsard and the Pinot Noir are elegant and quick-maturing, the Trousseau giving a wine with more colour and *goût de terroir*. The rosés, pleasant and dry, have less character than the reds. The little commune of L'Etoile has its own *appellation* producing only white wines, but the finest of the region. The marriage of wine and food in the Jura is perfect. Both bring out the best in each other. Nothing is as good with a *coq au vin jaune et aux morilles* at the Hôtel de Paris at Arbois than a dry white *vin d'Arbois*.

The two most remarkable wines from this region are not strictly table wines. They are *vin jaune* and *vin de paille*, and they are both miracles of wine-making. The *vin jaune*, of which the best is Château Chalon, is made from very late-picked (often in December) Savagnin grapes, slowly fermented and then racked off to spend a minimum of six years in oak casks with no topping-up allowed. In principle, the wine should turn into vinegar but, in fact, turns into a golden-coloured wine with a curiously heady bouquet and a distinctively nutty finish. It gives something like the impression of a dry sherry but is more interesting. The *vin de paille* is a dessert wine made from grapes which have been dried and concentrated on round straw mats until the Christmas following the vintage, then pressed to obtain a rich amber-coloured nectar. The lucky priests in the Jura used to serve *vin de paille* as altar wine.

In case one is ever at a loss for an *apéritif* in France, one of the most curious is Suze, made from the gentian.

Above This region is the source of a rare and remarkable wine: *vin jaune*. It matures in the cask for six years, and becomes golden in colour. In this cellar near Arbois, the bottles are sealed with distinctive wax caps. The best *vin jaune* comes from the Château Chalon (**left**).

Poitou-Charentes

A region of plains, Poitou-Charentes comprises green stretches of pasture land, expanses of gentle hills swept by warm Atlantic breezes, and red-tiled roofs. It also embraces the elegance of La Rochelle on the coast, its timbered houses covered with slate tiles to protect them against the salt air, the sweep of marshes and sand and the offshore islands – the Ile d'Oléron (largest of France's islands after Corsica), the Ile de Ré and the Ile d'Aix.

Each of these islands is different. On the Ile d'Oléron the biggest industry is oyster-farming. The Ile de Ré, the 'bright' island, is so-called because of its brilliant sunshine. Small whitewashed cottages laden with climbing roses and overhung by fig trees

Introduction

give it an almost Mediterranean look. It used to be famous for salt and wine but now is more or less given over to market-gardening, with asparagus one of the specialities. There, some of the older women still occasionally wear a head-dress known as the *quichenotte* or 'kiss not'.

The Ile d'Aix is where Napoleon spent his last days in France before giving himself up to the English. Mother-of-pearl provides the basis for local crafts. The mainland fringe is known as the Coast of Light.

From Les Sables d'Olonne to Esnandes and stretching as far as Coulon is the *marais poitevin*, the marsh of Poitou. The watery region of 'Venise Verte' (Green Venice) lies inland. Near the coast is open land interrupted by dykes. Drainage work has been going on for hundreds of years but most of it was undertaken in the seventeenth century.

'Venise Verte' is a world of quiet canals overhung by elms, willows and poplars, where black-and-white cows graze on small islands. As islets arose from the swamp, tradition allowed anyone to take possession, providing a hut was built complete with roof, a fire was lit in the hut and the owner-to-be spent the night there. In winter the canal water is almost black. In summer every canal is a tunnel of complete greenness, for the trees meet overhead and weed covers the surface of the water.

All transport in the marshes is by boat and the flat-bottomed iron craft are pushed along with poles. Even the cows and hay are taken from place to place in this way and one of the sights of the *marais* is a marriage party, the bride in frosty white, punting to church in splendour through an arch of leaves.

The marsh-dwellers are traditionalists, proud of being different and well aware of the photogenic charm of their pretty little houses reflected in canal water, each one with a miniature landing for the boats. Small eels and a type of white bean called *mojettes* are typical of their cuisine.

Cognac, to the south-east, produces sterner stuff, for most of the great brandies of France come from here (rivalled only by Armagnac). The river Charente flows through the region and the finest brandy-producing area is around the town of Cognac itself. The whole thing was an accident in the first place for, some 300 years ago, surplus wine from a succession of good harvests proved an embarrassment as much as a blessing. It was distilled, to make it less bulky for storage, then placed in old casks of oak from the Limousin and forgotten. Some years later the owners sought out and reopened the casks, tasted the contents, *et voilà* – cognac! Ever since no one has dared vary the magic technique and the liquor is still aged in casks of Limousin oak which must, themselves, be mature first, since new wood spoils the brandy. Thirty to forty years is the period during which it continues to improve. After that there seems to be no further progress. Brandy, unlike wine, will not age in the bottle.

Some important historical events have taken place in Poitou. It was in this old province that Clovis, King of the Franks, defeated the Visigoths under Alaric in AD 507. Even more significant for European history was the battle in which Charles Martel withstood the Saracens under Abd-er-Rahman in AD 732. This was the furthest point of Arab penetration into Europe. Had Martel failed, the history of Christianity in the West would have taken a different turn.

Parts of the area have, at times, fallen under English domination, with the marriage of Eleanor of Aquitaine to Henry II of England and with the Black Prince's victory over King Jean le Bon in 1356. The medieval chronicler, Jean Froissart, has described the battle – how Jean le Bon defended himself with a battle-axe and finally surrendered to a young knight from Artois who was fighting on the English side because he had been banished from his own country. Froissart has also described the supper after the fight when the Black Prince himself served the vanquished king's table, proclaiming himself unworthy to sit at it and eat alongside so valiant a foe.

Above 'Venise Verte' (Green Venice) is a region of quiet waterways overhung with trees; small islets of grazing land; and marsh-dwellers punting in flat-bottomed boats.

Right Sparkling sunshine warms the Ile de Ré, the 'bright island', lying off the Charente-Maritime coast.

Towns and Villages

For many people, La Rochelle is the most delightful town in western France, a kind of maritime Bruges, a city of infinite elegance. It was a Protestant stronghold for many centuries and was an important centre for the brotherhood of religious knights, the Templars, founded in the twelfth century. Again and again it has been the victim of siege, the most famous being that against the armies of Louis XIII, when Richelieu built a massive sea wall to stop the citizens receiving supplies by sea. Much of the wall still exists as do the two fourteenth-century towers at the harbour entrance, from which a massive chain once hung to prevent the entry of unwanted vessels. The harbour traffic was until recently confined to fishing craft, and La Rochelle is the fifth biggest fishing port in France. Now, with the construction of the new Richelieu Harbour, commercial trade is growing.

The Renaissance Hôtel de Ville is the most attractive town hall in France, and all around it are narrow streets lined with pavement cafés. La Rochelle today is famous as 'the ecology-minded town of France'. With its celebrated mayor as its moving force, this city has become an example of what can be done to improve the quality of life. The old town has been tastefully restored; a major annual contemporary arts festival has been instituted, a new Maison de la Culture and Museum of the New World are under way. To solve the car problem, many streets in this ancient town have become traffic-free zones; 700 free municipal bicycles are provided for public use.

The town of Niort stands on the edge of the *marais poitevin*, the lush canal-crossed pastureland where you can ride in flat-bottomed boats called *plattes*. The town is dominated by the remains of a château-fortress built by England's Henry II, where a collection of local costumes is housed. A major industry of this sizeable town is the curing of soft chamois leather and the manufacture of gloves. Poitiers, formerly the capital of the ancient province of Poitou, was the scene of two major battles: the defeat of the Visigoths in AD 507 and the defeat of the Saracens in 732. The town fell into decline after the Wars of Religion, but today its university has become an important centre once again, and industry has brought prosperity.

Strategically placed on a high plateau, Angoulême, the 'town built on a balcony' is protected by immense ramparts. The making of water-marked paper was a major industry here in medieval times

and today there are several paper factories. Another traditional industry still continuing is the manufacture of *pantoufles charentaises* (felt slippers). An experimental industrial scheme has begun at Angoulême, now the site of heavy engineering works, in which factories are built in country areas to provide a healthier life-style for the workers. Factories are small and workers collaborate with management in decision-making.

Further down the Charente is Cognac, a pleasant, bustling, little town with a delightful park in which stands the ruined château of the royal Valois family. From the castle above the town you can look down on the brandy sheds and cellars that stretch along the river banks, repository of the twenty million bottles made here every year. Visits are allowed, but are carefully controlled, for Cognac must be matured in near-darkness, silence and a constant temperature. Cognac is an ideal centre from which to visit Saintes, which has some remarkable Roman remains.

For visitors preferring a seaside resort, that part of the coast known as the Côte de Beauté, just north of the Gironde estuary, is ideal. Small resorts, sheltered by woodland, stretch around the peninsula. At La Rochelle there are ample yachting facilities, with an international regatta held annually during the first week of June.

Above Fourteenth-century towers flank the entrance to La Rochelle harbour, once the major port for trade with Canada. It remains an important fishing port today, and is also the finishing point for an annual yacht race from Plymouth.

Opposite Rebuilt after World War II, Royan is a popular seaside resort, with long sandy beaches. The building in the background is the remarkable church of Notre-Dame, designed by Guillaume Gillet.

Top right The succulent oysters of this region are grown in farms along the coast. Here tiles with spats (oyster spawn) attached are threaded on a line, to be replaced in the sea.

Below Colourful dances in the street are a feature of local festivals.

Châteaux and Churches

Like Limousin, Poitou-Charentes is a land of transition, a bridge between north and south, which is rich in Roman remains, fine Romanesque churches (the legacy of medieval pilgrimages to Compostella in Spain), and castles, reminders of centuries of warfare between the English and the French, the Catholics and Protestants.

All along the Gartempe river between Saint-Savin and Montmorillon there are so many churches and secular buildings decorated with fifteenth-century murals that the area is known as 'the valley of the frescoes'. The most famous, though, are the twelfth-century scenes from the Bible at the abbey-church of Saint-Savin, painted in yellow and red ochre. Full of life and movement, they are precious examples of Romanesque art.

Châtellerault, to the north, has a famous sixteenth-century bridge, the Pont Henri IV with fine twin towers. Poitiers, where the advance of Islam was halted in a famous battle in 732, is the site of a vast number of churches. The ornate façade of the Notre-Dame-la-Grande Cathedral, covered in carvings and sculptures represents the pinnacle of Romanesque Poitevin art; inside, its columns are adorned with a variety of gaily-coloured geometric patterns. Poitiers' riches do not stop there, however: the nearby brick Baptistry of Saint-Jean dates from the fourth century and is probably the earliest Christian building in France; the impressive Gothic Saint-Pierre Cathedral with three naves and a vast apse, still retains its original thirteenth-century carved choir stalls. The church of Saint-Hilaire-le-Grand is unique in France with its seven aisles and nine cupolas, a forest of pillars and elaborately carved capitals ornamented with beasts.

Thouars is another walled town that has preserved its Gothic bridge and fortified gate, a number of corbelled and half-timbered brick houses and the fifteenth-century Saint-Médard church, a Romanesque building combining several unusual features: an ornately-carved façade, a Gothic rose-window and the north door which shows Moorish influence.

At Sanxay, south-west of Poitiers, an entire Roman town was unearthed in the nineteenth-century, which dates from the first to the third century and comprises a theatre which could seat 10,000 spectators, a temple, forum and baths.

The medieval walled town of Parthenay was considered to be impregnable and could only be entered by way of the Pont-et-Porte-Saint-Jacques (built in 1202), a narrow stone bridge with a solid, twin-towered gateway. The main street and its medieval houses have hardly changed since the era when Parthenay was an important stopping-place for pilgrims on their way to Compostella.

Farther north is one of the finest Renaissance châteaux in France, Oiron, where Madame de Montespan (mistress of Louis XIV) lived out her life after her fall from royal favour. It is famous for its grand arcaded gallery and its splendid murals with scenes from the *Iliad* and the *Aeneid*, framed by allegorical *trompe-l'oeil*

Left The Roman Arch of Germanicus, Saintes. The architecture of southern France often shows the influence of Roman buildings, in contrast to that of the north.

paintings.

At Niort, not far from the house where Madame de Maintenon (another of Louis XIV's mistresses) was born, stands the twelfth-century keep built by Henry II and his son Richard the Lionheart. The silhouette of its massive square, twin towers looms above the river. Today, it is a museum housing a collection of regional costumes.

At Aulnay a splendid example of Poitevin Romanesque stands in the midst of an old cemetery surrounded by cypresses. This is the splendid church of Saint-Pierre-de-la-Tour, built of lovely pale stone and sumptuously ornamented, with friezes, again with a trace of an eastern influence.

Despite its unprepossessing appearance, Saintes has a long history both as a Roman city and as an important place on the pilgrim's route to Compostella, and it has a rich architectural legacy to show for it. There is the first-century Roman Arch of Germanicus, the ruins of a huge amphitheatre and baths.

Above One of the great French Renaissance buildings, the Château of Oiron was once the home of Madame de Montespan, mistress of Louis XIV.

Below left Surrounded by water, this curious oval fortification looks virtually impenetrable. It is the Napoleonic fort Boyard, lying off the coast of the Ile d'Aix.

Left The Tour Saint-Nicolas and Tour de la Chaîne at La Rochelle. A great chain used to stretch between them when the harbour was closed to ships.

Above The portals of Notre-Dame-la-Grande, Poitiers. The intricate carvings and patterns on this façade represent the quintessence of Poitevin Romanesque.

Cuisine

Though the terracotta-tiled roofs, the vineyards and the bright, broad skies of Poitou-Charentes speak of the distant Mediterranean, the people of this region are more northerly in nature: the farms, the dialect and the traditional cuisine are all akin to those of the Loire Basin and, beyond it, Normandy. Dairy cattle are numerous, providing vast quantities of milk for butter and cream; the soil is still light enough for cereals and vegetables, there are many small farms with pigs and fowl, and the hills are rich with game.

The coastline is sandy and flat. Many of the fishermen who once plied this shore have emigrated to Canada and other more prosperous places. The oyster beds remain, however, and many kinds of fish and shellfish are to be found at the fortified port of La Rochelle. Two specialities here are deep-sea bass stuffed with eggs, spinach and herbs (*bar farci*) and mussels in a white wine and cream sauce (*mouclade charentaise*). Eel is also popular and in the spring, when the young ones return from the spawning grounds off the West Indies, they are plentiful and cheap. You will find them boiled in a *court-bouillon* of white wine and vegetables (*chaudrée*) or stewed in butter (*fricassée d'anguilles*). At Le Faisan in Richelieu you can also enjoy fresh-water eels, cooked in the local Vouvray wine.

Of the rich variety of fowl, duck is commonest, usually dressed with herbs and slowly roasted (*canard rôti au four*) or baked with oranges in an earthenware pot (*terrine de canard à l'orange*). Duck liver has a rich, delicate flavour and is served with bilberries. Other good dishes on the

Above An old woman grilling eels in the market.

Centre Harbourside restaurants in the old part of La Rochelle serve excellent *fruits de mer*, particularly oysters fresh from the offshore oyster-beds.

menu are mussel soup (*soupe aux moules*); capon cooked in old local wine (*poulet au vin*) and a fine cheese board.

The main cheeses of the region come from the east, where goats and sheep are pastured on the foot-hills of the Massif Central. Most of them are sold fresh, and few are available outside the region. If you find them, try the Fromage de la Mothe, dried for two weeks between vine leaves; the Chabichou and Carré de Saint-Cyr, made from goat's milk; and the delicious triangular sheep's milk cheese, l'Aunis. Any of these may be used in the traditional cheese tart (*tourteau fromager*). Charente butter is the best in France, along with that of Normandy.

The eggs of Poitou are marvellous. Here the chickens are mostly free to peck around the farmyard, instead of being cooped up in factory batteries, and it shows in the flavour. Some of the more interesting egg dishes are boiled eggs with tripe (*oeufs à la tripe*); poached eggs on fried bread with meat sauce (*oeufs pochés à l'huguenot*) and, by the sea, poached eggs with mussel sauce (*oeufs du pêcheur*) and mussel omelette (*omelette aux moules*).

Towards the south, the nut tree estates grow larger: chestnuts, almonds and walnuts begin to take their place as everyday cooking ingredients. Salads may be dressed in vinegar and walnut oil (*salade à l'huile de noix*); goose stuffed with chestnuts (*oie de Poitou aux marrons*) becomes a popular Sunday lunch; and the desserts are flavoured with almond paste or chestnut purée. The nougat, made from ground almonds and sugar, is another excellent speciality of the region.

Charles Barrier, masterchef

Charles Barrier is one of the older generation of master chefs, and his route to success has been long and hard. His restaurant, Chez Barrier in Tours, was once a coaching-inn called Le Nègre, where he worked for two years as a young man. 'I could tell that the place was not well run and I told them that one day I would be *patron*. They all laughed at me, of course, but I knew it.' Independent and single-minded, Barrier has risen to success simply by the continual practice of his art; he has had to do without good luck, good connections and good timing. 'The quality which distinguishes my cooking,' he says modestly, 'is honesty. I have a great respect for produce. I remember once seeing an American chef putting paprika on sole. I asked him what on earth he was doing: he said he thought it looked nice. What a monstrous betrayal.' To eat at his table is to experience the pleasures of simplicity, harmony and good taste.

Wines and Spirits

The northern edges of the departments of the Deux-Sèvres and the Vienne touch the vineyards of the Loire. The wine made there is almost all dry white, *appellations* Anjou and Saumur, and a little rosé. Otherwise, the country is excellent for grazing but not for wine.

In the last few years, however, there has been a resurgence of wine-making in northern Poitou. The wines are known as *les vins de Haut-Poitou*, the *appellation* is V.D.Q.S. and they are red, white, rosé and sparkling. The types of grape used are more interesting than one might expect from such a 'non-wine' area: Chardonnay (from Burgundy) and Sauvignon (from Bordeaux and the Loire) for the whites, not blended so as to keep their individuality; Pinot Noir (Burgundy) and Cabernet, Gamay and Cot (Loire) for the reds and rosés; and Chardonnay for the Champagne-style sparkling wine.

The departments of the Charente and Charente-Maritime are given over to making a thin, acid wine which is distilled into Cognac. (Any wine which is distilled is a brandy.) Cognac itself has to come from the very strictly controlled region centred around the town of Cognac. The climate is similar to that of the Loire, although hotter in summer. The grape is Ugni Blanc from Provence and the soil is best where there is the most chalk. Cognac grapes are purposefully over-produced to make a wine light in alcohol and without much apparent character. But since this wine is reduced seven times by distillation, the character of the soil comes through. Cognac is distilled twice, in the traditional Charentais pot-still, the double distillation allowing better control. The liquid emerges colourless at around 70 degrees. It is then run off into Limousin oak, with the year of the wine and its provenance written on the casks, to go through the ageing process. This is partly through unavoidable evaporation, the casks being watertight but not airtight, to the degree of 3% per year, the spirit rising unseen through the tiled roofs of the *chais*, blackening the roofs and walls with a sort of fungus and partly through the acquisition of colour and oakiness through the wood. Unfortunately, it would take too long for Cognac to evaporate its alcoholic level down from 70 to the usual 40 degrees (and there would be precious little Cognac left) and sometimes too long for it to acquire the correct golden-brown colour. So almost all Cognac is cut with a little distilled water and some of the commercial blends are darkened with the addition of caramel.

While the grape variety is standard throughout the region, the particular areas in Cognac are very different. There are seven areas in Cognac: Grande Champagne, centred on Cognac, and the other important little town of Jarnac, for richness and smoothness; Petite Champagne, for finesse and delicacy, the perfect foil for a Grande Champagne; Borderies, just north of Cognac, for its rather rustic character, a good support for lighter blends; Fins Bois, quick-maturing but with enough finesse to stand on its own; and then the more fertile regions of Bois Ordinaires and Bois à Terroir producing very dull Cognacs. The skill is in the selection and blendings.

Above Cognac, the finest French brandy and much-loved by Napoleon, is distilled twice before being left to age in Limousin oak. From this wood the brandy draws its special character and mellow colour.

Left At the Saint-Antoine agricultural college in Saint-Genis-de-Saintonge, students are trained in every process of wine production.

Limousin

This region consists of a green, hilly landscape. Yet the mountainous area in the north-east around the Millevaches Plateau is monotonous, softened in autumn by the mauve and gold of heather and bracken but still a desolate, empty land where a few sheep or cattle graze and introduced pine forests bravely reclothe hillsides which were razed 400 years ago, during the Hundred Years' War.

Monedières Massif to the south is mountainous, too, with long, cold winters. These forests also suffered some destruction. Once they offered refuge to the druids who tried to resist the surge of Roman invasion. To rid himself of the problem, Caesar ordered firing of the trees. They burned for months. Much later the monks replanted. Again the forest was fired, by a Catholic baron at odds with his Huguenot neighbours. This century again, patient work has resulted in large acreages of pines. Settlements are small and the granite houses seem to cling together for company and warmth. Above the furze and heather, bilberries offer seasonal employment.

Many rivers begin in these rain-soaked, stony heights, among them the Creuse, which runs through a narrow valley to Argenton. George Sand, the French woman novelist, often wrote of it. For her it was the subtlety of the landscape which was satisfying: the folded hills, sudden unexpected vistas and patches of tawny, wind-shaken bracken. Théodore Rousseau and Claude Monet were among the painters who chose to spend some time here.

The river flows past the town of Aubusson, famous for its carpets and tapestries. Weaving has been going on for at least 500 years. The fifteenth-century tapestry of The Lady and the Unicorn, most popular exhibit at the Cluny Museum in Paris, is thought to have been woven at Aubusson and the craft continues.

West of the mountains lie the plateaux of Haut-Limousin where the image of a verdant, undulating countryside comes true. The climate is damp. Beeches and oak trees thrive. Bellac is a typical town, looking out over the Vincou river. The playwright Jean Giraudoux, probably best known for *The Mad Woman of Chaillot*, was born there in 1882. He described his native countryside as one of streams and hills, fields and chestnut trees. North is the Marche area, where

Introduction

hermits lived in the Middle Ages. South is Bas-Limousin where the climate is mild, the light suddenly warmer and richer with a foretaste of the Midi, and walnut trees grow thick in the valleys.

The Dordogne river begins to the east, in the Massif Central, and for part of its upper course it runs through the Limousin. Snows in the Millevaches Plateau sometimes cause it to flood but dams constructed along the upper Dordogne control it fairly well without disfiguring the countryside. Further down, around Argentat, the river spreads and the landscape offers an appealing variety.

Capital of the region is Limoges, inseparable from its traditions of enamel and porcelain.

Enamelling seems to have grown up around the Abbey of Saint-Martial where gold and silversmiths reached a high level of skill. They turned to enamelling, a technique by which powdered glass is fixed to a sheet of metal, in this case, copper. In the twelfth century they began concentrating entirely on *champlevé*, for which hollows worked into the copper are packed with powdered enamel and fired.

The Limoges porcelain story began in the town of Saint-Yrieix-la-Perche, situated in the cattle-raising district of the Haute-Vienne. Kaolin, a white clay, is essential for the production of hard-paste porcelain and the Meissen factory in Dresden was already making its fortune through the discovery of deposits. Until then, hard-paste porcelain had been an Oriental prerogative. The rich deposits of kaolin near Saint-Yrieix were discovered when a chemist engaged in conducting experiments to find a suitable material became friendly with a surgeon whose wife made use of a local clay to whiten her washing. Porcelain works were set up in the town in 1771, in Limoges soon after, and the industry has gone on ever since.

In two departments of the Limousin – Haute-Vienne and Creuse – every seven years there are festivals known as *Ostensions*. They revolve around the exhibition of the holy relics of saints who lived in the area and the custom goes back to the tenth century. In those days the relics were brought out as a plea for pity in times of epidemic or as the town's symbolic welcome to eminent visitors. A flag, hoisted to the top of the church belfry marks the opening, then the relics are transferred to their shrines for veneration. The shrines are often superb examples of gold and silver work. There are flowers and banners, singing and dancing as the processions wind through the village streets. National costumes are given an airing and craft guilds join in, all decked out in their traditional regalia. The celebrations start the Sunday after Easter and a big closing ceremony is held in the small town of Le Dorat.

Right From the confining gorges of the Massif Central, the Dordogne river spreads out at Argentat, into a wide and beautiful valley.

Towns and Villages

Right An old mill at Saint-Léonard-de-Noblat, not far from the twentieth-century industrial sprawl of Limoges.

Below Bucolic tranquillity on a quiet waterway, Limousin.

Far right The *vicomté* or lordship of Turenne remained independent of France for several hundred years. Now only the bare bones remain of the once-mighty fortress crowning the hill.

Opposite, far right Known as a *quercy*, this little building was a dovecote, kept for the collection of guano in the Limousin/Midi-Pyrénées area.

Limoges began its history in the Gallo-Roman period, when the town was little more than a ford across the river Vienne. Known as Augustorium, it spread out in an amphitheatre along the right bank of the river. Only in the Middle Ages did the ecclesiastical and commercial elements of life here separate, with the city itself around the cathedral and the town in the shadow of the powerful Abbey of Saint-Martial. Today both are united in an industrial sprawl reaching far along the river banks. The cathedral remains a major tourist sight, while the National Museum in Avenue Saint-Surin boasts a fine collection of porcelain.

Today Limoges is a thriving, twentieth-century commercial city. Besides the porcelain industry, shoe-making is an important business and there are major uranium-processing and hydro-electric power plants nearby.

Near Limoges is the interesting hill town of Saint-Léonard-de-Noblat, named after the sixth-century hermit Léonard whose miraculous healing power made him one of Limousin's most popular saints. In November he is remembered at the festival of Quintaine when a small wooden fortress is trampled down by riders on horseback armed with wooden clubs. Today the town is a centre

of small industry and agriculture.

Further east is the pleasantly situated town of Bourganeuf, famous for its tower, once part of a fifteenth-century castle. Known as Zizim's Tower, it commemorates the imprisonment here of a Mohommedan prince whose exploits are still spoken of. It contains some remarkable timber ceilings and offers a fine view of the surrounding countryside.

Two places mark the scene of grim but important events in recent history. A memorial in the industrial town of Tulle, and the remains of the village of Oradour-sur-Glane stand as stark reminders of two of the worst atrocities of the Nazi occupation of World War II.

A happier place is Aubusson, celebrated for its tapestries, situated in the narrow, picturesque valley of the Creuse, surrounded by wooden hills and rocks. Legend has it that the weaving workshops go back to the Saracens in the eighth century, though the local tapestries only became famous in the fifteenth-century. There is an annual exhibition of tapestry from 1 July to 30 September.

The 2000 feet high (610 metres) town of Ussel has fine views over the Millevaches Plateau and the Cantal heights. Though offering little of interest in itself – save a group of well preserved sixteenth-

century houses – Ussel offers easy access to Saint-Angel, with its surprising fortified church: the nave and aisles have some elegant ogive vaulting.

Travelling south-west down the Corrèze valley you approach a fertile area of fruit and vegetable farms, of which the capital is Brive-la-Gaillarde. The suffix 'La Gaillarde', meaning 'the Bold', derives from the courage displayed by citizens on the many occasions when Brive was besieged. It is a busy, thriving town with a most interesting museum, housed in an elegant Louis XIII mansion. The museum contains a large collection of

prehistoric and Roman remains, and two fine galleries of ethnography and folklore. You can get a good view of Brive from the Grottes-de-Saint-Antoine.

Still more charming than Brive is Uzerche to its north. 'He who has a house in Uzerche', runs the popular saying, 'has a castle in Limousin.' Bell-turrets, watchtowers and pepper-pot roofs vie with each other for airspace over this old fortified town. Apart from the Porte Bécharie, there is little of the fortifications left, but the splendid strategic position of the town, over the River Vézère, remains unchanged.

Châteaux and Churches

'A land of streams and hills, a patchwork of fields and chestnut groves', is how Giraudoux described his native land. A region of transition between north and south, its architecture is likely to be of either tradition. The pink granite Church of Saint-Pierre at Le Dorat, one of Limousin's finest, with its Moorish-style receding porch and splendid cupola with Romanesque windows flooding the noble interior with light. In contrast, the Cathedral of Saint-Etienne at Limoges, a solemn edifice of grey granite, belongs to the northern tradition of great Gothic cathedrals.

Limoges is most famous for its porcelain and enamel work. The Municipal Museum, located in the sober but elegant eighteenth-century Palais Episcopal, has an excellent collection of enamel work dating from the twelfth century on, and the Musée Andrien Debouché is renowned for its vast collection of china and porcelain of all periods.

Farther south lies Saint-Yrieix-la-Perche, source of the soil rich in kaolin, which made it possible to manufacture hard-paste porcelain and led to the flourishing Limoges porcelain industry.

Aubusson, to the east, is an old, pretty town known throughout the world for its tapestries. These were famous as far back as the fifteenth century; recently a tapestry based on Rouault's *Les Fleurs du Mal* (made in 1932), and others based on works by Lurçat, Picasso and Braque, have revitalized the industry.

Above Aubusson tapestries have been prized for centuries, and the art continues today, with well-known artists contributing designs. The one shown here is *Vierges Folles de Saint-Saëns*.

Near Evaux-les-Bains, at Chambon-sur-Voueize, stands one of the most imposing of Limousin's Romanesque churches, a severe eleventh-century edifice built of granite whose slender unadorned pillars force the eyes upwards to a soaring vaulted roof.

The unusual church at Moutier d'Ahun, between Guéret and Aubusson, is in fact the remaining part of an earlier, larger one. There is a garden where the nave used to be and the building now forms the background for a magnificent array of seventeenth-century carved choir-stalls, twenty-six in all, each with a profusion of flowers and animals.

At Bort-Les-Orgues to the south there is a spectacular giant dam, one of a series created to provide the area with hydro-electric power. Since the time it was put into operation, the nearby fifteenth-century Château of Val has been surrounded by water, which reflects its romantic pepperpot towers.

A picturesque sight to the west is the ancient walled town of Uzerche whose old, turreted houses hug a steep hill like so many barnacles. Farther south a sprinkling of delightful old towns may take you back several centuries. One of them is Turenne, whose turreted fifteenth and sixteenth-century houses stand guard around the dignified ruins of a once-formidable château. Another is Collonges-la-Rouge, a unique ancient township, rose-red in colour, as its name suggests. Its ornamented houses with their turrets and mullioned windows are all built of purplish-red sandstone. In the square the twelfth-century tower of Saint-

Sauveur church is typical of Limousin Romanesque architecture.

At Beaulieu-sur-Dordogne to the south-east stands the twelfth-century abbey-church of Saint-Pierre, surrounded by old streets. The splendid carvings on its south porch, representing the Last Judgement and an assortment of winged beasts, are the work of craftsmen of the School of Toulouse who worked on other Périgord churches such as the one at Moissac.

Not far from Argentat are the Towers of Merle, whose dramatic ruins consist of a fourteenth-century family compound of seven strongholds, impregnable until the advent of artillery. Their crumbling remains are spread out romantically over the hilltop, mute survivors of a beleaguered past.

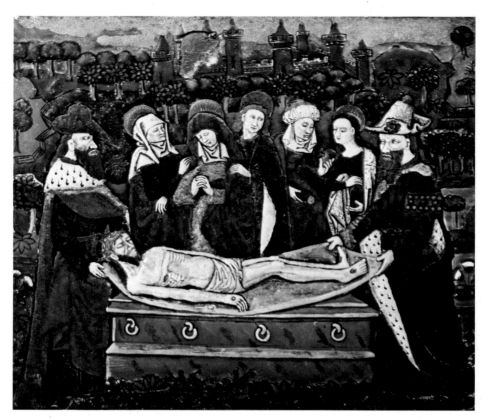

Left There is a northern flavour about the great Saint-Etienne Cathedral in Limoges, with its flying buttresses and truncated Romanesque belfry.

Top Among the works to be seen in the Limoges Museum is this painting, circa 1807.

Above Le Manoir de l'Ussinhac, at Collonges-la-Rouge. This picturesque town is unique in that all the buildings, mostly dating from the sixteenth and seventeenth centuries, are built of the same rose-red stone.

Cuisine

For centuries, the graceful city of Limoges has produced exquisite porcelain and its delicately-painted dinner services have carried many a royal meal in the palaces of Europe. For simpler citizens and smaller purses, there are undecorated plates and in Limousin they will bear you meals, if not rich in cream and black truffles, still fit for a king. The beef is particularly good and, at the Hôtel Frantel, there is always a fine roast fillet (*rôti de contrefilet*); the kidneys stewed in wine with mushrooms (*rognons de boeuf à la limousine*) are also excellent.

The mushrooms of Limousin are not those tasteless button mushrooms which fill the modern supermarkets, but wild from the pastures and woodlands. Ceps (*cèpes*) are the commonest and you can buy them dried from any grocer's shop, but there are also the golden *chanterelles* (*girolles*), *morelles (morilles)* with their curious maze-like tops and earthy flavour and, if you are fortunate and feeling adventurous, giant puff-balls (*vesses-du-loup*).

The green rolling landscape is crisscrossed with small farms, most of them bustling with chickens, pigs and geese. There are many delightful pâtés here – of veal, pork and, in particular, fattened goose liver (*pâté de foie gras*). At La Crémaillère in Brive-la-Gaillarde the goose pâté is exceptional, as is the stuffed goose neck (*cou d'oie farci*) served with red cabbage.

Cabbage grows well in the red soil and is available throughout the year. Braised in lard, it forms the basis of the thick vegetable soup (*brejaude*) which is served with rye bread. Two other local cabbage dishes are partridge with cabbage (*perdrix au chou*) and red cabbage braised with chestnuts (*chou rouge à la limousine*).

Wherever there are cabbages, there

Top left Chestnuts grow prodigiously in Limousin, and are used for both sweet and savoury dishes. You can also buy them roasted from braziers in the street, like this one in Limoges.

Left The fine spread of food at the Hôtel Château de Castel Novel, near Brive, includes garlic and egg soup (*tourain a l'ail*); hot chicken breasts served with endive and garnished with nuts, mushrooms and eggs; kidneys in wine with leeks (*rognons rotis au vin rouge et aux poireaux*) and finally small pear tarts (*flognards*).

are also rabbits and hares: if you do not see them by the road, you will meet them at the table. A traditional dish of hare is *lièvre en chabessal*: the animal is stuffed with veal, pork, aromatic herbs and spices, then trussed into a circular shape for roasting. The *chabessal* is a rolled circle of cloth once worn by women on the head when carrying a heavy load. Tractors take the strain these days, but the name lives on.

Walnuts and chestnuts grow prodigiously here. Every patron has his stock of walnut oil, and most will be happy to dress your salad with a French dressing (*vinaigrette*) made with this fine, sweet oil. As for chestnuts, they are added to ragouts of veal and pork, to sausages and pies and – as a purée – to confectionery.

Above the farmlands, filling most of the region and stretching away into the mighty granite mound of the Massif Central, are the plateaux. The rivers that flow from these stony heights are rich in trout, pike and eel. In Limousin, there are also crayfish, which are customarily boiled in white wine and vegetables (*écrevisses à la nage*). Much of the trout is not, however, from the rivers but from the fish ponds on the plateaux. Here, where little grows but bracken, there are ponds dating back to the Middle Ages – an inspiration of the early missionaries.

On the plateaux, the winds are strong and the winters long and cold: a splendid place for a military camp! The remains of the vast camp on the Plateau de Mille-vaches only leave us wondering what they could have eaten there. For the *mille vaches* are not cows (*vaches*) – which do not thrive here – but springs, from the celtic word *batz*. The traveller would be well advised to bring his own lunch – perhaps bread, pâté and a cherry tart (*clafoutis*) from Limoges.

Above The Place de la République, Limoux. The food market is an important focal point of every village and town.

Left The watchful eye of the master chef oversees all food preparation at the Hôtel de Truffe-Noir, Brive.

Wines and Spirits

The departments of the Creuse, the Haute-Vienne and the Corrèze, are agricultural but not viticultural. Vines prefer poor, usually stony soil, hardly survive over 1,200 feet (366 metres), so the Limousin is not for them. But there are two reasons why this area is connected with wine. The first is folkloric: the farmers of Corrèze used to make regular trips to Paris to sell their hams and other produce, stopping off in the Loire to pick up some wine to add to their selection.

The second reason is responsible for much of the livelihood of the area: Limousin oak. In earlier centuries, oak from the Limousin forests was used exclusively for building ships at La Rochelle and for maturing Cognac. The slow growing-season in the Limousin, extremely cold winters and rather wet summer, produce very regular oak with a dense grain. The resulting barrel dovetails perfectly with no glue, the dense grain keeping oxydation to a minimum. This is good for Cognac, where evaporation has to be kept low since the spirit is so valuable, and good for wine since the 'breathing' helps evolution. The other important attribute of oak (apart also from being a container) is the flavour the wood imparts. The experts have analyzed 120 aromas of oak, the most common being vanilla. The 'oakiness' of a barrel is quickly used up, as the wine or cognac literally sucks it out of the wood. Cognac is matured over several years and is then blended, so the oak is never present or even encouraged, but it can be dominant in a young wine which has spent more than a few months in a new cask. Oak thus adds another dimension to wine.

Above These great staves of Limousin oak are from a huge Armagnac barrel which has been dismantled for treatment. Besides being an ideal wood for containers, the oak imparts a special flavour to the brandy.

Left Here, distilled spirit is decanted into casks of Limousin oak, before being stored for the five years needed to turn it into Cognac.

Auvergne

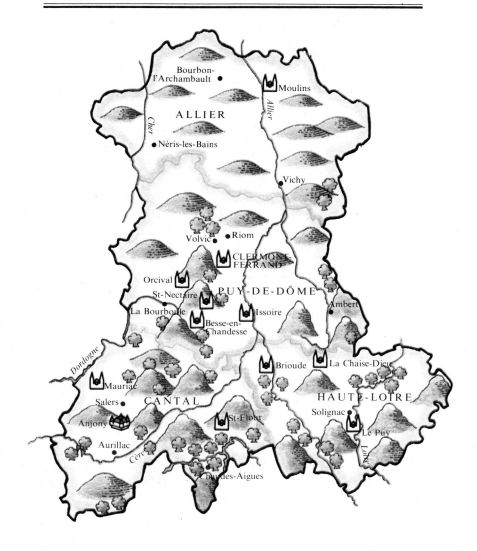

The Auvergne is the heartland of the Massif Central. The landscape is verdantly green like Ireland, yet with patches of dark. Black lava has contributed to the appearance of the towns, for this was an area of volcanic activity. The earth has been buckled into crags and craters. Rich volcanic ash supports stretches of agriculture.

Officially the region includes the modern departments of Allier, Puy-de-Dôme, Cantal and Haute-Loire. Major rivers are born in these highlands, including the Loire, the Cher, the Dordogne and the Lot. The temperatures, in true inland fashion, range from very hot to freezing,

sometimes in the course of a single day. The higher roads are often impassable from December to as late as May. Spring sets the streams bubbling with water from the melted snow and wild flowers embroider the pastures. Salmon rise in the Allier river.

Not an easy landscape but a supremely impressive and beautiful one. The Auvergnats themselves seldom escape from its spell. Traditionally poor, their activity hampered by harsh winters, they have always headed for Paris in their thousands where they become fuel merchants or set up small cafés and restaurants, or they do both at once. These little places, called *bougnats*, usually family-run, combine the business of

Introduction

selling firewood, coal, gas and heating oil with a normal café trade. Not many of these little *bougnats* still survive today, but you can find a few in old quarters such as the Marais.

The Auvergnats are probably Celtic in origin. All those British jokes about the canny Scotsman are turned in France to stories about the penny-pinching Auvergnat. There may be some truth in them, since the department known as Puy-de-Dôme was about to be called Mont d'Or (Mount of Gold) when a quick-witted citizen pointed out that the tax collectors might misconstrue the name and come in search of the carefully accumulated funds which Auvergnats are reputed to squirrel away in their houses. Their natural mistrust of strangers still, to some extent, includes a suspicion of banks.

More convincing proof of Celtic origins is the fact that they play the *cabrette*, an instrument resembling bagpipes. They play a kind of viol, as well, and are often seen with it in old illustrations. It is worked with a handle, like a hurdy-gurdy. The two together accompanied the typical dance, a Celtic jig or *bourrée*. The land is grave and majestic. It has made them silent, cautious, touched them with poetry and formed in them an enduring loyalty.

Vercingétorix was an Averne (the ancestral race of these people). He defeated Julius Caesar in 53 BC on the Plateau of Gergovie, a few kilometres south of Auvergne its present-day capital, Clermont-Ferrand. The tide was reversed later at Alésia. Vercingétorix exchanged himself against his men, was taken to Rome, imprisoned and, six years later, strangled. The Auvergnats became finally united with France only under Louis XIV.

Hot mineral springs still rise from the underground volcanic activity which gave birth to spa towns, vastly appreciated by the hygiene-conscious Romans. A good deal of France's bottled water also comes from here and is exported all over the world. Vichy, most celebrated of the spas, was already fashionable in the time of Henri IV and became even more so when Napoleon III began taking the cure there. Its elegant Great Thermal Establishment has arching ironwork, potted palms and conservatory gardens.

Nearby, at Super Besse, an important ski resort has developed with cable cars to the top of Puy-Ferrand, 4,790 feet high (1,846 metres). Besse-en-Chandesse is the home of the Black Virgin. At the beginning of summer when the herds are taken up to the high ground she travels with them all the way to the mountain Chapel of Vassivière and descends with them again only in the autumn, a Christianized goddess of the soil.

All the *puys* and *plombs* of the region are peaks, formed by the flaming volcanoes hurling their tons of molten lava then cooling to lunar strangeness. Sometimes the craters cup lakes of eerie beauty. Pascal's theory of air pressure was tested on top of the Puy-de-Dôme in 1648.

The town of Le Puy lies east, surrounded by spires and cones. The highest is the Rocher Corneille topped by an immense statue of the Virgin, made from cannons melted down after the battle of Sebastopol. Clenched to another fist of rock, the late eleventh-century Chapel of Saint-Michel-d'Aiguilhe is as firm and fortress-like as the stone on which it is set. Its triple arches echo the contours of the environment.

Polignac, only a short distance away, was the home of an Oracle of Apollo. Prayers used to be said at the foot of the rock, after which the Romans would climb to the top and the god's mask would miraculously give answers to the very questions they had been praying over – without them having to repeat them. They were never disenchanted, but later generations discovered a hidden chimney which had carried the whispered entreaties to the ears of the priests.

In the heart of the Massif Central, volcanic activity has shaped the landscape (**above left**), giving rise to hot springs and enriched the soil. Villages such as Orcival (**above**) nestle in valleys or cling to rocky outcrops.

Left Dramatically placed on a volcanic peak, the Château d'Anjony looks out over pasturelands, home of the famous Cantal cheese.

Towns and Villages

The spectacular town of Le Puy, in the south-east of the Auvergne, is a testimony to how succeeding generations have made the most of an extraordinary site. Surrounded by mountains, this town of 30,000 has grown up in what, before volcanic upheavals shifted the course of the Loire, was a vast lake. Various outcrops remain; on one, at the top of 268 steps, is the eleventh-century Chapel of Saint-Michel-d'Aiguilhe, built where once was a Temple to Mercury. On another is an imposing statue of Our Lady, built by public subscription in 1860 from cannon captured at Sebastopol.

Further down is a spectacular Romanesque cathedral, showing strong Byzantine influence, and surrounded by the picturesque houses of the old town: it makes a fine backdrop to the Saturday morning market. Le Puy has a long tradition of lace-making, and the Musée Crozatier houses examples of the craft since the sixteenth-century. The famous Theodolph Bible, a Carolingian masterpiece, is kept at the cathedral.

Throughout the region the geographic peculiarities make a constant theme. Aurillac is a city known for considerable carnage in the Wars of Religion and as the birthplace of a genius who started his working life as a shepherd-boy but ended up in AD 999 as Sylvester II, the first French Pope. It has a fine museum on volcanoes. The small town of Volvic is still a quarrying centre for the black lava, and three towns in the region make particularly spectacular use of this unusual building material: Besse-en-

Above The village of Saint-Paul, Maronne valley, Cantal.

Right The rural life predominates in this mountainous region. Roads are poor and often steep, so oxcarts are still used.

Chandesse, Mauriac and Riom.

Lava from Volvic was used in the construction of the great Gothic cathedral at Clermont-Ferrand, which dates from 1248. With more than 300,000 people, this conurbation is the one major industrial centre in the area, a dull, rather solemn town. First settled before the Roman invasion, Clermont was colonized by Romans, and sacked by Franks, Vikings, Normans and Danes. In 1638 it merged with its nearby rival Montferrand. The seventeenth-century writer Blaise Pascal lived there, as did the niece of a nineteenth-century Scots inventor who, inspired by her uncle's researches, used rubber balls to amuse her children. Her husband and their descendants (a family by the name of Michelin) developed the idea, and it led to the city's subsequent and continuing importance as a centre for the rubber industry. Michelin still has its main factories here.

Another feature of the region – the riches flowing under the ground – is also to be seen at Clermont-Ferrand, where there are twenty-two mineral springs. Most of them surface in the Saint-Alyre and at the Grottes du Pérou are some interesting examples of petrification. Springs and spas abound in the Auvergne: the waters of La Bourboule, which have a high deposit of arsenic, are considered beneficial for respiratory ailments, skin diseases and allergies. Chaudes-Aigues, set in a picturesque ravine and 2461 feet (750 metres) high is famous for hot waters, which can be as hot as 87 degrees centigrade, and are con-

sidered good for rheumatism and sciatica. The waters of Bourbon-l'Archambault are recommended for arthritis, those at Mont-Dore for asthma.

Best known of the spas, of course, is Vichy where the local state-owned factory bottles the water for exporting throughout the world. Popularized by, among others, the daughters of Louis XV, Napoleon's mother, and Napoleon III, it

has since become famous for a different reason: between 1940 and 1944 it was the seat of the collaborationist Pétain government; it was the capital of the unoccupied southern zone of France until the Germans moved in and took over the whole of France in 1942. Vichy is today a major conference centre as well as a popular and cosmopolitan spa town, with a wealth of hotels and restaurants.

Left The Auvergnats are a distinctive people, probably Celtic in origin. At festivals they play a type of bagpipes called the *cabrette*.

Above With infinite care, the lace-maker pursues her delicate craft. This tradition has been carried on for centuries at Le Puy, and the Musée Crozatier contains a collection of lace through the ages.

Châteaux and Churches

Auvergne is a land of huge dams, fortress-towns perched high like eagles nests, Roman remains and Romanesque churches. In the more southern regions the Romanesque style makes use of old Roman architectural features and is characterized by richly decorated façades and fine carving.

Brioude is the site of the eleventh-century Saint-Junien Basilica, the largest Romanesque church in Auvergne and a fine example of the Auvergnat style, with its band of red and grey mosaic patterning decorating the exterior. The reddish sandstone of the interior gives an impression of warmth and light. The splendid twelfth-century Abbey of Saint-Austremoine at Issoire is one of the most perfect Auvergnat churches of the period. It, too, has decorative mosaic designs on the outside of typical, finely-carved capitals in the choir and transept.

An important stopover on the pilgrims' route to Spain in the Middle Ages, the buildings of Le Puy are built on a series of steep outcrops of volcanic rock. One needs to be a steadfast climber to reach the colourful Notre-Dame Cathedral with its many Byzantine features, which include the stripes of light and dark stone and the row of cupolas along the nave. The curious Chapel of Saint-Michel-d'Aguilhe is also dauntingly placed on a soaring pinnacle. The façade, with its swirling arabesques and black, white and grey zig-zag patterns, is distinctly Oriental.

Clermont-Ferrand has a great Romanesque basilica, and the extraordinary Gothic Cathedral of Notre-Dame-de-l'Assomption, which is built of local black lava, so strong that the pillars and arches could be made unusually slender, thus increasing the effect of lightness and height.

Other major churches in this region include the beautiful Notre-Dame at Orcival; the abbey-church of Chaise-Dieu, set on a windy plain; and the Cathedral of Moulins, which houses one of the region's major treasures, the luminous triptych by the unidentified 'Master of Moulins'.

The dark lava appears again in the town of Salers, one of the prettiest in Auvergne, perched on a hill. Here, the famous Grande Place is lined with fifteenth and sixteenth-century houses soberly constructed of lava and topped with round or polygonal corbelled turrets.

Poised on a steep bluff stands a typical fortified town, the once-impregnable Saint-Flour, of which it was said that only the wind could take it by force. Other ancient strongholds built in inaccessible places include the brooding ruins of the once-powerful fourteenth-century castle of Tournoël, pondering its violent past high above the landscape, and the picturesque red ruins of the thirteenth-century Murol, once a brigands' lair.

George Sand called La Rochelambert, a fifteenth-century manor house, 'a jewel mounted in greenery'. This romantic château of fawn-coloured local stone set into the basalt hillside was the setting for her novel *Jean de la Roche*.

Anjony, with its round towers and machicolated battlements, rears up from a rocky outcrop like a fairy-tale castle. It has in fact, been witness to a long and bloody past of family vendettas.

The thermal spa of Néris-les-Bains has been an important health resort for centuries, as its Roman and Merovingian remains testify. The Romans have made their mark elsewhere, too, near the Puy de Dôme peak, where a huge temple of Mercury once stood. From this lofty peak one can appreciate the true splendour of this remote and mountainous region, as numerous volcanic peaks spread out all around, as far as the eye can see.

Left This spectacular building is the eleventh-century Chapel of Saint-Michel-d'Aiguilhe, which seems to balance precariously on a slender pinnacle of a lava rock.

Above left These colourful Renaissance murals and rich decorations can be seen in Clermont-Ferrand.

Above right A masterpiece of Romanesque design, the church of Notre-Dame-du-Port at Clermont-Ferrand has a series of little chapels fanning out from the central block.

Left The Château of Rochelambert, in the Haute-Loire department, was the setting for a novel by George Sand.

Cuisine

The ancient, undulating, volcanic plateau of Auvergne is not a fertile place. For centuries, a hardy breed of farmers have eked out a simple living here, and their traditional cuisine reflects this simplicity. Cheap cuts of beef and pork, some game and fish, hearty soups and rich, nourishing cheeses are the basis of the mountain diet.

Cows are kept wherever the pastures are rich enough and though most of the beef is sold in the lowlands, it is available in all the tourist restaurants. Local specialities include roast kidneys with leek sauce (*rognons rôtis aux poireaux*) and veal in cream sauce (*blanquette de veau*). An excellent *blanquette*, rich in onions, may be found at the Restaurant au Cerf in the mysterious volcanic city of Le Puy; other dishes on the menu include tripe in wine sauce (*tripes à l'auvergnate*) and duck in orange sauce (*canard à l'orange*).

Apart from ducks, the wild game includes partridges, which are roasted over an open fire (*brochette de perdrix*) or stewed in white wine, butter and herbs (*perdrix à l'auvergnate*). But the best wild flesh comes from the rivers, for the Massif Central is the water tower of France, and her many streams provide trout galore. At Le Livradois in Ambert, they are grilled, fried in butter and – from time to time – baked into an ethereal trout soufflé. Salmon is also sometimes available. Further north, in and around the splendidly decadent resort of Vichy – famous for its sparkling waters – you may also find crayfish on the menu. They will be expensive, but seize the opportunity: freshwater crayfish (*écrevisses à la nage*) are fast becoming a delicacy of the past.

Auvergne is the home of many fine cheeses and two have become world famous: the blue-veined Bleu d'Auvergne and the full-cream, semi-hard Cantal. Nowadays, most of the Bleu is factory made, but an authentic mountain variety is still to be found in the Thiézac area. Its succulent, aromatic flavour is quite distinct. Cantal comes from the volcanic pasturelands around Aurillac, taking its name from the largest volcano in Europe. Since Roman times, herdsmen have made these vast drum-shaped cheeses here in the mountains. Twice each season, they carry the ripened Cantal to the markets below. Some fresh and slightly cured Cantal-type cheeses are also made in the factories of Saint-Etienne, where they are known as *tommes*: they are used in the local cheese, bacon and potato pancakes called *trouffades auvergnates*, which are not to be missed.

Most small-holdings contain a pig or two, and pork plays an important part in the local cuisine. Larded meatballs (*fricandeaux*) are usually made with pork though veal may also be used, well seasoned with herbs and bound with egg; pickled pork is added to the local variations of thick vegetable soup (*potée*); pork, flavoured with fennel and rum, fills the black pudding of Auvergne (*boudin*), which is served with russet apples; and there is a marvellous range of hams and pork sausages (*salaisons*).

Vegetables are relatively few but lentils are popular and easily available. They are at their best in the winter pot of sausages and lentils (*saucisses aux lentilles du Puy*), but they also appear in summer. In Moudeyres, they are served as a salad with spring onions, herbs and a local sausage called *cervelas* (*salade auvergnate*).

In the lava valley of Limagne, north of Clermont-Ferrand, the land is once again fertile enough for cereals, vegetables and fruit. Here you will find some delightful desserts, including a black cherry pudding (*milliard*) and a batter pudding with apples and pears (*flognarde*). All in all, the gourmet will not be disappointed in the Auvergne.

Above Hearty, wholesome fare is characteristic of Auvergne. This warming pot of sausages and lentils (*saucisses aux lentilles du Puy*) is an ideal winter meal in this mountainous region.

Top An appetizing meal prepared in Salers: *trouffade auvergnate*, which is a type of pancake made with bacon, cheese and potatoes, served with mountain ham sliced finely.

Left Maize, depicted here on an early fresco, was once a staple of cornmeal dishes. Today it is fed to poultry, resulting in rich *foie gras* and the prized yellow-fleshed chickens.

Above The cheese-press in a *fromagerie*, Puy-de-Dôme. Cantal cheeses from the volcanic pasturelands around Aurillac have been made since Roman times.

Wines and Spirits

Auvergne makes up a large part of the Massif Central, better known for its grazing than its grapes. But everything tastes so good in the fresh clean air of the central plateau that the rather rustic Auvergne wines seem the only possible thing to drink with *saucisson sec*, *la potée* and aged cheese from the Cantal.

In fact, the only wines, Saint-Pourçain from the Allier and Côtes d'Auvergne from the Puy-de-Dôme, are classified as *vins de la Loire*. In character, they are nothing of the sort. The whites have a faint resemblance to the lesser Burgundies and the reds are like Beaujolais with an agreeable *goût de terroir*.

The Saint-Pourçain wines come in white, rosé and red. The biggest producer, and far from the most expensive, is the local *Cave Coopérative*, but the most individual wines come from the growers. The basic grape used is the Tresallier, to a minimum of 50 per cent, mixed with the Aligoté, Sauvignon and Chardonnay. It is these last three, particularly the Chardonnay, that give finesse and panache to the pale, often greenish-tinged, whites. The Saint-Pourçain vineyards are ranged along the banks of the Sioule, Alliér and Bouble rivers.

The reds and rosés which come from the Gamay and the Pinot Noir are cheerful and easy to drink. The light rosés have a singular success in the local spa resorts.

Whereas the wine of Saint-Pourçain used to grace the tables of the kings of France, and now has to be satisfied with a local reputation, the Côtes d'Auvergne wines had no such renown, yet are making great efforts to improve themselves. The main area is found south of Clermont-Ferrand, where the locals find the legendary red from Chanturges and the pale rosé from Corent the best wines in the world, around Issoire, where the *cru* Boudes has a special *cachet*, and from Riom, the *cru* to look for being Châteaugay. They are at their best from several months to two years old. The Auvergne whites are dullish and rather acid.

Except in the many Auvergnat restaurants in Paris, most of the production is consumed locally. In their unpretentious way, these simple country wines are worth looking out for.

Below The vineyards of the La Roche-Blanche area of Auvergne.
This mountainous region produces rather rustic wines. The white wines are produced from a blend of the Tresallier grape with the Aligoté, Chardonnay and Sauvignon (**bottom left**). Reds and roses come from the Gamay (**bottom right**) and the Pinot Noir.

Rhône-Alpes

The Rhône begins in Switzerland, in the Rhône glacier, and sets off with spirited purposefulness south-west to Lyon where it meets with the Saône coming down almost directly from the north. It never doubts its majestic destiny all the way to Avignon. There it splits into many waterways. The Little Rhône and Great Rhône delimit the triangular, watery desert of the Camargue.

It is a solid, sensible waterway; a great river and, at times, a beautiful one. The Romans knew it well. The town of Orange, at the southern limit of the Rhône Valley, tried to fight them off and killed 100,000 of them, but then succumbed. The Roman tide left a great many buildings to substantiate the fact, as it did at Valence, at Vienne and at Lyon, which was the capital of Romanized Gaul.

Most travellers today move down from Burgundy, through the Beaujolais region. The area on the edge of the Massif Central is rough and mountainous in the west, forest country with poor soil. Then comes

Introduction

the Roanne plain and, after more rolling landscape, the rich slopes of Beaujolais on the right bank of the Saône river.

West and south of Villefranche is Lower Beaujolais, a tiny section of the countryside described as the *pierres dorées* because of the harmonious glow of its old stone buildings. To the east is the fertile, grain-growing plain of Bresse where reedy ponds and lakes reflect the sky. Bresse produces the best chickens in France and you can recognize their blue blood for the legs, wattles and combs have an indigo tint. In case of any mistake, each one is banded with its breeder's number. The town of Bourg-en-Bresse is noted for its pre-Christmas poultry market. The region is gastronomically celebrated, so it is fitting that the birthplace and home of Jean Anthelme Brillat-Savarin should be only a short distance away. He was a lawyer and judge, more famous as the author of a well-meditated work on gastronomy – *Physiologie du Goût* – and was born in 1755 in the aptly named township of Belley, to the east.

Gastronomic pleasures in Bourg can be followed by a visit to one of the finest Flamboyant Gothic churches in France, the church of Brou. Marguerite d'Autriche commissioned it to house the body of her deeply-loved husband, Philibert-le-Beau – and handsome he was, judging by his portrait in stained glass. The church, part of a monastery, was begun in 1506 and finished about twenty years later. Marguerite was fulfilling the vow of her mother-in-law when she undertook its construction. She saw only the plans of the building and died two years before it was completed. For this church, dedicated to Saint Nicholas of Tolentino on whose feast day Philibert died, the glimmering stone of Revermont is carved into delicate, effortless fantasy, an exuberant expression of human love. Philibert, his wife and his mother lie at the East of the church. The linked initials of Philibert and Marguerite his wife appear time and again in the interior.

The city has always held an important geographical position set at the confluence of the Rhône and the Saône. Already there is the feel of the Midi, the South, about it expressed, too, in the Lyonnais accent. Winters can be cold but sometimes the heat, held close to the ground by a heavy sky, is brassy and oppressive. An affluent, down-to-earth town of hard-working burghers who invest with foresight, embellish their town with dignity and are circumspect in displaying their wealth.

The river below the city and further south still, between Valence and Montélimar, is a waterway of maturity, sure of its place in the sun, a characteristic it may have picked up from Lyon on the way.

Another river flows to meet the Rhône: the Ardèche, with quite a different character. It drifts, melancholy and romantic; descends through canyons of towering beauty; is reflective and passionate by turn, sometimes carving strange shapes into the cliffs or tunnelling formations like the Pont d'Arc,

sometimes an expanse of watered silk shot with green and grey. Vallon-Pont-d'Arc is the centre for visits into the area, which should take in the Aven d'Orgnac, an extraordinary underworld of limestone formations.

The other part of this major area of France consists of the Savoy and Dauphiné Alps and the country rising to them. Here is some of the most magnificent scenery in Europe and some of the finest winter sports areas in the world. Mont Blanc, with its crown touching 15,771 feet (4,807 metres) lies on the Franco-Italian frontier. On the French side it offers a gentler perspective than from Italy, where it appears grimmer and darker.

Chamonix is 3,402 feet (1,037 metres) high; it was from here that Mont Blanc was first scaled in the late eighteenth century. Now it has everything that goes to make a great winter resort with cableways running to high points from which the Alps appear in all their glittering splendour – timeless, wrapped in white silence. The first Winter Olympics were held in Chamonix in 1924. Since then, other resorts have proliferated throughout the area, including sophisticated, debonair Megève and Courchevel. From Chamonix you can rise almost to the summit of the Aiguille du Midi, using the highest cableway in the world and travelling in fifteen minutes to an altitude of 12,796 feet (3,900 metres).

Most spectacular of all the sights is the Mer de Glace, a great frozen curtain which you take a cable railway to visit. The carriages negotiate a triple bend before they arrive before the largest glacier in France, sparkling with crystalline colours, scattered with granite. This river of ice grows a little shorter every year. Now it extends for 3,418 miles (5,500 kilometres).

The Vanoise massif lies between the Tarentaise valley in the north and the Maurienne in the south. The village of Val d'Isère and the nearby resort of Tignes are popular winter and summer and offer excursions to the Parc National de la Vanoise, extending over 130,568 acres (52,839 hectares), 19,768 of which are glaciers. Animals and flowers are strictly protected and fishing is controlled. Chamois, ermine and eagles roam in peace and spring awakens thousands of alpine flowers.

The Lake of Annecy is one of the loveliest in the French Alps, surrounded by pretty little villages.

The pre-alpine area of Vercors and Chartreuse is an isolated landscape of scored peaks, high pastures, forests and waterfalls and a playground for speleologists and ski-trekkers. The Vercors Massif was a major stronghold of the French Resistance, and the scene of bitter fighting in 1944. Cemeteries and memorials to the fallen are numerous.

Grand indeed is the setting for Grenoble, with peaks rising on three sides of it. It lies quite close to the Monastery of the Grande Chatreuse, founded in 1084 by Saint Bruno. A city of life and bustle, with the mountains always in the distance pulling the eye upward.

Opposite The great Rhône river curves past Tournon in the Rhône valley, with its abundant fruit and vegetable gardens, and of course, numerous vineyards. The ones near Tournon produce Hermitage wines.

Right *La vie sportive:* the French Alpes are dotted with excellent ski resorts, such as Val-d'Isère and Chamonix.

Towns and Villages

Top One of the many attractive old villages in the Rhône Valley.

Above left The Benedictine Abbey of Hautcombe stands on the shores of Lake Bourget, near the popular spa town of Aix-les-Bains. This area is a busy centre for water sports.

Above right The skyscraper metropolis at the heart of modern Grenoble. This thriving city is a centre for industry and scientific research, with an important university. Its economic progress since World War II has set the pace for the rest of France.

Celtic legend has it that when the princes Momoros and Atepomaros had completed the foundations of their new town at Lyon, a flock of crows came down and enveloped them. When Julius Caesar invaded Gaul, he chose the town as his base camp and its Roman name because Lugdunum (hill of crows). Since then the city, situated at the meeting point of the rivers Rhône and Saône and at the centre of a network of roads, has grown and grown; now, with more than a million inhabitants, Lyon is the second largest conurbation in France.

Its history is a bloody one: there was a particularly violent massacre of early Christians from which has grown the city's special observance of the Feast of the Immaculate Conception on 8 December; during the French Revolution, the opposition of Lyon provoked the Committee of Public Safety to make the famous declaration that 'Lyon exists no more'. Such a prediction proved wildly inaccurate: with an economic base originally coming from the silk industry, and from banking, it is now a flourishing industrial centre, with chemicals, metallurgy and Berliet trucks. The university is well known for medicine, there is an annual trade fair, and in 1978 the city's first *métro* line was opened.

Yet history remains: the Place Bellecourt with its imposing façades; the Place des Terreaux, scene of so many executions during the Revolution, and the cathedral with its four square towers, Romanesque choir and thirteenth-century stained glass. There are Roman amphitheatres, a good Fine Arts Museum in what was a seventeenth-century convent for young ladies, a fine rose garden in the Parc de la Tête d'Or, and museums on puppetry and the resistance during World War II. Opera and music flourish in Lyon, where there are some of the best theatres in France.

Yet in many ways the richness of the past can be better seen in some of the smaller towns in the region. To the south of Lyon is the tiny village of Thines, with its beautiful Romanesque church. Nearer the city is Vienne, with its Roman Arch, Temple to Augustus and Livia, and Roman amphitheatre, the biggest in France. Then there is Perouges, a well preserved example of a medieval fortified town. Originally colonized by Italians from Perugia, time and (more important perhaps) the railways have passed it by.

Further to the east, among the peaks and lakes of the Alps, are a string of attractive resort towns: Aix-les-Bains, an elegant spa on the shores of Lake Bourget, has a bust of Queen Victoria, who once came to stay, a casino (said to be the first casino in France) and a summer season known for its festivals and galas. Annecy, a town of 50,000 on the lake that bears its name, combines a charming old quarter (with associations of Saint Francis de Sales and Rousseau) with thriving industries in razor blades, costume jewellery and ball-bearings, and an unusually active cultural life. Evian is on Lac Léman, the largest lake in Europe which stretches from Geneva to Montreux; the town is famous for its non-sparkling mineral water.

To the south is Grenoble, lying on a flat plain at the junction of three mountain valleys with high peaks all around – a majestic setting. Grenoble is a legend in France, the pace-setter of the nation's post-war economic revival. From a sleepy town in 1945, it has become a skyscraper metropolis, a thriving industrial, scientific and university centre; France's leading nuclear research centre is based here. 'What Grenoble does today, the rest of France does tomorrow', as the saying goes.

In 1968 the town was host for the Winter Olympics, which produced a flurry of town-planning; but the boom has not entirely destroyed the charming old quarter around the Place Grenette.

Left People have sought the curative waters at Aix-les-Bains since Roman times, and today the spa town is a busy resort, with lively festivals being held during the summer.

Above Narrow canals intersect the old part of Annecy, built on the shore of a beautiful lake of the same name.

Châteaux and Churches

This is not an area of great houses, but of attractive villages, each with a fine Romanesque church; modern cities with remnants of an ancient past; adventurous new architecture found side by side with important Roman excavations.

Such a contrast can be seen in the Nantua area. The giant Génissiat Dam is a spectacular piece of modern engineering that provides the area with hydroelectric power. Not far away, the church at Brou, in a suburb of Bourg-en-Bresse, is a powerful example of Flamboyant Gothic art, a symphony of finely-carved, mellow-hued stone. To the south stands the Benedictine abbey of Ambronay with its beautiful fifteenth-century courtyard, cloister and charter-house.

Lyon, a city that for centuries has thrived on industry and commerce, has nevertheless conserved 'Le Vieux Lyon', a maze of narrow alleys and splendid houses dating from the late Gothic and Renaissance periods. Here, the remains of a Roman theatre, the oldest in France,

of an odeon with a lovely pink, green and grey tiles floor and an amphitheatre all bear witness to the city's importance as a Gallo-Roman capital as do a number of aqueducts in the surrounding area. The design of these aqueducts, which supplied the city with 2,500,000 cubic feet of water a day, was not only a highly sophisticated system of hydraulics, but also aesthetically pleasing. At Beaunant, south-west of the city, one can see the spectacular forty-odd remaining arches of the Chaponost aqueduct. Lyon is famous, also, for two museums: the Musée Historique des Tissus which houses a unique collection of ancient Oriental and European fabrics, and the Fine Arts Museum.

West of Lyon, near Feurs, stands the Italianate, early Renaissance manor house of La Bastie-d'Urfé. This manor, with its exquisite painted and gilded stucco ceilings, its grotto whose walls are decorated with coloured shells, pebbles and bas-reliefs of pagan figures, provided the background for Honoré d'Urfé's

novel *Astrée*, the first of its genre.

Valence is rich in treasures, such as the Maison des Teles and the Renaissance Maison Dupré-Latour. Nearby, on the edge of a cliff, are the famous ruins of the castle of Crussol, and that mind-boggling folly, the 'Ideal Palace' of Postman Ferdinand Cheval, representing a lifetime's work. In his own backyard, he has created an astonishing universe of stones and pebbles wrought into Oriental, Arab, and medieval shapes.

Grenoble is the site of some excellent modern architecture created at the time of the 1968 Winter Olympics, such as its remarkable Maison de la Culture. In contrast, the most outstanding among the historic buildings in the old quarter is the Palais de Justice, a fine edifice of Flamboyant and Renaissance styles.

At Chambéry, the former capital of the Dukes of Savoy, whose great eighteenth-century château now serves as the Préfecture, there is also the fifteenth-century church of Saint-Pierre;

its ninth-century Carolingian crypt with its octagonal baptistry is moving in its simplicity. The Fine Arts Museum contains a fine collection of Italian, primitive and Renaissance paintings, including Paolo Uccello's *Portrait of a Young Man*, dating from the fifteenth century.

At Contamines-Montjoie, near Chamonix, stands the church of Notre-Dame-de-la-Gorge built in 1699 on the site of a much earlier sanctuary. The present church is one of the finest examples of Haute-Savoie Baroque with a breathtaking altar-piece of carved and painted wood, exuberant yet harmonious. Contrasting with this traditional church is the remarkable church of Notre-Dame-de-Toute-Grace, on the Plateau d'Assy, built by Novarina between 1938 and 1945. The mosaic of the facade is by Fernand Léger, the vast *Apocalypse* tapesty by Lurçat, the stained glass windows by Chagall and Rouault, with other contributions by Bonnard, Matisse and Braque.

Opposite The ruins standing out against a backdrop of the Rhône Valley are the remains of a great feudal fortification, Rochemaure.

The town of Vienne is rich in Gallo-Roman remains, including a large theatre, and the portico of the forum (**above**).

Right This well-preserved mosaic, depicting Herakles being received on Mount Olympus, is Gallo-Roman and dates from the first century.

Top The Renaissance Château of Grignan. The daughter of Madame de Sévigné lived here, and it was she who received so many of her famous letters that chronicle life in seventeenth-century France.

Cuisine

This is a large and varied region, encompassing the wild game and fruits of the Vivrais on the eastern flanks of the Massif Central, the varied high cuisine of Lyon in the Rhône Valley, the famous poultry of Bresse to its east, and the rich mountain cheeses of the Alps. Nowhere in the world is there a richer choice of wine and yet it does not dominate the cookery as in Burgundy.

Lyon, sometimes called 'the fountainhead of French cookery', is at the gastronomic heart of the region: no city has produced as many inventive dishes or as many famous cooks. The streets seem to be lined with restaurants, and their names are legendary: Mère Brazier, Nandron, Café Neuf, La Tour Rose. Here you will find the finest ingredients – Bresse fowl, Charolais beef, game from Dombes, fish from the lakes of Savoie and fresh produce from the valley of the Rhône – all prepared with simple pride and loving care. Even the smallest bistros (locally known as *bouchons*) take a pride in the local tradition.

How closely love and culinary pride are bound together in Lyon can be seen from the story of Poulet Célestine, a traditional dish of chicken and mushrooms. The year was 1860 and the widow Célestine was owner of the Restaurant du Cercle in Lyon. Her chef, young Rousselot, fell in love with his *patronne* but she, alas, failed to respond. In desperation, Rousselot allowed himself to be taken by the culinary muse: he cut his chicken, browned it, added mushroom caps and peeled, seeded tomatoes, then stewed them all in dry white wine, meat stock and (such inspiration) a glass of liqueur brandy. Perhaps it was the brandy, perhaps the cayenne pepper, which won the widow's heart.

Women are said to be originally responsible for much of the fame of Lyonnais cooking, and many *mères* still thrive to support the claim. Mère Brazier is the acknowledged queen, and some of her best dishes are the simplest: clear soup (*consommé*) enriched with egg; fried sole (*sole meunière*); skate with black butter (*raie au beurre noir*); creamed chicken (*poulet à la crème*). Her version of the Lyonnais speciality pike *quenelles* (*quenelles de brochet*), in which the fish is mashed, blended with cream and egg into finger shapes, which are then poached until they swell up into small soufflés, is quite astonishing. The sauce is flavoured with crayfish.

Rather starchy *quenelles* tend to appear in the cheaper restaurants and yet the Lyonnais tradition is also evident here in grilled tripe with tartar sauce (*tablier de*

Paul Bocuse

Paul Bocuse, sometimes called the modern Messiah of French cooking, is the eleventh generation of his family to run a restaurant at Collonges-au-Mont-d'Or near Lyon. With great respect for tradition and simplicity, he administers his three-star kitchen with the charm of a musician, the enthusiasm of a true patriot and the authority of a great chef. His restaurant stands on a busy main road and drivers are welcome to stop off for the simplest of meals. There are few formalities for those who do so: 'red wine' says Bocuse with a grin, 'goes perfectly well with fish'.

He has been accused of being too commercial, of serving raw food as *haute cuisine* and of plagiarizing other chef's creations, but he takes these comments as the inevitable hazard of success. As a member of France's illustrious Légion d'Honneur, and organiser of State luncheons on more than one occasion, he has no reason to be modest. 'When I travel to demonstrate my art,' he says, 'I go to publicize French cooking *and* to spread the name of Bocuse.'

sapeur), grilled pig's trotters (*pieds de porcs panés*), and the Lyon salad which contains both trotters and tripe as well as boiled beef and sausage, all dressed in a shallot and parsley *vinaigrette*. The sausages of Lyon are mostly studded with little cubes of fat, like salami: the best known is *cervelas*, made of lightly cured pork, which is eaten sliced as an hors d'oeuvre, poached with potatoes or stuffed into a piece of rolled, boned beef.

This region is very rich in *charcuterie*, especially among the craggy valleys of the Vernais and the Ardèche to the south-west. In Lamastre, at Mère Montagne's shop, there are sachets of

Cuisine

boned ham stuffed with fresh pork meat (*jambonettes*); rissoles of pork, cabbage and spinach (*cayettes*); snails stuffed with parsley butter (*escargots farcis*); truffled pâté of duck (*pâté de canard Lucullus*), and fine local hams. Any of these are likely to be served at the nearby Hôtel du Midi, followed by partridge and cabbage (*perdrix au chou*), thrush with grapes (*grive aux raisins*) or turkey stuffed with chestnuts and apples (*dindonneau farci aux marrons*). Apart from chestnuts, these valleys produce apricots, peaches, pears and cherries, which are cooked in a variety of pleasant tarts and mousses.

The chickens of Bresse have juicy flesh and – because they are fed on corn – soft, yellow livers. One traditional dish celebrates this fact: *gâteau de foies blonds de volaille* (blond chicken-liver cake), of

which Robert Courtine has written: 'Centuries of true epicurean aristocracy, of nobility of taste, of housewifely science, have gone into the elaboration of this wonder never to be found in textbooks.' It is served at the Hôtel France in Bourg-en-Bresse with a simple egg and cream sauce; chez Bocuse in Lyon, it is presented in a crayfish sauce.

Other, more common Bresse chicken dishes are in a wine and cream sauce (*poulet à la crème*), or with a vinegar sauce (*volaille au vinaigre*). Both are served at Le Mas Pommier in Bourg-en-Bresse, along with excellent pepper steak (*steak au poivre*), jugged hare (*civet de lièvre*) and that most delicate morsel of a dish – frogs' legs (*cuisses de grenouilles*).

Savoie is famous above all for cheese, and two in particular: Gruyère de Beau-

fort (in contrast to that of Comté) and Emmenthal. The Gruyère is made from that creamy milk produced by the high-meadow cattle of Tarertaise and Maurienne, and its smooth, delicate, aromatic charm is known throughout the world. Emmenthal, though Swiss in origin, is largely made in the French Haute-Savoie, and all of this is eaten in France. Mild and rather sweet in taste, it is softer than Gruyère, with larger holes. Both are ideal for the local melted-cheese pot (*fondue*), flavoured with white wine and kirsch, as well as the cheese sauces that are often served with vegetables (*légumes au gratin*). Other cheeses are the very soft Tomme de Savoie, sometimes rolled in herbs or raisins before ripening; Saint-Marcellin, ripened in chestnut leaves; and a tangy goat's cheese called

Above Typical Savoie dishes arrayed at a hotel in Aix-les-Bains. In the foreground *gratin de queue d'écrivisses* (crayfish tails in a cheese sauce) is a classic local dish; also shown are cheese fritters and an almond tart.

Right Tommes de Savoie cheeses set out on a market stall. The fat content is marked on the boxes. This region is famed for its cheeses, which included Emmenthal and Gruyère de Beaufort.

Bossons Macérés, ripened with alcohol, olive oil and herbs.

Savoie was, until 1860, an independent state, with its capital at Chambéry. This attractive old town enjoys the best of local lamb, cheese and fish. At La Chaumière you will find excellent trout; a remarkable truffled pâté of lake fish and two dishes of char, a delicious mountain lake fish, one hot in a tomato sauce (*omble chevalier au four*), the other cold in a light herb dressing (*sauce ravigote*).

Savoie produces a reputable honey, which is added to some of the *pâtisserie*, such as the light cakes called *pognes*, and pine-kernel croissants (*croissants aux pignons*). Other delicacies are raspberry soufflé (*soufflé aux framboises*); baked apples with cheese sauce (*pommes au gratin*) and peaches (*pêches gratinées*).

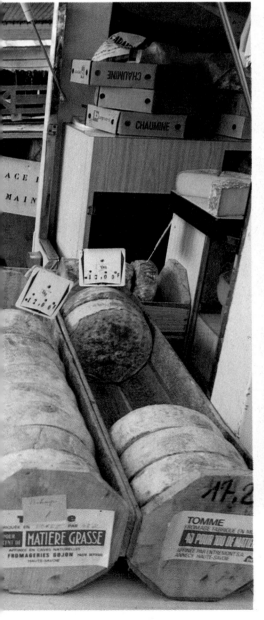

Top In this region of fine cuisine, many an old inn, such as the Hostellerie Gérouges, or quiet restaurant will offer splendid fare.

Above Vegetables grow well in the fresh air of the Rhône-Alpes region, and fruits such as apricots, cherries and pears abound in the valleys.

Wines and Spirits

Top One of the best Rhône wines is *vin blanc* from the Château Grillet. this tiny estate, perfectly situated beside the Rhône, is the smallest vineyard in France to have been awarded its own *appellation controlée*.

Above Vineyards of the Rhône Valley.

Right Three people are needed to push the bar on this press.

Top The *co-opérative* of Fleurie produces a delicious *grand cru* Beaujolais: light, fruity and fun to drink.

Above The *vigneron* fills a *tastevin* to sample new Beaujolais, one of France's most delightful wines. This *vin de l'année* is produced very quickly and drunk within a few weeks.

If one links the produce of the Rhône Valley to that of the ancient provinces of the Dauphiné and Savoie, one has enough variety for a lifetime. From the carefree Beaujolais north of Lyon to the majestic Côte-Rôtie and Hermitage to the south, the simpler country wines from the departments of the Loire and Ardèche, the solid reds from the middle Rhône, the sparkling whites from Clairette de Die to the tangy whites of Savoie, the range is unparalleled.

To start with the Beaujolais, the wines really belong with the Burgundies but the department is the Rhône, the vineyards running from just south of Mâcon to the outskirts of Lyon. The production is vast, 150 million bottles in plentiful years and almost all red. The little Beaujolais Blanc there is actually made in the Mâconnais (Saône-et-Loire) from the Chardonnay grape and to avoid confusion with the red, it is usually sold under the *appellation* Saint-Véran. The white is wonderfully stylish and refreshing, better than a Mâcon Blanc, less good than a Pouilly-Fuissé. The red is made from the Gamay grape, also planted in Auvergne and along the Loire, but which gives its best on the granity slopes of the Beaujolais. Vines, over 40,000 acres of them, are planted up to 1,800 feet (549 metres) overlooking the Saône Valley. The basic Beaujolais is bright, fruity, charming and refreshing, the perfect carafe wine. To appreciate the fruit, Beaujolais has to be drunk young, not more than a year old and always cool. Beaujolais Nouveau (or Primeur) is drunk not even two months after the harvest and is the least solemn wine imaginable. Many Lyonnais and Parisians talk of and drink little else in the week which follows the release date of 15 November. But the fresh grapeyness of the new wine from the southern end of the vineyard (or Beaujolais Bâtard, as it is known locally) gives little hint of the quality and individuality of the wines from the north. Here, the *appellation* Beaujolais-Villages, from around thirty-five villages, gives wines fruitier and a little sturdier. The best come from the nine *crus*, each with its own character: from the north to south, one has Saint-Amour (full but with a light bouquet); Juliénas (bigger and a little racier than Saint-Amour); Chénas (fruity and generous); Moulin-à-Vent (the biggest of the Beaujolais, and able to age marvellously); Fleurie (the queen of the *crus* with superb style); Chiroubles (soft and charming and must be drunk very young); Morgon (fuller and meatier and can age

like a Burgundy); Brouilly (typically Beaujolais with its charm and fruit), and Côte de Brouilly (a superior Brouilly). The best way to sample all the *crus* is to follow the *route du vin* through the villages stopping at the local *caveaux*, or converted churches in the case of Juliénas and Morgon! Nothing is so much fun as a trip through the Beaujolais.

East of the Rhône, and on the way to Switzerland, is the department of the Ain. The wines here are known as *les vins de Bugey* and are neatly situated both in geography and style between those of the Beaujolais and Savoie.

To the west of the Rhône is the Loire department, where a considerable amount of pleasant red wine is made. The *appellations* are Côtes du Forez, Côtes Roannaises and Coteaux du Lyonnais. As might be expected, the Lyonnais wines very much resemble the Beaujolais in style, as do the Côtes du Forez. Only the Côtes Roannaises make serious wine, blending up to 50% Pinot Noir with the pervasive Gamay and making a wine with some depth and character. They are excellent wines for drinking on the spot and as a change from the more expensive Beaujolais.

It is as though the Gamay regions of the Rhône and the Loire were sandwiched as a relief to the palate after the superb Burgundies to the north and the very serious and great Rhône wines to the south. The seriousness starts at Vienne, or rather Ampuis, with the vineyards of the Côte-Rôtie. Here the vineyards are terraced at incredible angles, often only fifteen feet wide. The soil is arid and stony, all work is done by hand. But the base of this superb wine are the grape varieties: Syrah, and to a 20% maximum, the white Viognier. Côte-Rôtie is full, almost purple in colour, has a particular bouquet of violets and raspberries, and on the palate is as sumptuous as a Châteauneuf-du-Pape, but more elegant. On its own, the Viognier produces the marvel called Condrieu, a white wine with an unctuous bouquet and a flavour of dried apricots, and the even more rare Château Grillet.

Moving down the Rhône river, we come to Tain l'Hermitage, the centre of the northern Rhône wine trade. Here, the terraced vineyards rise high above the river planted with the famous Syrah for the reds and Roussanne and Marsanne for the whites. The red Hermitage (and the 'minor' Crozes-Hermitage) are the 'manliest' wines of France, powerful and generous. They are at their best after ten years and can rival a wine from any part of France. The whites, full and fine at once, are particularly aromatic. From the same soil and same grape, but opposite Hermitage, come the wines of Saint-Joseph. Dark in colour, full-bodied, they are a little rough when young but soften with age. There is also a little rosé and white in the *appellation*. Further south from Saint-Joseph on the outskirts of Valence is the tiny vignoble of Cornas. The wine is only red (from the Syrah), less noble than the Hermitage, but a very genuine wine. South of Cornas is Saint-Péray, an *appellation* producing excellent dry white wines with a scent of violets. In the region, much of the Saint-Péray is drunk *champagnisé* or sparkling.

Still in the department of the Drôme, although very much to the south, one finds the best-known sparkling wine of the Rhône Valley, La Clairette de Die. The variety of grape is the Clairette with a touch of Muscat which gives the wine its bouquet and particular character.

There are virtually no grapes growing in the department of the Isère and it is almost a surprise to find such a selection on the foothills of the Alps in the Savoie and Haute-Savoie. Most of the wines are white, almost colourless, sprightly with a touch of acidity. The reds are light in colour, soft and fruity. The most prestigious wine in the region is the Crépy, grown on the edge of Lac Léman. It is made from the Chasselas grape (seen also in Pouilly-sur-Loire and in Switzerland) and is delicious, very dry, low in alcohol and often still slightly *spritzig*. The other famous wine is the Seyssel, made only from the Roussette and produced in tiny

quantities. It is softer and more elegant than the Crépy, but less fun. Recently, many Savoie wines have been awarded *appellation controlée* status, a move up from the V.D.Q.S. Thus, if a wine is made from any single variety (Altesse, Apremont, Chignin, Roussette for the whites; Mondeuse or Gamay for the reds), the wine may carry the *appellation* Vin de Savoie. This makes the range of wines most appealing, since each variety has its own characteristics.

Below The wine-maker uses a hydrometer to test the gravity of the 'must'. This measures the sugar content and ripeness of the grapes – an important process in determining the quality of the wine.

Bottom Wines of the region.

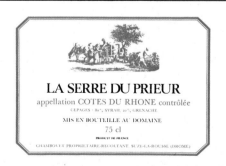

Aquitaine

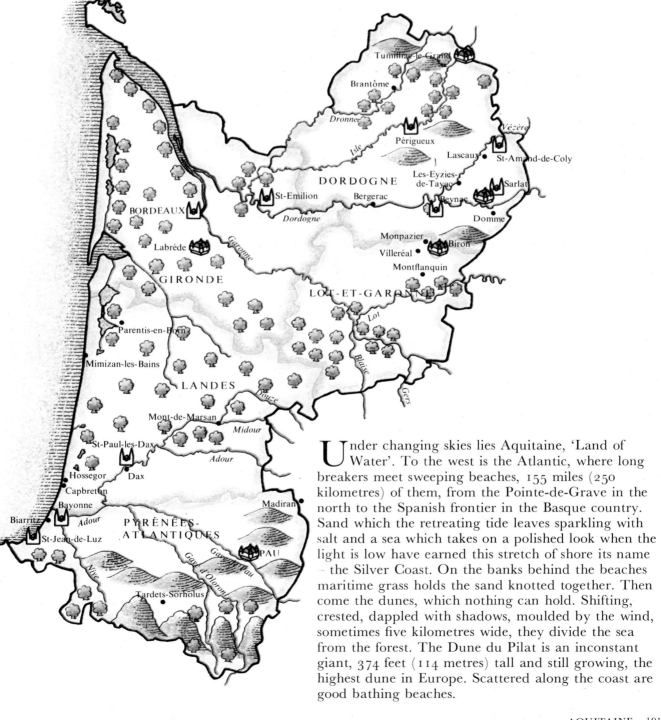

Under changing skies lies Aquitaine, 'Land of Water'. To the west is the Atlantic, where long breakers meet sweeping beaches, 155 miles (250 kilometres) of them, from the Pointe-de-Grave in the north to the Spanish frontier in the Basque country. Sand which the retreating tide leaves sparkling with salt and a sea which takes on a polished look when the light is low have earned this stretch of shore its name – the Silver Coast. On the banks behind the beaches maritime grass holds the sand knotted together. Then come the dunes, which nothing can hold. Shifting, crested, dappled with shadows, moulded by the wind, sometimes five kilometres wide, they divide the sea from the forest. The Dune du Pilat is an inconstant giant, 374 feet (114 metres) tall and still growing, the highest dune in Europe. Scattered along the coast are good bathing beaches.

Introduction

Inland from the dunes stretches the area known as Les Landes. In the nineteenth century pines were planted to stop the encroaching sand which even threatened inland vineyards. Before the pines there was nothing but a semi-desert of pools and rushes, marshy in summer, parched in winter, where the shepherds wore stilts to move about looking, as the French poet Théophile Gautier put it, like walking compasses measuring the land. The seedling pines took root and now this is one of the largest introduced forests anywhere, and the source of much of France's timber.

Inland again, to the north-east, is the rolling countryside of the old province of Périgord, corresponding more or less to the department of the Dordogne. Best-known is the stretch from Argentat via Sarlat to Bergerac where the river runs in loops through valleys and between cliffs. Trees often grow right to the water's edge, small villages cling to the heights, the land rises and falls in green waves and the bare faces of limestone have weathered to a myriad of colours.

Far to the south, from Biarritz inland to Tardets is the French Basque country, with more excellent beaches alternating with rocky headlands. Here, relatively rare in Europe, surfing is a popular sport.

On the lower slopes of the Pyrenees, villages nestle among hills which support flocks of rugged Pyrenean sheep and equally rugged shepherds who have their own ideas about individuality and independence, marked by long periods of smouldering discontent and occasional flashes of violence. Until the eighteenth century many of them used to earn their livelihood by whaling in Arctic waters. The port of Saint-Jean-de-Luz was a whaling town and is still the home of a fishing fleet as well as a popular seaside resort and, surprisingly enough, the scene of Louis XIV's wedding in 1600 to the Spanish princess, Marie-Thérèse. The church is still standing but the door through which the couple passed was walled up after the ceremony and has never been used since.

Spain seems very close in this part of the world where *espadrilles* (rope-soled shoes), berets and bull-baiting are common and the game of *pelote* is a favourite sport. With an eye to the tourist trade, Basques still perform their famous, lively folk dances. Symbol of legendary Basque male pride is the *makila*, a walking-cane presented to a boy on his reaching adulthood. Bayonne is the principal town of the area.

Capital of Aquitaine is Bordeaux, which has given its name to great wines – some would say the greatest in the world. The Latin poet Ausonius was born here

in AD 310 and his memoirs contain descriptions of life in the city.

Five departments in all go to make up the Aquitaine region: Dordogne, Gironde, Lot-et-Garonne, Landes and Pyrénées-Atlantiques – and they offer almost as many contrasts as anyone could hope to find compressed into the corner of one country.

It was the Romans who called Aquitaine 'Land of Water' but parts of it had already been inhabited centuries before by prehistoric people. They hunted and fished for a living and took refuge in natural formations, under overhanging cliffs or in caves. There they embellished the walls with pictures of the animals they hunted. This is man the artist, relentless hunter, loving the thing he kills.

Bison, deer, mammoths and horses are among the animals depicted in the caves of the Dordogne. Some of the paintings go back 30,000 years and doubtless had religious or magical significance, otherwise they would not have been created in such numbers and with such care. How awesome these underground frescoes must have appeared to Stone-Age peoples in the flickering light of primitive lamps.

Strangely, too, there are modern cave dwellings, where houses and churches have been built back into the limestone. Some of the houses are still inhabited. In Saint-Emilion, at the mouth of the Dordogne river, the church of the same name was formed by enlarging existing caves and carving deeper into the rock. It is the work of twelfth-century Benedictine monks.

After the Romans came the Visigoths and then raids by the Norsemen. Mostly, though, Aquitaine remembers the English. Much of the area spent a long time under their rule when Henry Plantagenet became Henry II of England, with Eleanor of Aquitaine as his queen.

To Rome goes the credit for planting the original vineyards and to England some of the credit for appreciating, praising and buying the resultant wines. The Englishman who could afford it always loved his claret – and still does. Wine traders from the area were often seen in England in the Middle Ages.

Opposite Médoc, Bordeaux, Saint Emilion: Aquitaine is the home of some of France's greatest wines, and has a fine cuisine to accompany them. These vines belong to the Château Ausone vineyards.

Below The southern part of France is distinctively Spanish in flavour. Bullfights are a feature of the summer festivals, such as these revelries in Bayonne, principal town of the French Basque area.

Towns and Villages

A quarter of Aquitaine's population lives in the regional capital, Bordeaux, and its suburbs, which leaves the remainder of this big region rather sparsely populated, except for the newly-industrialized vicinity of Pau, and the Basque coast.

As Burdiglia, Bordeaux was inhabited by a Celtic people, the Bituriges Vivisci. The Romans came later, and an amphitheatre, and parts of the old city wall remain from that era. Since the earliest times, trade with Spain and Britain has flourished, and the area, at the time of Henry II of England was under English rule. This left its mark on Aquitaine in the form of châteaux – more than a thousand of them in Dordogne alone.

The urban renewal of the eighteenth century made Bordeaux the fine city it is today. It prospered from the triangular trade between Africa, France and the Americas, and the Marquis de Tourny (1690–1760), Intendant of Guyenne, graced it with splendid buildings and squares. The Grand Théâtre, with its statue-topped colonnade, is outstanding, and Garnier later imitated its imposing double staircase and cupola in the Paris Opera House. An international festival

Top left The picturesque buildings of La Roque-Gageac cluster at the foot of a massive cliff, with the Dordogne flowing in front.

Left Shepherds in their traditional flowing capes were once a familiar sight in the Landes department, striding about the marshy countryside on tall stilts.

of music and dance takes place in Bordeaux in May, and in June the annual art exhibition draws crowds from all over the world.

Today, Bordeaux is a busy commercial and administrative city, with three universities, the sixth largest port in France, and an industrial centre too, (petrochemicals, oil refineries and a big Ford car factory). In recent years, much has been done to modernize this sedate and conservative town, and bring in new industry and new ideas.

The department of the Landes is a vast pine forest planted on swamps and sand-dunes reclaimed in the 1800s. Today, the Landes region is better-known for its outstanding *foie gras* and asparagus. The oil wells at Parentis make France an oil-producing country, though a minor one.

The Landes is one of the strongholds of French rugby, but Spain as well as Britain has imported its sport, and at Mont-de-Marsan there is a famous *corrida*. Just outside Dax, the church at Saint-Paul-les-Dax contains a twelfth-century apse, and a frieze reputed to be one of the most interesting examples of eleventh-century wood sculpture in southern France. Dax itself, another town

well known for its rugby and totally unconnected mud-water cures, was a bishopric as far back as AD 400.

Further to the south lies the picturesque Basque Coast, with a more ancient tourist tradition. Biarritz, 'the Queen of resorts and the resort of Kings', and Saint-Jean-de-Luz were patronized by the cream of Second Empire society; and by later generations too. Biarritz was popular with the Empress Eugénie, then with Edward VII and many other royals, followed by filmstars. The aura of thirties glamour still hangs over the place, and one half expects a slinky Hispano Suiza to glide up to the hotel door at any moment.

The Spanish flavour of the Basque region is evident in numerous festivals and bull-fights that take place in June,

July and August. During the celebration of *Toro del Fuego* in Saint-Jean-de-Luz, a fire-spitting, papier-maché bull is paraded through the streets.

East of Bordeaux the ground begins to rise and fall as in a motionless ocean swell, and the Landes becomes the Périgord, which covers much of Dordogne and Lot-et-Garonne. In summer the markets of the fortified medieval towns of Lot-et-Garonne: Monflanquin, Villeréal, or the arcades of Villeneuve-sur-Lot are filled with delicious sweet tomatoes, melons bursting with sugar, and the famous prunes of Agen.

In the Dordogne department, Périgueux, Brantôme, and Sarlat, with their well-preserved medieval centres, are among the most attractive towns in south-western France.

Above Spanning the broad Garonne river, the great city of Bordeaux has found a new prosperity, with the continuing growth of its port and industries in recent years.

Above Brightly-patterned tents and umbrellas testify that Saint-Jean-de-Luz is as popular a resort today as it was during the Second Empire.

Châteaux and Churches

Aquitaine's architecture records its long history of relentless wars between the English and the French and the Wars of Religion that shook the land for centuries. Here there are many fortified towns known as *bastides*; great castle strongholds; even the churches are fortified.

On the Dordogne river, the dramatic fourteenth-century Castle of Beynac-et-Cazenac, whose crenellated keep and massive walls tower high above the village and command a bird's eye view of the landscape, overlooks the ruins of its arch-rival, the Château of Castelnaud.

Gentler in aspect is the fairy-tale Castle of Jumilhac-le-Grand in the north of the Dordogne, whose ochre, ambre and pink walls, and steep roofs with clusters of pepperpot turrets, inspired the artist Gustave Doré. At Périgueux stands Saint-Front Cathedral, a huge Byzantine structure, the earliest of the domed churches built in the Middle Ages along the old Roman road from Rodez to Cahors and Saintes. Breathtaking, with its five glittering cupolas, elegant minarets and soaring bell-tower, it stands in the midst of an old quarter of the town.

The town of Les Eyzies-de-Tayac, is also known as the 'capital of prehistory', for all along the banks of the Vézère river are prehistoric caves, the famous Lascaux ones among them, whose walls are covered with amazingly sophisticated and well-preserved engravings, drawings and paintings. Horses, bisons, stags, mammoths, wild boar and deer are all depicted with great vitality.

Directly south of Monpazier, on top of a hill, stands the great Château of Biron, a lumbering mass of towers, high walls and battlements built between the twelfth and seventeenth century. The severity of its medieval exterior is offset by the grassy courtyard that was used as a haven for beleaguered villagers and their livestock in times of trouble, by its fine Renaissance chapel and splendid kitchen whose floor consists of huge slabs of stone.

The age-old fortified town of Saint-Emilion is the site of a subterranean monolithic church, an amazing ninth to twelfth century edifice created out of earlier caves and the most important of its kind in France. It is located on top of a veritable warren of caves and catacombs. The town itself is most picturesque with its steep cobbled streets and ancient grey and ochre stone houses set in the midst of a landscape of vineyards.

Bordeaux is a historic city rich in Roman, Merovingian, Romanesque and Gothic monuments. In the eighteenth century, it became one of France's most beautiful due to two great architects of the period: Victor Louis who designed the Grand Théâtre famous for its harmonious proportions and sober elegance, and Jacques Gabriel. They were re-

Above Domes and minarets towering over Périgueux recall the splendours of the East. The Byzantine influence is strong in this Cathedral of Saint-Front, built on the plan of a Greek cross surmounted by five glittering domes.

sponsible for the grand avenues and elegant mansions for which Bordeaux is known. Among its outstanding churches are Saint-André Cathedral, a part-Romanesque part-Gothic structure built over a 400-year period and renowned for its fine thirteenth-century carvings; fourteenth-century Saint-Michel basilica, a great edifice badly damaged in 1940 but successfully restored and known for its modern stained-glass windows by the celebrated designer Max Ingrand; and Saint-Seurin, an eleventh-century church whose main interest lies in the eleventh century Romanesque crypt and ornate sixth-century sarcophagi.

Down in the Basque country, the interior of the Church of Saint-Jean-Baptiste at Saint-Jean-de-Luz, where the marriage of Louis XIV to Maria Teresa of Spain took place in 1660, is typically Basque in style, with many statues and colonnades, a three-tiered gallery and painted panelling. At Bayonne there are two outstanding museums, the Musée Basque which has a fascinating display bearing on all things Basque, and the Musée Bonnat which has an excellent collection of paintings and drawings by Dürer, Goya, Ingres and others.

Left Contained in this gold statue are the remains of Sainte Foy, once the object of pilgrimages to the abbey at Agen. Covetous monks from Conques infiltrated the monastery to steal the relics, which are now in the splendid church at Conques (Aveyron).

Below and **bottom** Cave paintings at Lascaux. Powerful and sophisticated, these vivid depictions of various animals are a remarkable legacy from prehistoric times.

Below left Religious upheaval and turbulent times led to great fortified châteaux in southwestern France. The Château of Les Milandes, however, was built as a *château de plaisance*.

Cuisine

Truffles

In Périgord, there are also the best truffles in France. Sometimes called 'black diamonds', these subterranean members of the mushroom family grow on the roots of certain trees, especially the oak, from which they are sniffed out by specially trained dogs or pigs. 'The fragrance of the truffle,' writes the gastronome Robert Courtine, 'spreads itself abroad with the November frosts: sometimes a mere sniff can make the head spin.' The very high cost of truffles, tends to reinforce this over-enthusiasm, but the flavour *is* unusual and most agreeable. Whether used in small amounts to scent a chicken or an omelette, or served in their own right – bound in light pastry (*truffe en feuilleté*), or baked in the embers of a fire (*truffe sous les cendres*), truffles are worth pursuing in Périgueux.

Aquitaine remains France's greatest repository of country cooking. From the broad sands of the Landes, where Atlantic rollers beat against the shores, to the fertile farmlands of the hinterland and up into the hills of Périgord and Béarn, there is a vast supply of foods and an ancient tradition of preparing them for the table. The styles change but there is always the flavour of authenticity.

The Landes are magnificently bleak and still. Offshore the oyster beds provide a constant supply of this delicacy for the tables of Aquitaine. The French like to eat them at any time of day, ice cold and raw, washed down with dry white wine. On the Bordeaux waterfront, outside the restaurants, you can see them being cleaned and opened, and the sight draws you inside. Here the patron serves them with small spicy sausages. Mussels are also abundant, served with a red wine and tomato sauce, or in a creamier sauce called *mouclade*.

Fish is abundant along the coast, but for the best of it, the traveller is better off in Bordeaux. Here you will find red mullet baked with chervil (*petits rougets au cerfeuil*), lamprey in a leek and wine sauce (*lamproie aux poireaux et au vin rouge*) and fresh sea bass with mushroom sauce (*escalopes du bar aux cèpes*). Ceps are one of the many mushroom varieties which pepper the inland woods in autumn: they are canned for use at other times of year but if you find them on the menu in season, ask the patron to prepare them *à la bordelaise*, stewed in olive oil with parsley and garlic.

Wine is the *leitmotif* of Bordeaux, and food plays a secondary role. The best restaurants, like Clavel, Dubern and the Château Trompette, all boast splendid cellars. The cuisine is rich, perhaps a trifle ostentatious, but several dishes will always be rooted in local tradition. Try fattened buntings (*ortolans en caissettes*), a succulent bird which migrates across the Landes in spring and autumn, and – if they are available – venison or pheasant,

the best of the wild game of Aquitaine. Rabbits are also ubiquitous. Beef and lamb are not always of the best, though at the Château Trompette the steaks are excellent: here the chef prepares a true *entrecôte à la Bordelaise*, marinated in oil, salt and pepper, rubbed with shallots, beef-marrow and butter, then grilled.

Once out in the hills, you will find a simpler, more reliable cuisine. In Périgord (an area known sometimes as the Dordogne), where fresh streams run down from the Massif Central to the valleys of the Aquitaine basin below, there are many small villages with friendly, cheap restaurants serving fine food. Among the many traditional dishes are soups flavoured with sorrel or saffron; eggs baked with aubergines (*oeufs à l'agenaise*); beans with salt pork (*haricots à la couenne*) and duck with onions (*canard aux oignons*). Often there are freshly-caught trout, perhaps marinated in olive oil, lemon and thyme (*truite marinée*) or stuffed with duck (*truite farcie au confit*).

Opposite top These shrouded figures are not taking part in a sacred rite, but merely enjoying a meal! The flavour of the *ortolans* (buntings), is thought to be so special that every aroma must be savoured – hence the head-cloths.

Top *Salade périgourdine.*

Above One of the delights of Aquitaine: succulent oysters from the Landes region are washed down with a glass of dry white wine.

Right Not for the faint-hearted: garlic bulbs roasted and eaten whole.

Cuisine

Every village *charcuterie* in Périgord is lined with colourful jars of *confit*, preserves of goose or duck or pig which are used instead of butter. Many fish and meat dishes will contain their delectable flavours. Snails are also preserved in this way, but for the authentic experience of this delicacy, ask for *escargots frais*: they are only available in the spring and summer, but then any patron will be happy to serve them in his own version of a wine or garlic sauce.

Montaigne was born among these lush, green hills, an influential writer of the sixteenth century, his philosophical works stand today as a symbol of the hearty way of life here. 'The value of life,' he wrote, 'lies not in the length of days but the use we make of them.' Four centuries later, his name is still remembered in one of the fine local wines and in a confection made of almond paste and cherries called *la Montaignette*. Almonds, along with walnuts, chestnuts, peaches and plums, grow in abundance in the valleys, and the Périgord desserts make good use of them.

Further south, where the plain of Gascony rises into the Pyrenees, there is another, quite different but no less fascinating, style of country cooking.

This is Béarn, much influenced by its proximity to Spain: the food is spicy and the folk tales about it equally sharp. As in Périgord, goose dripping is the primary cooking fat, and the Béarnais say it gives them potency. It certainly enriches their table, and – judging from the swarthy features of these people – perhaps it does more. Goose fat is used to cook eggs, a *daube* of beef, a leg of lamb and even trout from the mountain streams. Tarragon, also said to be an aphrodisiac, is used in the Béarnaise cuisine, where it takes a prominent place in the famous *sauce béarnaise*, along with vinegar, white wine and chervil.

Another speciality of Béarn is *garbure*, a thick bean soup with potatoes, cabbage and salt pork. Haricot beans were once the main ingredient, for they grow well among the maize fields which once covered Aquitaine, but nowadays *langots plats* are used, which are a little like navy beans. *Garbure* is a meal in itself, an incomparable end to a day's walking in this picturesque part of France.

The Basque people, who occupy the south-west corner of Aquitaine, also have their version of *garbure*, as indeed they have their version of almost every aspect of life. Their individuality is remarkable,

as their ongoing struggle for political autonomy demonstrates. Their cooking reflects this quality. They hunt wood pigeon in the hills and make it into a delicious stew (*civet de palombe*). They use olive oil, which is otherwise rare in Aquitaine; they add *piment basquais* – a spicy red pepper resembling chillies but less hot – to many dishes; and they are the only cheese-makers of the region. The best known of their cheeses are Orrys and Castillon, both strongly spiced with pepper and *piment basquais*.

A sea-going people for centuries, the Basques have many fish dishes, prepared without pretention. Cuttlefish (*chapirons*), angler fish (*baudroie*), octopus (*gambas*), squid (*chipirones*), prawns, *langoustines*, fresh sardines fried in olive oil – the list is vast and varied. At the Restaurant Euzkalduna in Bayonne is a delicious version of the Basque fish stew, as well as several dishes which contain the famous local Bayonne ham. Another common Basque dish is *pipérade*, a kind of omelette with tomatoes and peppers.

As for Basque desserts, they are somewhat rough but always of good flavour: one of the best is *martuxa*, an iced jelly of soft fruits, usually raspberries and blackberries, which grow in abundance here.

Left People shelling walnuts in the Dordogne. An important ingredient in many dishes, such as the *salade périgourdine*, the nuts are also crushed to make oil (**centre left**). Mixed with vinegar, this makes a delicious *vinaigrette* for salads. **Bottom left** This Basque version of a *paella*, topped with fresh seafood, was served in Ainhoa. **Below** the perfect answer to a hearty appetite, this regional dish from Béarn is called a *garbure*. Potatoes, salt pork and beans make a filling soup.

Left Although not a great cheese-producing region, ewe's milk is used for some. The Basque people make two cheeses – Castillón and Orrys – both spiced with peppers.

Wines and Spirits

In the ancient province of Aquitaine, the presence of Bordeaux and its wines is overwhelming. Bordeaux is the largest *appellation* in France and the grape varieties used throughout the province are generally attributed to the Bordelais. But it would be quite wrong to think that wines from the Gironde are all that the Aquitaine has to offer.

While the grape varieties are often associated with the Bordeaux region, some of them originated elsewhere in France. The skill in Aquitaine is in the diverse planting according to the soil and blending in the vinification vats. The red grapes are: Cabernet Sauvignon, the principal grape of the Médoc and the Graves, deep-coloured, austere wines developing incomparable finesse with age; Cabernet Franc (known as the Bouchet at Saint-Emilion, the Bouchy at Madiran and the Breton in Touraine!), good fine colour, a little softer than the Cabernet Sauvignon and often with a bouquet of violets; Merlot, less deep in colour but rich in fruit; Malbec, rather rustic and hard; Petit Verdot, used in small quantities for blending. The whites are: Semillon, for flavour and softness; Sauvignon, for finesse and body and Muscadelle, used in small quantities for its heady scent of muscat.

The Aquitaine region runs from the Charente to the Spanish border. In the north is the department of the Dordogne (otherwise known as Périgord) where wine-producing is centred around the historic town of Bergerac. The reds are fruity, not too hard and repay investigation, especially Pécharmant, a sort of

Top left Saint-Emilion produces some of the greatest red wines of France. Wine is even stored in cellars cut into the limestone below the church.

Left Half-barrels of grapes being delivered to the *chais* (the sheds where the wine is stored), at the Château Magdelaine, at Saint-Emilion.

Right Beynac, not far from Bergerac, a great centre of wine production. The best *appellation* is Monbazillac.

Bergerac Supérieur. Bergerac whites used to be semi-sweet, but are now generally dry, the driest being from Panisseau where the grapes are harvested especially early. The sweeter whites have their own *appellation*: Rosette, an original wine, full and semi-sweet: Montravel, sweeter with great charm and Monbazillac, the pearl of the Dordogne, golden in colour, honey-scented and wonderfully luscious. There is some pleasant rosé made around Bergerac.

Farther south in the Lot-et-Garonne, to the south-east of the great vineyards of Sauternes and Barsac, the red wines from the Côtes de Duras are a little tougher than the Bergeracs and the whites very good, a little softer but not fully sweet. Next door, the Côtes de Marmandais offers dry, white, fruity whites from the Sauvignon grape and good reds, mostly from the Cave Coopérative de Cocumont (translation: 'cuckold's mount'), a name which amuses the French. The best wines in the Lot-et-Garonne, however, come from the Côtes de Buzet, most expertly vinified at the Cave Coopérative by an ex-*régisseur* from Château Lafite-Rothschild. The extra wood-ageing given to the Cuvée Napoléon makes this the wine to look out for.

If one heads north-east into the department of the Gironde, one discovers the Bordeaux vineyards at the outskirts of Langon. Apart from the sand-dunes on the Atlantic coast and the pine forests on the edge of Les Landes, vines cover most of the department. The basic *appellations*, Bordeaux Rouge and Bordeaux Blanc, represent well over half of the

Top Grapes from the Château Coutet at Barsac, the largest of the five *communes* producing Sauternes. These grapes have reached the state of over-maturity known as the *pourriture noble* (noble rot), which gives a sweet, heady wine.

Above An *eau-de-vie* distillery near Sarlat, in the Dordogne.

Wines and Spirits

production, the rest being split into three main areas: the meaty reds from Saint-Emilion, Pomerol and Fronsac and Côtes de Bourg on the right bank of the Gironde, the elegant Médocs and Graves on the left and the Sauternes and other sweet white wines from the Langon region. The range is wider than any other wine area in France, from the simple everyday reds to the intense, complex wines of the great Châteaux, from the driest of dry whites to the rich long-lived Sauternes, not to speak of a little rosé and some *vin mousseux*.

To take the right bank first, if one were driving south from the Cognac area the first vineyards one comes to are the Côtes de Blaye, pleasant wines, both red and white. A little farther along the Gironde, the *vignerons* of the Côtes de Bourg, underlining the fact that they are just across the river from Margaux, make a better wine than the Blayais. And, as you follow the river, the wine improves still more. The Côtes de Fronsac and the superior Canon-Fronsac have been described as 'classic old-fashioned claret', quite elegant, deep-coloured, long-lasting wines, not so well-known and always good value. Fronsac is next to Libourne, a small market town which is second only to Bordeaux in importance for its wine business. On the other side of the town are Pomerol and Saint-Emilion. The latter, grown around the medieval town of Saint-Emilion are generous, warm, sturdy wines with an excellent colour. Often referred to as 'the Burgundies of Bordeaux', this over-simplification gives some impression of the velvety softness from a high proportion of Merlot grapes. Saint-Emilion is divided into wine from the vineyards on the slopes around the town (les Côtes) and those from the flat, gravelly land on the way to Pomerol (les Graves). Château Ausone is the best known wine from the Côtes and Château Cheval Blanc from the Graves. Saint-Emilion should be drunk at five to ten years old, more for great vintages. One of the back roads to Libourne separates Saint-Emilion from Pomerol, yet the wine is different. It is more velvety, if anything, than Saint-Emilion, has the same ruby colour and full flavour but perhaps has more finesse where the other has more vigour. It is often thought of as an autumnal wine and is supposed to have a bouquet of truffles. Here, Château Pétrus is the star.

The main road to Bordeaux brings you back to Libourne where you cross the Dordogne River and enter the vast region of Entre-Deux-Mers. Here the wines are, for the most part, white, the *appellation* Entre-Deux-Mers applying to dry, white wines which are good with fish and particularly good with oysters. Red wines in the area are sold under the Bordeaux or Bordeaux Supérieur label and despite the lower *appellation* are more expensive than the whites. Along the banks of the Garonne are the Premières Côtes de Bordeaux, with the white and fairly sweet wines, notably Loupiac and Sainte-Croix-de-Mont, in the south end by Langon, and the rather sinewy reds grown in the north towards Bordeaux.

Most wine-lovers consider the great wines of the Médoc to be the finest in the world; those who disagree consider them to be the next finest. They have a special 'Médoc' character, partly due to the gravelly soil, mostly due to the Cabernet Sauvignon grape. They are wines of an intense colour, austere, even stand-offish when young, giving way to elegance and finesse combined with great depth of flavour and perfect harmony. Driving north from Blanquefort, there are four main communal *appellations* each with its own character: Margaux for elegance and finesse; Saint-Julien for pure breed, 'quintessential claret'; Pauillac for Médoc at its most extreme and Saint-Estèphe for robustness and longevity. The lesser *commune* of Moulis is smooth and full-flavoured, while Listrac is fine if a little less generous. These are in the Haut-Médoc, the Bas-Médoc from north of Saint-Estèphe producing similarly excellent wines of perhaps less overall distinction. The typical Médoc property is larger and more cohesive than elsewhere in France, generally with a grand Château to justify the name on the label. In 1855, the wine brokers of Bordeaux classified the better known Châteaux (admitting Château Haut-Brion from the Graves and Château d'Yquem from Sauternes) into first, second, third, fourth, and fifth Great Growths (*crus classés*). The Château Margaux (Margaux), Latour and Lafite-Rothschild (both Pauillacs) were awarded first Growth status and these three were joined by Château Mouton-Rothschild (also Pauillac) in 1973. While the classification is still adhered to, there are many Châteaux making wine superior to their classifications and a few who no longer justify inclusion. Considered just below are the excellent *crus bourgeois* which often produce wines of astonishing quality.

The main way out of the Médoc is back down to Bordeaux. At the south-

Above A view of the Médoc vineyards of Lafite-Rothschild, Pauillac. Classic French clarets are produced in this area.

Left An array of superb wines from the famous Château Lafite.

Right Wine labels of Aquitaine.

Top right Tying new vines to stakes, Gironde department. This area produces huge quantities of wine, all Bordeaux.

Wines and Spirits

west edge of the city starts the region of the Graves. This area, which takes its name from the gravelly soil, has the distinction of producing both white and red wines of quality. White wines can be made in the Médoc, Saint-Emilion and Pomerol regions, but they may only carry the simple Bordeaux *appellation*. The greatest Graves come from the north, around Léognac, the lesser, although very pleasant wines, from the south around Langon. The reds have great finesse, are less intense than the Médoc but with a touch of the softness of wines from the right bank, sometimes with a definite hint of roses in the bouquet. The whites are the best dry white wines of the Bordeaux region, the greatest on a par with the Montrachet family in Burgundy, if allowed time to develop. The difference between a Graves Grand Cru Classé and a plain Graves is marked, but so is the price.

While the southern Graves region circles Langon and rejoins the right bank of the Garonne, the centre of interest here is the great, sweet white wines. At Cerons, and especially Barsac and Sauternes, the sometimes semi-tropical micro-climate allows the grapes to attain a state of over-maturity known as the 'noble rot'. The density of sugar in the grapes (which are harvested bunch by bunch, if not berry by berry, over a period of several weeks) gives a natural, sweet wine of incomparable flavour and bouquet. It is golden in colour, sometimes a little heady when young and improves with age almost without limit. The best known is Château d'Yquem.

The most illustrious wine in the Pyrénées-Atlantiques is Jurançon (near Pau). While some of the white wine is now made dry, the reputation rests on the luxurious sweet wines with a touch of spice in the bouquet and a refreshing point of acidity. It ages well, being almost as indestructible as Sauternes.

Left Bordeaux: the very word brings to mind the finest wines of France. The British-owned Château Loudenne, where these grapes are being sorted, makes a light, minor Médoc.

Below Resplendent in the livery of the Confrérie du Bontemps, an expert samples the wines of Médoc.

Midi-Pyrénées

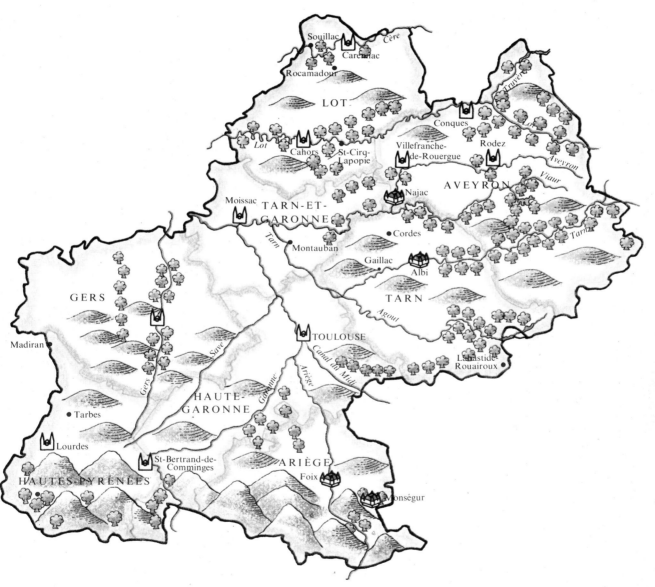

This large south-western stretch of France is full of diversity, both the landscape and the people. There are places in the department of the Lot which seem magical. Not the magic of watered-down modern fairy-tales but an old, dark brooding business which generations have either drawn from or imposed on the countryside. The feeling is strong in the Célé valley. In this region there are two distinct life-styles, depending on the geography. There are the tough shepherds of the chalky *causses* (highlands), where the ground is poor and stony, covered with straggling oaks; and there are the valleys where the oaks grow into copses and villages are built against cliffs, for protection, and sometimes to conserve every inch of fertile soil for cultivation. The mountain people are less communicative, as is often the case.

In summer it is hot. Even the sound of the cicadas is like a weight in the air. Some of the farmers wear

Introduction

wide straw hats. It is a good area for camping, or for hiring one of the horse-drawn caravans available for slow exploration.

The old, upland province of Rouergue, to the east, corresponds roughly to the department of the Aveyron. It is broken countryside, formerly fairly poverty-stricken, but it contains two treasures at least – the draughty caves near Roquefort-sur-Soulzon where Roquefort cheese is matured, and the church of Sainte-Foy in Conques.

The Romanesque church of Conques clings above a ravine and has been a pilgrimage point for 1,000 years. It was built to house a reliquary containing the bones of the child martyr, Sainte Foy. No one seems to know much about the life of this little girl, burnt and beheaded under Diocletian, but her bones were considered precious enough for a monk to undertake the business of stealing them from the abbey at Agen.

Conques monastery was poor, things showed no hope of getting any better, so the no-nonsense abbot sent off a certain Aronisdus and told him to gain confidence with the monks of Agen. He did the job extremely well. It took him ten years to gain a position of trust which finally included guarding the remains of Sainte Foy. One night when no one was around he pushed the lot into a bag and made off. Crime paid. Pilgrims flocked to Conques as they had previously flocked to Agen. The monastery became rich. The miracles continued without diminishing in number and strength and soon the monks could afford to make a splendid idol to contain the relics and build a magnificent church to house it. The statue is of wood, covered with gold and jewels.

The department of the Gers, inland from Les Landes, is a place where forests and vineyards thrive. A statue of d'Artagnan in the town of Auch is a reminder that someone of this name really existed before Alexander Dumas made him larger than life in his romantic novel, *The Three Musketeers*. Auch is in the brandy-producing region of Armagnac.

Toulouse, historically the capital of Languedoc until the Revolution, is today the capital of the Midi-Pyrénées region. Despite its post-war industrial expansion and its pre-eminence in aviation and electronics, the city remains relatively unmarred by its long march into the twentieth century – a very long march indeed, since it has been inhabited since prehistoric times. It sits astride the Garonne river, *la ville rose*, so-named because of the colour of its faded bricks, which glow pink in the early morning, red in the full light of the sun, mauve in the evening.

South-west is Lourdes, where Bernadette Soubirous saw her first apparition of the Virgin in 1858. In all, the 'Lady', as she called her, appeared to Bernadette eighteen times. Crowds began following the fourteen-year-old girl to the grotto where her visions occurred. On the ninth occasion they watched her scratch at the soil with her hands and a stream of water trickled out. This is the spring to which many pilgrims come

and the Massabielle grotto is the centre of a large religious city, where the commercial exploitation of Christian Faith runs riot. The mountains are close and nearby are the Grottes de Bétharram, a series of caves formed by an underground stream.

The Ariège is named after a river which begins in Andorra, high in the Pyrenees, and it contains the old county of Foix, once part of Gascony. Right up to the end of last century, the waterway used to attract gold-panners. Nuggets weighing up to fifteen grammes have been found in it. The Counts of Foix were highly important personages in the thirteenth and fourteenth centuries. The châteaux of the area and especially Monségur recall the Albigensian crusade and the slaughter of the Cathars.

Below Balanced on an impossible rock, the village of Cantobre seems to encapsulate this region's strife-torn past, when towns were citadels and even the churches were fortified.

Left Pockets of France remain where rural ways are little changed.

Far left Ewes near Roquefort, home of the famous cheese.

Towns and Villages

Toulouse is one of the finest of the great cities of France, colourful beneath the Mediterranean sun, an important trade and cultural centre. Around the Place du Capitole in the city centre are many medieval and Renaissance houses, built of the characteristic local pink brick. Modern Toulouse has expanded since the war into a major cosmopolitan metropolis; it is the leading university town in the provinces, and a major centre for scientific research, along with Grenoble. Capital of the French aviation industry, it is the birthplace of Concorde and the Caravelle, and today the Airbus. The streets are packed with Spaniards, Italians, North Africans, repatriates from French Algeria, as well as other Europeans. In this hot southern city, the streets are animated until well past midnight.

North of Toulouse, at the foot of the Bas-Quercy hills, is the largest fruit centre in France, Montauban. In the summer and autumn, samples are given away to visitors free of charge. Birthplace of the painter, Jean Ingres, the town contains many relics of his life and work. Albi, to the east, contains a similar collection relating to the painter Toulouse-Lautrec, who was born here. To the north, up in the Aveyron, Rodez is an attractively restored old town with a fine pinkish cathedral and Flamboyant Gothic belfry towering on a hilltop.

Auch, the only town of any size in the wild and beautiful countryside between Toulouse and the Pyrenees, clings to the sloping hills beside the river Gers. Here, local charm is enhanced by the production of Armagnac.

South-west of Auch is Tarbes, a popular centre for those wishing to explore the mountains and return each evening to the comforts of urban life. Known as 'the town of the horse', it is famous for stud farms which have, in the past, produced some of the best warhorses of Europe. Today it is an aircraft-producing centre.

Further into the mountains lies the bizarre little town of Lourdes: unknown and poverty-stricken until a century ago, it is now one of the world's largest pilgrimage centres. The grotto where Bernadette Soubirous experienced her vision is the centre of outrageous commercial exploitation: the whole town is a mass of little shops selling religious souvenirs and kitsch knick-knacks.

Above Lourdes, high in the Pyrenees, lies the splendid resort of Cauterets where sulphurous springs have drawn ailing plains people since Roman times. Summer climbing is popular among the jagged peaks, while winter skiing has been responsible for the construction of many new hotels. Higher still lies the charming Pont d'Espagne, by which one can reach the astonishing Cirque du Gavarnie, a massive glacial amphitheatre high against the Spanish border.

There are many picturesque old villages in the Pyrenees, and some have become popular as work-centres for artists and craftsmen. Montbazens offers

courses in a variety of skills, including pottery, ironwork and weaving.

For those more inclined to explore, the massive caves around Foix offer a more adventurous playground. These curious underground palaces, notably the Mas-d'Azil, have been inhabited in the past by refugees from injustice. Foix itself is a town of 10,000 inhabitants: it is dominated by a rock on whose summit are the remains of the castle of the Counts of Foix. The Niaux cave has remarkable prehistoric cave-paintings similar to those of Périgord. Not far away are the unforgettable, haunting ruins of the château of Monségur, where one of the last episodes of the Albingensian Crusade took place when, after a gruelling siege, 200 believers were burned at the stake in a terrible massacre.

Cahors has a rich history as an important Roman city and medieval banking centre. Indicative of its former power is the great fortified bridges, Pont Valentré, with its three towers.

Left and **opposite** Two views of one of the most beautiful towns in the Midi-Pyrénées. Situated high on a rocky cliff above the river Lot, Saint-Cirq-Lapopie has been fought over many times, by the English and French, Catholics and Huguenots. The ancient craft of wood-turning once flourished here, although today it exists only for the tourists.

Top Saints, pilgrims and characters from history take to the streets of Estaing, at the annual pageant in honour of Saint Fleuret.

Above Left The Alpe d'Huez is a major ski resort, situated above the Romanche Valley, with a magnificent panorama of the Pelvoux Massif spread out in front.

Above right The deep Truyère river cuts a swathe through the mountains in the Aveyron department. The curving wall across its path is the great Barrage de Couesque, one of many hydroelectric dams in the area.

Châteaux and Churches

Top The architecture of this once turbulent region is defensive in character: châteaux and churches have massive walls.

Above left This great 'palm-tree' pillar in the Église des Jacobins, Toulouse, supports twenty-two brick arches.

Above right Carvings on the south porch of the church at Moissac, the work of the brilliant 'School of Toulouse'.

The scars left by the twelfth and thirteenth-century Crusades against the Albigensian heretics (also known as Cathars), are still visible in this land of simple villages, citadels, graceful Romanesque and proud fortress-churches.

At Conques in northern Aveyron, a medieval town whose lovely old houses line steep and narrow street, stands one of the finest Romanesque churches in all of France, the abbey-church of Sainte-Foy, famous for the richly carved tympanum, representing the Last Judgement. The spacious interior is severe in design, relieved by varied and decorative pillar capitals.

At Villefranche-de-Rouergue, a former French *bastide*, stands a fifteenth-century charterhouse, the Chartreuse Saint-Sauveur, which survived the French Revolution and is a fine example of Gothic architecture with its profusion of pointed-arch vaultings through the two chapels and cloisters.

The picturesque village of Carennac, east of Souillac, is famous for the white-stone carvings on the west doorway of its twelfth-century church which represents Christ in Majesty, the work of the School of Toulouse. At Moissac, further to the south-west, the twelfth-century church houses two of the finest treasures of French Romanesque art: its cloisters, and the carving on the south doorway. An oasis of tranquillity, the elegant cloisters with their richly ornamented capitals are well worth a visit. The carved doorway is the best-preserved example of work by the School of Toulouse, whose sculptures are found throughout the region (Cahors, Carennac and Beaulieu-sur-Dordogne).

Montauban, originally a twelfth-century *bastide*, is built almost entirely of the pale brick typical of the area. The museum here is renowned for the paintings of its native son Ingres. Another fortified hill-top town, Cordes, is dramatically situated with sweeping views of the surrounding valley. Its ramparts and fourteenth to fifteenth-century houses such as that of the Great Falconer, are carefully restored to their original state.

At Albi, the fortified cathedral of Sainte-Cécile, of soaring proportions and built of the same faded pink brick as the old part of town that surrounds it, is a beautiful but formidable reminder of the great thirteenth-century Inquisition against the Albingensian sect. The Palais de la Berbie, the fortified episcopal palace built in the thirteenth century of the same brick, holds a famous collection of works by Toulouse-Lautrec, who was born in Albi.

Toulouse, known as *la ville rose* because of its brick buildings, is an ancient city possessing many architectural treasures. The splendid eleventh-century Saint-Sernin basilica is the largest Romanesque church in the south of France. Its octagonal tower crowns the great stone and brick edifice; a huge barrel-vault, characteristic of the Romanesque style, starts twenty metres above the floor. The remarkable Eglise des Jacobins is one of the great masterpieces of Southern French Gothic art, famous for its 'palm-tree' pillar that alone supports all the vaults of the apse and whose twenty-two ribs fan out like palm branches – a remarkable sight.

The walled town of Saint-Bertrand-de-Comminges was once an important Roman capital; the remains of a Forum, thermal baths, theatre and temple, have recently been excavated here. The twelfth-century cathedral is known for its lovely cobbled courtyard with a magnificent set of pillars. Most famous, however, are the cloisters, for as you walk round the delicately-carved arcade you discover the south wall is open, presenting a breath-taking view of the valleys and mountains beyond.

Left A splendid Gothic octagonal tower and spire crowns the Romanesque Basilica of Saint-Sernin, Toulouse. This was a great pilgrimage church on the way to Spain.

Above The three massive towers of the Château de Foix, in the Ariège department. Once a mighty fastness, it withstood many a siege during the Albigensian crusade.

Cuisine

The roads that lead south-west from the Massif Central were once a constant thoroughfare for hungry travellers bound for the great shrine of Saint Jacques at Compostella. Many towns along the way also had their own shrines, like Rocamadour, which still draws pilgrims in its own right. There are numerous restaurants in these towns, serving simple, well-prepared country dishes: trout with almonds (*truite aux amandes*); saddle of hare (*râble de lièvre*); stuffed duck (*canard farci*) and an unusual sweet-savoury stuffed breast of lamb (*poitrine d'agneau farci*), filled with herbs, onions, breadcrumbs and locally dried prunes. Near Rocamadour, at the Lion d'Or in Gramat, there are also truffles, the famous black diamonds of Périgord (page 198), tossed into a bean salad (*salade aux haricots truffés*) or blended with ham and *foie gras* to stuff a fowl (*poularde demi-deuil*).

Toulouse is the main city of the region. One of its specialities is the long, red, spicy Toulouse sausage (*saucisse toulousaine*). Its most famous dish is *cassoulet*, a white bean stew containing tender pork and mutton, sausages, preserved goose (*confit d'oie*) and pork rind. Tourist restaurants sometimes omit the more expensive ingredients, which is a shame for the good name of the dish. If in doubt, go to the Rue Peyrolières, where – at Le Cassoulet – you are assured of the authentic pleasure. Also good is La Belle Chauvienne, a restaurant in a converted barge on the Canal de Brienne. Throughout the south-west and notably its home-town of Castelnaudary there are variations of the dish, some using lamb or even partridge: towards the Pyrenees, beer is also included. The best *cassoulet* is one that grows from week to week, like Mère Clémence's in *l'Histoire Comique* by Anatole France: 'She adds some goose occasionally, or some bacon from time to time, and every now and then more beans or sausage, but it is still the same *cassoulet* . . .'

The valley that separates the Massif Central from the Pyrenees is irrigated by the upper Garonne and its many tributaries. The soil is very fertile and thousands of acres are given over to fruit trees: plums, cherries, peaches, apricots. Montauban has one of the most colourful markets in the spring and must have been an inspiration to the great painter Ingres, who was born and raised here. Another fruit centre is Albi, where the plum tarts of the Auberge Landaise are worth sampling, perhaps as a dessert after the excellent local lamb and salmon that are served here.

The ancient pilgrim paths stretch on to the shrine at Lourdes, nestling at the foot of the Pyrenees. This is spectacular country, rich in wild game: rabbits, deer, pheasant and partridges. The pheasant cock is tender if hung for several days before cooking, but the hen is much sweeter and it is worth specifying your preference: simmered in red wine, Madeira and meat stock (*ragoût de faisan*), it is among the finest of all game dishes. Partridges are drier and less tasty, but cooked with vegetables – such as cabbage – and a little goose fat (*perdreau au chou*), they become softer and richer.

In the high Pyrenees, overshadowed by magnificent glacial rock formations, there are spring and summer pastures for sheep. Here the herdsmen make a fresh cheese which is sometimes available at the village restaurants, though most of it is exported to Roquefort to ripen in the famous caves. On the lower slopes, there are dairy cattle, where the milk is made into a drier, spiced cheese called Bethmale: well-ripened, it is hard enough to grate, which makes it ideal for flavouring omelettes, sauces and the local maize biscuits (*millais*).

Top left A common dish throughout France, but particularly in the Auvergne, is *chou farci* (stuffed cabbage) and *soupe au chou farci*. This version was served in Najac, in the Aveyron Gorges region.

Left In Villecontal, a cake is baked on a spit over the fire (*gâteau à la broche*).

Above Roquefort cheeses ripening in the caves of Combalou. The conditions in these caves, due to fissures in the limestone rock, create a micro-climate where the mould *Penicillium roqueforti* thrives. It is this mould which gives Roquefort cheese a distinctive flavour.

Wines and Spirits

While 'Le Midi' generally means Provence, it is, in fact, the middle area above the Pyrenees between the Atlantic and the Mediterranean. In France, it is referred to as the South-West, which also includes the ancient province of Aquitaine.

The best known wine of the South-West is, of course, Bordeaux, with an image and status of its own, but Bordeaux is not a typical *vin du sud-ouest*. Cahors, from the Lot, is, however. This deep crimson – almost black – earthy wine is at its best from five to ten years old, but it is generally drunk too young.

East in the Aveyron, to the north of Rodez, there are some interesting local wines. The grape variety is the Fer, grown all over the South-West. The name, meaning 'iron' in French, is said to come from the hardness of the vine stalks, but could as well have come from the tough fruitiness of the wine. The local wines to look out for are: Marcillac, les Vins d'Estaing and les Vins d'Entraygues et du Fel. There is a little dry white, all consumed locally.

In the Tarn, Gaillac is almost the only wine-producing area of interest. Here, just north of Albi, the best known wine is the sparkling white, made either by the Champagne method or the traditional Gaillac method, the latter leaving the wine more natural but slightly sweeter. The rosés are pleasant and the reds are lighter and less rough than others from the South-West, especially good at Cunac and Labastide. From December to March, you can drink Gaillac Nouveau (red and white), which has had a great success. The local vin du Pays du Tarn is lighter and probably better than those from farther south.

East of Gaillac are two wines to look for: Lavilledieu (V.D.Q.S.) from the Tarn et Garonne, a well-made red wine almost wiped out by the 1956 frosts, and the Coteaux de Frontonnais (V.D.Q.S.) from the Haute-Garonne, where the production is increasing.

From right across west, on the borders of the Hautes-Pyrénées and Les Landes, come the powerful red wines of Madiran, second only in reputation to Cahors in the South-West. The grapes are the Tannat, the Bouchy (Cabernet Franc) and the Fer, and depending on the mix, Madiran resembles a Saint-Emilion or a Cahors. The latter style is more appreciated locally and has become quite fashionable in Paris. From the same area comes the Pacherenc-du-Vic-Bilh, a white wine which used to be a semi-sweet and is now usually made dry.

However strong-tasting the wines from the Midi-Pyrénées may be, they are not heavily alcoholic, so there is often room at the end of the meal for the great *digestif* of the area, Armagnac, produced in the Condom area, near Toulouse. This brandy is more fiery and earthier than Cognac due partly to the grapes planted, the Baco as well as the Ugni blanc from Cognac, and partly to the difference in distillation techniques. Cognac is distilled twice, the rough edges or 'tops and tails' being eliminated, while Armagnac is distilled only once. Thus, it is a little harsh when young (but Calvados and the other brandies are even harsher) and needs age to gain real distinction. The best are from the Bas Armagnac; there are some interesting Armagnacs from the Ténarèze, and those from the Haut-Armagnac are used only for blending. Armagnacs may carry a vintage date, which Cognac may no longer, but buy these only from reliable sources.

Below An Armagnac distillery at Lajuzan, Gers department.

Languedoc-Roussillon

L anguedoc – the area curves around the south of a map of France, rich in the associations of a long and gracious civilization. The Cévennes mountains thrust into it. Far to the south, lying against the Pyrenees and already part of them, is Roussillon, with the Côte Vermeille dipping to the sea.

There are many memorable cities in this proud old region of southern France. Even though the castles stand broken-toothed and centuries have passed since the northern 'barbarians' conquered it, the people still remember a glory that depended not only on the courtesies and love poems and the troubadours but also on a struggle for freedom of thought. Nowadays, when Paris is the undisputed capital of the country and the more northern part of France has economic dominance, it is difficult to realize the importance the Languedoc once held.

Introduction

It was culturally superior, for its artistic achievements and for its tolerance. Phocaean Greeks had settled the southern coast 600 years before Christ. Herakles passed through the lower plain on his way west to seek the golden apples of the Hesperides. Hannibal moved east across it, elephants and all. Roman legions marched along the Via Domita, main highway from Italy to Spain. The Romans not only conquered, but deserted from their conquering armies to take up land and plant vines, seduced by a winsome, sunny land. The Saracens came and went. These North African people who crossed into France via Spain (they were finally defeated in the eighth century), brought the benefits of a highly-developed civilization which had already passed through the refinery of Greek influence. And the troubadours, romanticized as they have been, did sing: of the joys of courtly life, of peaceful times, and battles.

They fell silent in the thirteenth-century when the crusade of Paris and Rome against the local Albigensians scorched the land with the fires of religious intolerance. The open-minded southern nobility had permitted the growth of a new theology which originated in the Balkans but spread through northern Italy to this part of France. The Cathar or Albigensian theology was in opposition to a corrupt church. The English term is based on the name of a town, Albi, but the French only use the term 'Cathar'.

The crusade launched by the Pope and the King of France vowed to stamp them out and did so with a sadism that still echoes in folk memory. The whole town of Béziers was destroyed. Hundreds of people were tortured and burned. Carcassonne, seemingly impregnable, was taken. After and during the crusades came an Inquisition, weeding out Cathars through the denunciation of members of their own family or neighbours or frightened friends. As condemnation proceeded, the land of the heretics was, very conveniently, seized. In the south, orthodox Christians and Cathar heretics fought together in a united cause to defend their homeland.

The whole Cathar affair was paradoxical in that they themselves were ascetic and puritanical, and yet they flourished in the midst of a Languedocien civilization that was the very opposite, personified by the troubadours.

Some of the drama of history is written in the architecture, for here the churches are often more like fortresses and the fortresses themselves were built with desperation on almost unscalable outcrops of rock.

The landscape is sometimes harsh but not grim. The Cévennes mountains present a face of stony grandeur, broken with gorges and potholes, where ice sculptures the rocks in winter and pebbles rub to a polish in swift-flowing streams. Old castles, like those at the foot of the Black Mountain, blend with their wind-hewn background. Mont Lozère is a mighty haunch of granite rising to 5,474 feet (1,669 metres).

Between the mountains and the coastal plain is vine-growing land, broken by *garrigues*, the brush-covered foothills of the Cévennes. South of the mountains the climate is Mediterranean. Winds are warm. On the plains the sun is hot. The coast of Lower Languedoc, east of Carcassonne, was extended by silting many centuries ago and there is a chain of land-locked lagoons and marshes.

Roussillon is Catalan country, with separate traditions and a strong identity with Spanish Catalonia across the border. As you go towards the Côte Vermeille, fruit and vegetables flourish.

Collioure used to be called 'the pearl of the Vermilion Coast' in the days when its dramatically clashing colours – ochre, violet and green – attracted painters like Matisse, Derain, Dufy, Gris and Picasso. Now the coast has been developed for mass tourism.

Modern resorts such as Port-Barcarès alternate with fishing villages. The sailboats planing along the blue Gulf of Lions have their visual echo in the flight of waterbirds from the sleepy streams and lagoons.

Here, although modern motorways, resorts and factories are bringing much-needed prosperity to a formally declining area, one still gets an impression of Languedoc-Roussillon with summer sun beating on rocks and vineyards, of towns where the brick has weathered to rose, of cicadas drowning the air.

Right and **below** Villages nestle amongst some of the most spectacular scenery in France in this ancient region. Historical Languedoc was once the centre of a great and powerful civilization (the land of the troubadours) before the period of religious upheaval, and violent conflict between north and south.

Towns and Villages

As you drive along the new motorway from Toulouse towards Narbonne an apparition appears; a towered castle, squatting in the dusty plain. It is Carcassonne, serene and ageless, a Saracen city which still lives. Massive walls enclose many ancient houses, giving the visitor a vivid glimpse of how life might have been here centuries ago. They called the city 'The Virgin of Languedoc' because, through many sieges, she was never taken. Modern commerce and the motor car have slipped in like a Trojan horse, but they have yet to take the place. Among the fine buildings are medieval keeps and storehouses, and two notable churches – those of Saint-Vincent and Saint-Michel, which contain interesting sculptures and paintings.

Another town with a tradition of proud independence is Perpignan, which was once the capital of the kingdom of Mallorca. While Mallorca is now part of Spain, Perpignan remains essentially Catalan, closely identified with Spanish Catalan towns such as Barcelona.

The castle of the former Mallorcan kings still stands, together with other medieval buildings, interspersed with Catalan architecture and restaurants. Perpignan was once an important cultural centre as the local museums testify. There is a big Midsummer Festival held here in June. Today the city is the centre of France's rapidly-growing solar energy industry: the major solar furnace is in the hills to the west.

Another medieval city with a university is Montpellier. The faculty of medicine was one of the first and most important here, and it is still in the forefront of medical research. Other faculties have been developed over the centuries, making Montpellier a major academic centre today. A long line of celebrated artists and academics are associated with the university, beginning with the Roman poet Petrarch, who lived here from 1304 to 1374.

A prosperous, crowded town, Montpellier has many narrow, winding streets bordered by fine houses from the sixteenth, seventeenth and eighteenth centuries. Imposing fountains, an ancient and exquisite botanical garden, the Peyrou, and one of the best art galleries in the south, the Musée Fabre, have made this one of the most refreshing cities of the Mediterranean. The Musée Fabre is housed in a seventeenth-century theatre where the young Molière and his travelling company once played. From the man-made elegance of Montpellier it is but a short ride to the natural elegance of the grottos of Demoiselles, some distance north of the city. The extraordinary convolutions of stalagtites and stalagmites are reminiscent of a Gothic cathedral.

Nearby, the port of Sète is one of the most attractive on the south coast of

Opposite top Saint-Martin-de-Canigou is a Catalan abbey in Roussillon, an area which has strong links with Spanish Catalonia across the border.

Above The startling architecture of La Grande-Motte is part of a vast and forward-looking scheme to promote tourism along the Mediterranean coast.

Opposite below left The tourist resort coastline, which includes La Grande-Motte, stretches from the Pointe de l'Espiguette in the Carmague, to Maguelone.

Opposite below right Built on a sandbank between the Bassin de Thau and the Mediterranean, Sète is the second largest French port on this coast.

Towns and Villages

France. It is criss-crossed by many canals, giving it the air of a smaller Venice. On a hillside above the town is the famous sea cemetery where Paul Valéry, a native of Sète, wrote his great poem *Le Cimetière Marin*. He lies buried there, and nearby is an interesting Valéry museum.

Further north-east, towards Provence, lies the oldest Roman city in France, Nîmes. The famous Pont-du-Gard, built on the orders of Agrippa during the year I BC was actually part of a vast system to bring spring water into the city. Towering nearly 160 feet (49 metres) high, its three rows of arches are built largely on the dry-stone principle. Some of the stones used for the construction are six tons in weight. The city also boasts a colossal amphitheatre, one of the best preserved of its kind in the world. The exits were so cleverly arranged that the 20,000 people which the structure can accommodate could all leave within five minutes. The amphitheatre is still used today for bullfights, sports festivals and other performances.

Other Roman relics in Nîmes include the temple known as the Square House, La Maison Carrée, dedicated to the sons of Agrippa, and the so-called Temple of Diana. These ancient, classical structures contrast pleasantly with the more recent, neo-classical Fountain Gardens,

built in the eighteenth century, a popular place on warm summer evenings.

Languedoc is graced with nearly 124 miles (200 kilometres) of sandy beaches, marked by a few charming old fishing villages and some imaginatively conceived new resorts. La Grande-Motte with its dramatic ziggurat blocks and huge marina, and Cap d'Agde nestling incongruously beside an extinct volcano, are examples of the modern age doing its best to combine the needs of mass tourism with exciting futuristic development.

Aigues-Mortes, an unspoiled medieval city with bastions and ramparts that have stood for ten centuries, lies close to

the Camargue. Once a great port, it is now five kilometres inland as a result of the retreat of the sea. The main entrance, the Pont de la Gardetta, leads into a diminutive high street and past the crusader church to the main square.

This region is little known to the foreigner and, as a result, maintains much of the traditional ways of life. In June, on Midsummer's Eve, there are bonfires and dancing in many towns, while a few days later, on the 29th, there is a fishermen's festival at Sète. In the cities, there are two wine festivals in October: the annual harvest festival in Nîmes and the wine fair at Montpellier.

Above Encircled by double walls and a moat, the old city of Carcassonne is an impressive example of a fortified town. Its gateways are guarded by machicolations, a drawbridge and portcullis.

Top The medieval towns of Languedoc contrast strongly with the futuristic developments of its coastal resorts. Here, the tiled roofs of Saint-Michel-de-Cuxac stand out against a wooded background.

Left Easter celebrations in Perpignan have a distinct Spanish flavour. Hooded figures march in honour of Sainte-Saloustres.

Top Sainte-Enimie stands on the banks of the river Tarn, which flows down from the Cévennes mountains.

Above Snow-capped mountains rise steeply above the walled town of Mont-Louis. The Albigensian crusades led by Simon de Montfort wrought havoc in this area during the thirteenth century.

Châteaux and Churches

Languedoc-Roussillon has a rich heritage of architecture which encompasses Roman cities, Gothic churches, remote fortresses. It is also the birthplace of two major schools of twentieth-century painting.

Some of the earliest remains are found on a hill-top site near Béziers, which was already a thriving city in pre-Roman times. The Ensérune Oppidum is the site of a great sixth-century Gaulish town which once had 10,000 inhabitants. The archaeological museum here has an excellent display of pre-Roman Mediterranean artefacts.

Nîmes, once called 'the Rome of France', has many reminders of its early history. Among the most famous buildings are the amphitheatre, the best-preserved in France and still used today, for bullfights, and the Maison Carrée, a first-century B.C. temple built during the reign of the Emperor Augustus. Over the centuries it has served successively as a

Left Matisse, Dufy, Derain and other painters lived and worked in the seaside town of Collioure, the birthplace of Fauve painting. A collection of their works can be seen in the Hostellerie des Templiers.

Above The Tour Fenestrelle with its tiers of windows rising to a height of 33 feet (46 metres) is a fine example of Romanesque.

town-hall, private dwelling, stable and church. Narbonne, too, is rich in Roman remains, with fine examples of triumphal arches, temples and baths.

Stark reminders of the region's troubled past, and the dark days of the Albigensian Crusades, the ruins of ancient strongholds dot rocky outcrops throughout the area. Two such are the shattered eyries of Peyrepertuse and Quéribus, where a few remaining Cathar 'heretics' made a last desperate stand. The most impressive of the fortresses, however, is the old *cité* of Carcassonne, Europe's largest surviving fortified city. With its double walls, fifty-four towers and crenellated ramparts, it powerfully recalls the days of medieval sieges and battles.

Of the great churches of the region, Perpignan has a fine Gothic chapel, its red-and-white striped marble façade shows the Moorish influence. The large Gothic Cathedral of Saint-Jean contains some fine examples of Spanish Baroque art. There is another large cathedral at Narbonne, fortified as are many churches in this region, northern Gothic in style. This building is something of a curiosity: it is unfinished, and the bulk of the church, braced by flying buttresses, seems to end abruptly.

The fifteenth-century Château of Grange-des-Près, in the picturesque town of Pézenas, was known as 'the Versailles of Languedoc'. Many a royal host was magnificently entertained here, and Molière's plays were first performed here. Today many of the old streets seem little changed and the old houses have lovely courtyards. One of these is the Hôtel de Lacoste, remarkable for its fine staircase and Gothic vaulted ceilings.

In Montpellier, the lover of elegant town-planning will appreciate the Promenade de Peyrou, a wide seventeenth and early eighteenth-century avenue built in honour of Louis XIV. At the end of this fine boulevard stands a small masterpiece, an eighteenth-century water-tower called the Château d'Eau. This polygonal pavilion, classical in style, is the terminal of an aqueduct which, with its two tiers of arches, is reminiscent of the Pont du Gard.

The fishing port of Collioure was the birthplace of Fauvism, a school of painting that was to direct the course of modern art. Leading Fauves (or 'wild beasts', so called because of their revolutionary use of bold colour and flat patterns) included Matisse, Dufy and Derain. A small collection of their work can be seen here at the Hostellerie des Templiers. The small town of Céret was the home of Cubism. Following the example of the Spanish sculptor Manolo, a number of avant-garde painters and sculptors took up residence here. Matisse, Picasso, and Juan Gris among them. The style that led to the development of abstract painting can be seen in the Museum of Modern Art here.

Left This mighty aqueduct, the Pont-du-Gard, is one of the most impressive Roman buildings to be seen in France. The three great tiers of arches spanning the river Gardon once carried water from Uzès to Nîmes, a distance of 31 miles (50 kilometres).

Above With its garden stretching down to the edge of the river Tarn, the fifteenth-century Château de la Caze is set amid the spectacular canyons called the Gorges du Tarn.

Cuisine

Right The fresh seafood on this stall in Sète hints at the wide variety of fish dishes to be had in Languedoc, varying from tasty hors d'oeuvres to filling variations on the *bouillabaisse* theme.

Far right Good regional cooking is found in restaurants such as this one in the twelfth-century Château d'Ayres, now a hotel, in Meyrueis.

Lower Languedoc, the sun-baked coastal plain backed by stony hills runs from Carcassonne to the Rhône delta, is mainly an area producing cheap table wines. But the new irrigation networks, bringing water from the Rhône and from the streams of the Cévennes, have in recent years encouraged the planting of some orchards and fields of rice and vegetables.

The cookery shares much with that of Provence, to the east, where olive oil and garlic are the most important basic ingredients. To the south-west, in Roussillon, where the Catalan influence of Spain is strong, spices are also liberally used: paradoxically, they will help to cool you as you dine in the midday shade.

Fish and shellfish are abundant on the coast, and your hors d'oeuvres may well

be boiled prawns, ice-cold oysters or a bowl of anchovy paste, served with a chilled *vin du pays* and a hunk of bread. Other dishes on the menu will include lobsters in a spicy sauce (*langouste à la sètoise*), sea-bass roasted on a vinewood fire (*bar grillé au feu*) and mussels grilled on skewers (*brochette de moules*). Tuna fish are also popular: the fishermen of Palavas cook them fresh on the boat – in a mixture of wine and herbs – and sell them on the shore as *tripes de thon*. Elsewhere tuna fish are grilled or baked or added to the fish stew (*bouillabaisse*).

Throughout the region there are variations of the true Marseille *bouillabaisse* (see page 241). One of the best, surprisingly, is served inland at La Caravelle in Castres, on the western end of the Cévennes. The patron also serves a fine *cassoulet*, for here we are not far from Toulouse and Castelnaudary (see page 214), Languedoc sausages (*saucisses à la languedocienne*), fried in goose fat and served with a spiced tomato purée.

Up on the limestone *causses* of the Cévennes, there is a different feeling. Here, along the southern side of the Massif Central, there are herds of sheep as well as game and river trout. The

sheep provide milk for one of France's greatest cheeses, the blue-veined Roquefort, which ripens in the cool damp, limestone caves of the village of that name, near Millau. For twelve centuries, Roquefort cheese has been exported from these hills. One famous consumer was Casanova, who ate it with iced ham: it is also splendid with grapes.

The Cévennes also offer fine soups: cabbage and potato soup flavoured with salted pork (*l'oulade*); chicken soup with saffron (*bouillon de poulet au safran*, sometimes called *mourtrairol*); and, in the Bas-Cévennes, garlic soup (*aillo bouillado*). There are also wild mushrooms and truffles, notably from Hérault and Gard. Truffles are added to several local dishes including roasted guinea fowl (*pintade truffée*) and Nîmes salt cod (*brandade de morue nîmoise*), where they are put into the thick garlic sauce.

The southern part of this region is not Languedoc at all but Roussillon (French Catalonia). Here, as you might expect, the cuisine is more Spanish in flavour, and you may find dishes such as paella.

In the wild Camargue, there are, at Eastertide, delicious semi-sweet deep-fried pancakes (*preillettes*).

Left *Loup au vin vert* is not, as its name suggests, wolf in green wine, but a delectable sea-bass dish, served here at the restaurant La Balette, in Collioure.

Above Cherries ripen early at Céret, near Perpignan, and are often the first crop to be picked in France. The local cherry tart (*tarte aux cerises*) is delicious and worth a detour.

Wines and Spirits

Left Vineyards in the Hérault department, near Mazamet.

Below left This statue commemorates the 'Saviour of the Vine', who developed a way of combating phylloxera, a disease which threatened to wipe out the vineyards.

Below right The Cellier des Aspres, Roussillon, is a small but interesting wine museum.

Opposite below right Harvesting grapes on the rocky slopes near Banyuls-sur-Mer, an area which produces dessert or *apéritif* wines.

North-west of Avignon, in the Gard, the *appellation* is still Côtes du Rhône and some of it very good indeed. The soil here on the west bank of the Rhône is the same arid, stony, difficult-to-work terrain as on the east, but vines thrive on poor soil, forcing their roots down to catch the water and mineral deposits several yards below the surface. The villages of Laudun and Chusclan produced excellent, elegant Côtes du Rhône, rather leaner than those from east bank, while the best wines in this area are Tavel and Lirac. Tavel is the best known rosé in France, with a striking, pale-ruby colour, often with a violet tinge when young. It is said to age well, but should really be drunk within two years to catch the fleshy fruitiness of the Grenache grape. The rosés from Lirac are rather overshadowed by Tavel, but the reds are only eclipsed in the southern Rhône only by Châteauneuf-du-Pape and Gigondas. A Lirac red tastes like a lighter version of Châteauneuf and is one of the best bargains in the area. There is a little white Côtes du Rhône which has to be drunk young and cold.

Just south of Nîmes are the wines from the Costières du Gard, well-made wines with less stuffing than the Côtes du Rhône, but fruity and lively. The lesser *appellation*, Vin du Pays du Gard, make good table wines, getting better and better with improved plantings and vinification.

The same is true all over the departments of the Hérault and the Aude, the area producing the Great French Wine Lake. Forty per cent of all French wine comes from here, and well over half of all French cheap table wine. For a long time, this area was known in wine terms as the dustbin of France, making wines in immense quantities to be sold on their alcoholic degree regardless of quality. This is changing and the *vin du pays* are replacing the *vins ordinaires*, and the individual style of each *commune* is emerging from the morass of Gros Rouge. Just about every village has its *cave coopérative* to which most of the local growers belong. The best of the wines are grouped under the appellation Coteaux du Languedoc (V.D.Q.S.), often followed by the name of the commune. The reds and rosés are superior to the whites, which still are sold as *vins du pays*. A little farther west along the coast are the excellent wines of Minervois (V.D.Q.S.), famous since the Romans. They have a good, full red colour, are relatively fine and can age well, the best coming from the region north-west of Narbonne. As good as the Minervois, and better known, are the Corbières from the hills south-east of Carcassonne. Here again, the red wines are typical of the region and climate, deep in colour, chewy and solid with lots of fruit, so particular in fact that the Corbières are known as *le cru qui a de l'accent*. The best, Fitou and Côtes du Roussillon have their own *appellation*. While this is not a white wine area, mention should be made of the wine of La Clape (V.D.Q.S.), with their inhabitual freshness and fruit.

While there are good table wines from all over the south of France, by far and away the best *vin doux naturels* come from the Languedoc-Roussillon. There are two types: those made from the Muscat and those from the Grenache. The operation is the same, that of *mutage*, the addition of grape alcohol to the partially fermented must of grape juice, to give a wine (*apéritif* or dessert), which has kept the fruitiness of the grape, a natural sweetness balanced against a firm fortified backbone of alcohol. The

Wines and Spirits

Muscats, especially fine from Frontignan (near Sète) and Rivesaltes (near Perpignan), are golden and honey-scented. The Grenache is good at Rivesaltes, but reaches supreme heights at Banyuls, on the Spanish frontier. It is one of the hardest vineyards to work in France, almost perpendicular terraces of slaty soil, for one of the least known wines. Banyuls is the French answer to Port, and Banyuls Grand Cru, with an obligatory two-and-a-half years ageing in wood, achieves an extra raciness and complexity. Vintage Banyuls is remarkable.

South of Carcassonne, the little town of Limoux produces the Blanquette de Limoux, a white wine made sparkling by the *méthode naturelle*. It has been well known since the sixteenth century, but has seen a tremendous increase of popularity in the past few years or so and is marketed all over France. Many people drink it as a cheaper alternative to Champagne – though it is not the same!

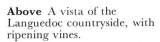
Above A vista of the Languedoc countryside, with ripening vines.

Top A pattern of vineyards near Ensérune, in the Hérault department, where vines have been planted since Roman times.

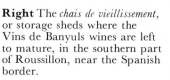
Right The *chais de vieillissement*, or storage sheds where the Vins de Banyuls wines are left to mature, in the southern part of Roussillon, near the Spanish border.

Provence-Côte d'Azur

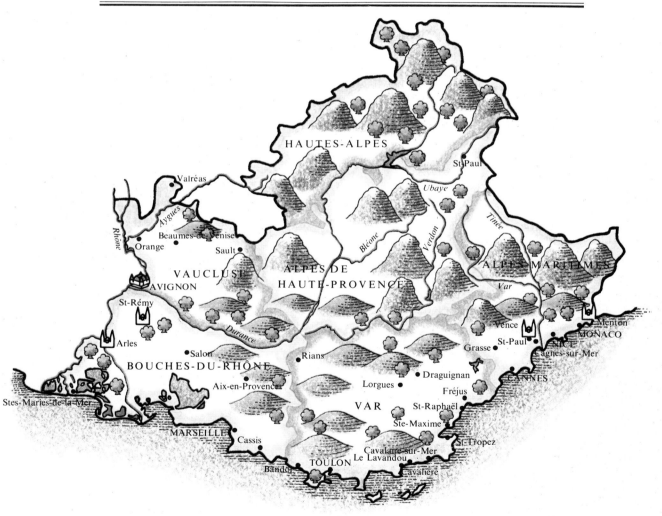

The South of France seems to mean something different to everyone who goes there. Whatever they do to it, it remains beautiful. However hideous the apartment blocks, noisy the cars or crowded the beaches, that is not the memory that lingers. This coast is bigger than its conquerors. Still the Mediterranean swirls cobalt or pearl-grey or opal against rocks of vivid rose. Still the ancient olive trees, their trunks twisted like the hides of prehistoric animals, ruffle silver in the breeze. There is a tang of eucalyptus along with the salt and a heavy whiff of expensive perfume mixed with the two, for the visitors who come continue to make this the most glamorous length of coastline in the world.

The name 'Riviera' should really be confined to the southern strip from Nice to Menton in France (and from Ventimiglia to Genoa in Italy) but the term 'French Riviera' has been stretched through

Introduction

common usage until now it is often applied to the whole Côte d'Azur, the Azure Coast, from Marseille all the way to the Italian border.

Wrapped around by France on three sides is the minute sovereign state of Monaco, only half a square mile (one-and-a-half square kilometres) in size but known for its casino at Monte Carlo, its car rally, its prince with his film-star princess, its maritime museum and fading Edwardian splendours. It is also known for its flower shows, just as Menton, the closest French town to the Italian frontier, is famous for its Lemon Festival.

In touristic terms, the English were responsible for 'discovering' Menton, as they were for adopting the whole of the Riviera. At first they came in winter for the sake of their health as far back as the eighteenth century. Menton acquired its English reputation in the late nineteenth century. Queen Victoria visited it in 1882. Its reputation as a resort for the sick gave rise to an unfortunate saying that Cannes was for living, Menton for dying (and Monte Carlo for gambling). The New Zealand short-story writer,

Katherine Mansfield, spent some time living in Menton and the city has preserved her room.

Nice is the capital of the Riviera, and the Promenade des Anglais is a reminder of English affection for this city, too. The English colony financed construction of the boulevard in 1822 to provide work for men who had suffered loss of employment when heavy frosts destroyed the orange orchards. The promenade now runs for four miles around the Baie de Anges, stretching westward to the Cap d'Antibes. Tobias Smollett, the English novelist, stayed here in the eighteenth century and was very taken with the idea of sea-bathing – which women should, of course, eschew for reasons of modesty. Not an opinion which would carry much weight on the Riviera today, where peeling it all off is becoming more and more a matter of course. The two-week pre-Easter Carnival at Nice is famous and so is the Marc Chagall museum, housing a permanent exhibition of the artist's works.

Festivals and all-year-round elegance characterize Cannes where the Lord Chancellor of England, Lord

Brougham, built himself a house in 1834. He returned there regularly for the next thirty-four years, and was responsible for Cannes becoming fashionable.

Saint-Tropez is a little port. Which, of course, says nothing at all about what it really is, except in winter, when it seems very small and quiet. Once it was a pirate village.

False cynicism cannot deny the town's attractiveness, nor the fact that a great many wealthy or celebrated people go there and a great many people live in hope of meeting someone wealthy or celebrated while they are there. Guy de Maupassant, the French writer, was one of the first people to 'discover' it, the woman novelist Colette lived a mile or two away from 1923 to 1936, and Brigitte Bardot has added to its fame: Saint-Tropez is chic, it's fun, it's cosmopolitan, it's brash and outrageous – it is, quite simply, the experience of Saint-Tropez.

Further west, between Toulon and Marseille are the beautiful fjords or *calanques* which bite into the coastline near Cassis, and still further on, beyond the Rhône delta, is the Camargue. In this haunting, watery world flamingo still breed in the Etang de Vaccarès, a huge lagoon sanctuary rich in bird life. The sturdy white horses of the Camargue are the main way of getting around the area which is half marshland. Horses and fighting bulls are raised in the south. The northern part has been turned into desalinated paddy fields for rice.

Every spring pilgrims flock to Saintes-Maries-de-la-Mer. They are mainly gypsies, come from all over Europe to venerate the statue of their patron saint, Sara of Egypt. Story has it that Mary, the Virgin's sister; Mary, the mother of John and James; and Mary Magdalene, together with other saints and a maid called Sara, sailed to Marseille and came to this spot. Mary Magdalene and most of the others went on, but the two Maries and their black servant remained.

Flamingos and casinos; wild bulls and topless bathing; orange groves, Roman ruins and gypsy rituals: the South of France is all these things. It is irreplaceably, and in spite of bad moments, seemingly everlastingly itself.

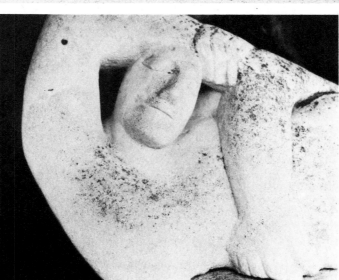

Just some of the varied riches to be discovered in Provence: wild horses roam over the wide Carmague swamplands. (**far left**); the beach at Beaulieu, one of the many sophisticated resorts along the Riviera (**above**); a sculpture from the Musée Picasso at Antibes (**left**).

Towns and Villages

Right Menton is the setting for a citrus fruit and tropical flower show, the Lemon Festival, when millions of oranges and lemons are used to decorate floats for a big parade.

Far right The Nice Marina, Baie des Anges. Called the Capital and Queen of the Riviera, this exciting city is a lively resort.

The most dramatic way to enter Provence is by air, landing at the sun-bleached airport of Nice, in the heart of Europe's most celebrated playground, the Côte d'Azur. Here you are suddenly confronted with magical light and soporific odours, shimmering sea and, beyond the town, a backdrop of jagged, snow-capped mountains. Flowers add colour to the terminal buildings, and flowers are a constant feature of Nice itself, whether sprouting from traffic islands, adorning the pleasant gardens or piled in massive bunches at the famous flower market. There are even battles of flowers here, during the summer. A major two-week long carnival precedes Lent, with vast processions and firework displays.

Once a favourite retreat of the English, after whom the sweeping beach-side Promenade des Anglais is named, Nice is a bustling cosmopolitan city, with every kind of diversion: an opera, fine restaurants, nightclubs, interesting shops, and a university (its two famous casinos went out of action in 1980). But, like many of these beautiful southern towns, it has been overrun by motor cars, which can make life unpleasant in the height of the season: newly-made pedestrian precincts happily make it possible to saunter calmly through a few of the town's lively streets. The old town, Italian in character, with a maze of narrow streets, is a delight: one might almost be in Naples.

The motorcar disease has struck Provence with some force. Antibes, for example, a charming port of cobbled streets and squares, rich in artistry and colour, restaurants and delightfully de-lapidated houses is eaten away with years of pollution. For the best impression of the town, leave your car on the outskirts, stroll through the old town and onto the seafront by way of the Avenue Amiral de Grasse. On the way you will pass the Grimaldi Museum, which contains a magnificent collection of the works of Pablo Picasso.

Nearby, on the plateau of Valbonne, the French government is building the most important 'scientific park' in Europe a centre for advanced research and high technology.

Further west along the Côte d'Azur is Cannes, which oozes wealth. Elegant apartment buildings are interspersed with expensive shops, and the marina is packed with the most ostentatious motor-boats and yachts imaginable. In the old town is the Church of Notre-Dame-d'Espérance, with a bell-tower which gives a fine view of palms, sea and for most of the year, a broad pale sky. For an aviator's view go to Super-Cannes: there is a 1000-foot (305 metres) observation tower. Cannes is famous also for its film festival, held every May, and for its great hotels along the smart La Croisette promenade, overlooking the sea.

Opposite top Defensively placed high above the sea to deter Saracen raiders, the old town of Eze is accessible only on foot.

Above The port of Monte-Carlo, Monaco. This tiny principality is famed not only for its casino, but its musical festivals and gruelling Grand-Prix car rallies.

Right Large lavender plantations cover the hills of Upper Provence. The production of lavender essence is an important industry, much of it being sent to Grasse, home of the French perfume industry.

Towns and Villages

Most of the coastline has been heavily exploited, and though there are many fine beaches and quaint, winding towns, the tourist boom has filled many a sweet-smelling pine glade with concrete box hotels. The conurbation of Saint-Raphaël and Fréjus offers Roman remains, a fine cathedral with a fifth-century baptistry, and wonderful swimming, but in summer there is hardly room to breathe. The coastal road traffic, though much is now diverted by the motorway, still presents a formidable barrier to safe transit from town to beach. Further south, at Sainte-Maxime, at the infamous and elegant port of Saint-Tropez itself, marine traffic adds to the tumult. But nothing can change the marvellous hues of sky and sea and hills, which have attracted painters for the last hundred years. Signac, Matisse and Bonnard all worked around this delightful bay, and some of their best paintings are collected at the Musée de l'Annonciade in Saint-Tropez.

Further west lies a string of smaller resorts like Cavalaire, Cavalière and Le Lavandou which offer a good deal less old-world charm, but somewhat more of the original landscape. In the season they are very busy. Not until you have travelled beyond the naval base of Toulon, and the great port of Marseille, is there a truly calm spot in summer.

Marseille itself is the third biggest city in France. The Canebière, a broad short street that runs down to the port, is the commercial centre, and the nearby Quai de Rive Neuve, at the old port, is the bohemian centre. Noisy and colourful, this is the heart of an otherwise workaday industrial city. It is the largest port on the whole Mediterranean, and it is strongly Levantine in character, an exciting melting-pot of races and a centre of mafia-type gangsterism, and 'French Connection' drug-trafficking. There are, however, many museums with examples of some outstanding local art and craft-work, and the view from Notre-Dame-de-la-Garde, high on a hill outside the suburbs, is quite outstanding.

North of Marseille the hills are gentle, rolling and for much of the year very dry. Once you reach Aix-en-Provence, however, there are cool splashing fountains, graceful tree-lined streets, elegant seventeenth-century houses, and all the trappings of high culture. The university is one of the most popular with foreigners in France, and the museums house great art, including works by the painter Paul Cézanne, who was born and raised here. One of the most delightful squares is the Place de l'Albertas in the Rue Espariat, parallel to the bustling and delightful Cours Mirabeau: here you will find the Hôtel de Boyer d'Eguilles, which contains superbly decorated panelling and painted ceilings.

The region east of Aix has some lovely scenery and interesting little towns like Rians, Barjols and Lorgues, with its enormous eighteenth-century church. Further still is Draguignan, looking to all the world like a main street in Paris, but without the animated bustle of a city. Behind the tree-lined *cours* is the old quarter which is more characteristic of the local style. Draguignan has two excellent *pâtisseries* and a fine library, containing a fifteenth-century Book of Hours.

Above A vast panorama of the river valley and mountain ranges spreads out around the hilltop town of Gordes. The Renaissance Château here contains a permanent exhibition of work by Vasarely.

Top Bullfights are regularly held in the great Roman arena at Arles, once the setting for gladiatorial contests and fights between wild animals imported from abroad.

Above An open-air café in a side street in Antibes. This resort town is an important

centre for horticulture. Thousands of flowers, particularly roses and carnations, are grown for export as cut flowers.

Left Rising high in the French Alps near Briançon, the Durance river winds through Provence to join the Rhône.

Châteaux and Churches

The very names Provence and Côte d'Azur conjure up visions of ancient Roman ruins basking in the sun; old southern towns scarcely touched by time; the brilliant luminosity of the Mediterranean sky that attracted so many great painters. From the late 1800s, artists were drawn to this part of France: Matisse, Bonnard, Picasso, and Chagall, to name but a few. Museums displaying their work literally dot the area.

Arles, where Van Gogh painted in the 1880s, has retained many treasures from its long past. Roman remains here include a theatre, public baths, temples, a huge stone amphitheatre and the famous Alyscamps, a Roman cemetery consisting of a once-majestic avenue bordered by sarcophagi. The most beautiful of these have long since gone, but the enigmatic and peaceful atmosphere of the place lingers on. The Carolingian church of Saint-Trophime was altered several times during the Middle Ages. Its classically-proportioned doorway is a beautiful example of Provençal medieval art, with an exquisitely-carved tympanum. The superb cloister of mixed Romanesque and Gothic design is famous for its carved corner pillars and capitals. Similar carvings can be seen in the partly ruined abbey of Montmajour.

One of the major Roman settlements in Provence, Orange has the best-preserved theatre of the former Empire, one of the few to have kept its stage-wall, and a huge triumphal arch which is splendidly decorated with well-preserved sculpture. The excavations at Vaison-la-Romaine allow a glimpse of everyday life in Roman times: two *quartiers* have been laid bare with villas as sophisticated in design as those at Pompeii, with reception and private rooms, mosaics and sculpture.

Avignon's most memorable building is the vast Palais des Papes whose fortified walls dwarf the town. A forbidding reminder of the days when Avignon was the focal point of Christendom, its austere silhouette is tempered by the patina of its time-worn stone.

The list of painters who have lived and worked in Provence includes many of those who have directed and influenced the mainstream of twentieth-century art. Aix-en-Provence is the birthplace of Cézanne; Marseille lays claim to Honoré Daumier (and an earlier artist Pierre Puget). Their works can be seen in the excellent Musée des Beaux Arts.

At Saint-Tropez, the Musée de l'Annonciade is famous for its magnificent collection, which includes work by Signac, Bonnard, Matisse, Vuillard and Dufy. The Musée Fernand Léger at Biot is a splendid modern building, designed to catch the sunlight; it houses over 300 works by Léger. Antibes has a large collection of work by Picasso, who lived at nearby Vallauris.

Another excellent museum is that of the Fondation Maeght at Saint-Paul, a modern building set among pine trees, where twentieth-century works of art are displayed both inside and in the garden. Giacometti bronzes, and works by Miró, Bonnard and Calder can be seen.

Marseille is the setting for one of Le Corbusier's finest and most revolutionary works, the *Unité d'Habitation*, an apartment building which makes optimum use of space and light. Called a 'radiant city' by the architect, it was dubbed '*Maison du Fada*' (madman's house) by his critics.

The seemingly endless list of museums here includes those dedicated to the work of Fragonard, Renoir, Vasarely, and Chagall. The contrast between the staggering wealth of modern art and the imposing Roman remains found throughout the region makes Provence one of the most exciting areas of France.

Opposite A colourful work by Léger in the Léger Museum, Biot. This is one of numerous collections to be seen in the Provence – Côte-d'Azur area.

Top The Chapelle de Rosaire at Vence was designed and decorated by Matisse. Stained glass windows reflect on white ceramic walls.

Above left A detail of the richly carved porch of Saint-Trophime at Arles has columns resting on lions, with figures of saints.

Above right Colourful murals in the vast Palais des Papes, Avignon, recall the days when this was a splendid and powerful centre of religion.

Cuisine

Above A special dessert is prepared in Gordes: *crêpes souflées, flambées aux oranges.* These delicate pancakes, flavoured with orange, will have flaming liqueur poured over them before serving.

Top An *épicerie* (grocer's shop), Vence.

Top right Olive oil is central to Provençal cuisine, and the olives themselves appear in numerous dishes, such as the tasty *salade niçoise*, a delicious combination of tuna, anchovies and tomatoes.

For nine months of the year, Provence and the Côte d'Azur bask in the sun, offering up a cornucopia of Mediterranean foods. Terraces are lined with twisted olive trees and vines; valleys are lush with fruit and vegetables; there are abundant fish in the sea and wild game in the hills; and the air is sweet with the aromatic fragrance of herbs: thyme, sage, basil, fennel and the region's most important flavouring, garlic.

Central to Provençal cookery, almost a symbol of the traditional way of life here, is garlic, hot and pungent. 'Its heat' wrote the herbalist Nicholas Culpeper, 'is very vehement – in choleric men it adds fuel to the fire.' Crushed into a simple tomato salad (*salade de tomates*) or pressed into the sunday joint of chicken (*poulet rôti*), it is always included in a savoury dish. Nor is the value of garlic purely gastronomic: it also has medicinal

properties. 'It purges the head' wrote Culpeper, 'helps the lethargy and is a remedy for any plague.'

The basic oil is made – as it is throughout the south of France – from olives, pressed again and again to yield first the exquisite virgin oil, and subsequently thinner juices. Mixed with red wine vinegar and seasoned with salt, pepper and garlic, olive oil is the basis of the classical French dressing (*vinaigrette*), which is invariably served with a salad before the main course of a meal. Olive oil is also used in most cooked dishes.

As for the olives themselves, they find their way into many traditional dishes. The *salade niçoise*, which takes its name from Nice, is made of olives, anchovies, tomatoes, peppers, tuna and celery. When packed between two halves of a French loaf (*baguette*) the Niçoise becomes a *pan bagnat*, a favourite sand-

wich. The combination of olives and anchovies is also found in the local onion tart (*pissaladière*) and in Provençal stuffed eggs (*oeufs tapenades*).

The best of the meat comes from wild game, which is prepared in a thousand different ways, befitting an imaginative people. Guinea fowl pie (*croustade de pintadeau*), rabbit in red wine (*civet de lapin*), thrush pâté (*pâté de grive*), are the sort of dishes to expect at the many secluded and delightful restaurants inland, usually offering better value than the more touristy ones on the coast. The Hôtel Provence in Saint-Rémy is constantly dreaming up new ways to make the best of what is available.

Along the coast, fish provide the honours, freshly fried, grilled with herbs or stewed into the famous *bouillabaisse*. An authentic Marseille *bouillabaisse* contains three particular fish: *rascasse*, a

spiny rock-fish; *grondin* (red gurnet); and conger eel. Other fish and shellfish are added, according to what has turned up in the catch, and the whole is flavoured with herbs and served with fried or toasted slices of French bread (*croûtons*) and with a pungent garlic sauce (*rouille*). In acknowledgement perhaps of Spain, just along the coast, saffron (*safran*) is added as colouring, to give the stew its characteristic deep-red hue.

Although most of the fish is fresh, salted cod (*morue*) has also found a particular place in the Provençal heart. At the Mas d'Entremont at Aix, it is often on the menu, usually drenched with a wonderfully pungent garlic mayonnaise called *aïoli* (*brandade de morue*). This sauce has captured the imagination of gastronomes and poets for centuries. Mistral, who started a Provençal newspaper called *L'Aïoli* during the last century,

Cuisine

wrote of it, 'Aïoli is the quintessence of our table: it concentrates all the warmth, all the strength and the sun-loving gaiety of our people: and it also has a particular practical value – it keeps flies away!' Aïoli is served as accompaniment to hors d'oeuvres, soups, grilled meat – especially lamb – and fish: be prepared to surrender to its charm.

Provence supplies its northern neighbours with the first vegetables of the season, les primeurs, which grow mostly along the eastern valley of the Rhône, sheltered from the wind by rows of cypress trees.

Tomatoes, aubergines, courgettes and green peppers are the commonest, and all are included in the traditional vegetable stew (ratatouille). Each stands as a dish in itself when stuffed with meat and onions (farci) or baked with cheese

(gratin), deep-fried in batter (beignet) or simply steamed and served cold with a vinaigrette. At Les Florets in Gigondas, they make a wonderful dish of deep-fried courgettes, a perfect partner for the superb salmon mousse (mousse au saumon), garnished with crisp fresh endives, tomatoes and herbs.

Two other vegetables are even more celebrated: the artichoke and the asparagus. In the spring markets you can find the young tender artichokes which can be eaten raw, simply dressed with mayonnaise, while the asparagus needs only the lightest boiling to bring out its delicate flavour.

There are no great cheeses here, but the few that do exist are pleasant and tasty. Cachat, made from sheep's milk and eaten either fresh, or in a marinade of brandy, vinegar and local herbs, is one

of the best. Another is Banon, soaked in white wine and wrapped in chestnut leaves before being left to ripen in clay pots. Throughout the region, there are also Chèvres, goat's milk cheeses, some bland and creamy, others highly salted or – like Poivre d'Ane of Haute-Provence – sprinkled with herbs to give it the flavour of the countryside.

Provence is also the fruit basket of France, and there is no more uplifting sight for the traveller from northern rains and ice than to arrive here, even in winter. 'Once across the green mulberry-belt and into the olive zone' wrote Durrell in his novel Monsieur, 'one becomes reassured; for even in the grey winterset of early dawn the gold tangerines hang in thriving loads as if in some Greek garden of Epicurus.' In spring, the trees are loaded with cherries, apricots and peach-

es, and every *hôtelier* takes advantage of them at his table, where they are served at the close of the meal. Later in the year, the figs are ripe: the green ones from around Marseille – small, juicy and particularly sweet – are well worth seeking out. From the area round Cavaillon come delicious small melons, their flesh sweet and pink. Their season is July and August, when locally their price can fall to just two or three francs each.

And then there is the almond tree, which gives its blossom and the finest of nuts. Almond oil is highly prized and priced, for salads and massage alike, while the paste is used for confectionery. Ground with sugar it is made into *nougat*, a speciality of Montélimar and Sault, and it forms the flavouring for the almond cakes (*calissons*) of Aix and Salon – well worth trying.

Above Regular spraying with a copper sulphate and sulphur is necessary to control moulds and pests which attack the vines. Vaucluse.

Left Wine labels of Provence.

Far left Colour, scent and flavour: each must be studied to assess the wine.

Opposite Vaucluse, origin of the most important wines of Provence.

Just as Beaujolais in wine terms belongs to Burgundy, but is geographically in the Rhône, so the most important wines in this area come from the department of the Vaucluse yet they belong quite firmly with the Côtes du Rhône, not in Provence. They are, in effect, the 'heavyweights' of the Rhône Valley: Châteauneuf-du-Pape, Gigondas, Vacqueyras, and the *villages* of Visan, Valréas, Vinsorbres, Rasteau and Cairanne. These wines are full of sun and natural alcohol (since *chaptalisation* is forbidden here), but only the very best can rival the reds from the terrassed vineyards of the northern Côtes du Rhône.

If you leave the *autoroute* at Donzère and head south-west, you drive first through the relatively new Coteaux de Tricastin vineyards and then into the

arid stony country of the Côtes du Rhône. These are big, meaty wines and the style is very much dependent on the mix of grapes planted and used. Up to twenty varieties are allowed, principally the Syrah (from the north), Grenache, Cinsault, Mourvèdre and Carignan for the reds, and Clairette and Bourboulenc for the whites. The Carignan is a big producer from the south and contributes largely to the slight commonness or even bitterness of wines from the Languedoc.

The Côtes du Rhône with *villages* on the label are better than the simple Côtes du Rhône and the best are those from the particular villages mentioned above. Vacqueyras and especially Gigondas (where they have done away with the Carignan grape altogether) now have their own *appellations* and they have a

velvety smoothness and longevity which the others lack.

The best wine from the south part of the Rhône valley (although Gigondas comes near it from time to time), is Châteauneuf-du-Pape. Here the soil is not really soil at all, but a whole plain of smooth stones – the vineyard being the river bed of the Rhône in prehistory – which hold the sun's heat well past the evening to give the final wine an extra richness and density. Even with modern techniques, Châteauneuf-du-Pape is a little rough when young, while it is at its best between five and fifteen years. The sheer power in the wine keeps it intact for several decades.

There is a little white made in this part of the Rhône, including some excellent Châteauneuf-du-Pape, which must be drunk young. The Côtes du Rhône rosés are a little heady, the best coming from Tavel in the Gard, so on a hot day it is better to drink the lighter wines from the Côtes du Ventoux (now A.O.C.) and the Côtes du Lubéron (V.D.Q.S.). These two used to be made as *vins de café*, light thirst-quenching wines almost rosé in colour. Now they are more serious 'proper' wines but still light and refreshing, which the classic Côtes du Rhône certainly are not.

To the east of the Vaucluse are the Alpes de Haute-Provence where, before you get too high for vines to survive, there is a little *vin du pays* and the V.D.Q.S. Coteaux de Pierrevert, more like Côtes du Rhône than Côtes de Provence. To the south is the department of Les Bouches du Rhône, south of Avignon. There are the same grape varieties here as in Rhône, except that there is more Carignan. Around Les Baux, the Coteaux des Baux-en-Provence (V.D.Q.S.) are racy and elegant with a spicy bouquet of herbs of the region. Across the Route Nationale, in the Coteaux d'Aix-en-Provence, some proprietors are experimenting with the Cabernet Sauvignon grape from Bordeaux, especially Château Vignelaure which is almost a Médoc-sur-Durance.

South of Aix-en-Provence is the very small *appellation* of Palette, where the best and almost only wine is from the lovely eighteenth-century Château Simone, and the best place to drink it is on the terrace of the Café La Rotonde at Aix. The reds are harder than one would expect and rather serious owing to the addition of the Mourvèdre grape variety. The same grape, not grown outside Provence and the Rhône, comes into its own at Bandol, where it is planted on

Wines and Spirits

terraced vineyards running down to the Mediterranean. The high proportion of Mourvèdre, a deep coloured, low-producing variety, produces long-lasting elegant wines, without doubt the best red wines of Provence, if they come from a good grower such as Domaine Tempier. The rosés, pale and fruity, are almost as good as Tavel, but the whites are better a few kilometres along the road to Marseille at Cassis. Here, made from the usual Rhône white grapes of Clairette and Marsanne, the Ugni Blanc from Provence and sometimes a little Sauvignon from the Loire to liven it up, the wine is bone dry but without acidity.

While Cassis and Bandol make the best known wines in coastal Provence, the rarest (even rarer than Palette) is from Bellet, north of Nice. A selection of vines is planted up to 1,000 feet (305 metres) above sea level, as opposed to the plains of Provence, to produce fine, delicate reds and extremely bouqueted, stylish whites. Bellet is seldom seen outside the good restaurants on the Côte d'Azur.

Roughly between Nice and Marseille lie the Côtes de Provence, awarded *appellation contrôlée* status in 1977. There is steady improvement in this area, particularly amongst the domain-bottled wines. The basic Provençal wine of old was deep in colour (red, rosé and white), high in alcohol and very uninteresting and tiring to drink. New grape varieties, modern methods of vinification and con-

stant effort by new proprietors have given the area a new image. Even the fancy bottle *style Provençal*, which is about as indicative of quality as the raffia-covered carafes from Chianti, is being given up in favour of the *style Bordelais* or *style Bourguignon*. The wines have become more elegant and quite individual.

Below Grapes ripening in the warm Provençal sun.

Bottom In the autumn, after the vintage, the vineyards are ploughed so as to cover the bases of the vines with earth – a protection against frost in the winter months.

Corsica

Napoleon, Corsica's most famous son, found a job for nearly every member of his family. If he couldn't provide a good military or civil position he married them off for political reasons. Blood ties are strong on this island which hangs like a ripe fruit off the coast of Italy, directly south of Genoa. It is only 114 miles (183 kilometres) long but it has been fought over by just about everybody, including the Etruscans, the Romans, the Moors and the Genoans, who had it from the Middle Ages and sold it to the French in 1768. Napoleon was born just fifteen months later.

It is a place of dramatic contrasts, from the icy splendour of its inland mountains to its rose-tipped peninsulas pressing forward into the Mediterranean Sea. Much of the land is covered with *Maquis* (from the local term, *macchia*, meaning brush). The French Resistance borrowed the word in World War II. This is the hardy vegetation of an arid climate – thorn trees, gorse, arbutus, wild foxglove, myrtle and heather. The fragrance, mingling with pine resin and rosemary, lavender and eucalyptus, drifts out to sea so that when wind and weather are right, Corsica has every claim to its title of 'the Scented Isle'.

It lies only 112 miles (180 kilometres) from the southern coast of France and is separated from Sardinia by a mere strip of water, but maintains an air of isolation. Its inhabitants refer to the French mainlanders as *les continentaux*. Officially (and sometimes unwillingly) it is a region of France (divided into two departments) although the people are Italianate and so is their dialect.

The name, Corsica, seems to be a form of the Phoenician word, *korsai*, meaning 'wood-covered'. A particular kind of pine, the *laricio*, grows to extreme heights and many of Corsica's marauders had their eye on this ready supply of spas and masts for sailing ships. Nelson strongly advised Britain to take Corsica for that very reason.

In winter snow turns the trees into lofty spires of white – and snow lasts long in the high country, patching the mountainsides as late as May or even June. Chestnuts and olives thrive in some regions. Chestnut flour and the nuts themselves lend an idiosyncratic note to Corsican cooking. This is because the islanders grew so disenchanted with having their

Introduction

grain taken from them by a succession of invaders that they ceased planting and relied instead on the harvest of their forests. There were times when the inland inhabitants, cut off even from supplies of fish, were forced to survive on chestnuts. Nowadays, though, the best are sent to the south of France where they go up in the world to become *marrons glacés*. There are swift, cold mountain streams full of trout, plunging gorges and some beautiful beaches.

The people have a reputation for being hot-blooded. Vendetta is a Corsican word. Prosper Mérimée has written about it in his books *Colomba* and *Mateo Falcone*. The tradition for blood feuds is supposed to have died out but a nineteenth-century visitor recorded 28,000 vendetta killings in the space of twenty years. They are also fervent and superstitious Catholics. Barefoot pilgrimages still take place. Assumption is a particularly high holy-day because it coincides with Napoleon's birthday. There are processions, spectacular fireworks and a party that continues into the following day. Belief in the Evil Eye is current.

Memories of the Emperor are, of course, everywhere, especially in Ajaccio, the capital, and every other street seems to carry reference to him. The Maison Bonaparte can be visited and so can the sixteenth-century Renaissance cathedral where he was baptized. From the nearby Pointe de la Parata you can look out to the three russet islands known as the Iles Sanguinaires.

Bastia is the largest and busiest town. It contains two venerated objects, a silver statue of the Virgin carried in procession in August and a black crucifix, Christ of the Miracles, which was found in the sea in the fifteenth century and is made the object of a fisherman's procession in May. From Bastia it is easy to visit the 'stalk' of Corsica, projecting towards the mainland. The French novelist, Guy de Maupassant, was inspired by this area when he toured Corsica and retained a memory of wildly beautiful scenery and tiny ports.

Inland are quiet villages where shepherds tend flocks of sheep and goats. Pigs gourmandize on fallen nuts in the thick chestnut forests. Higher still, above

Porto Vecchio, are rugged mountain outcrops. Corte, the old capital, is a mountain fastness with a fifteenth-century citadel and one of the most superb views in the whole island. The Tavignano and Restonica gorges are nearby. Crowning them is Mont Rotondo, second highest peak.

An epic compressed into an island of 3,367 square miles (5,418 kilometres) with a landscape encompassing turbulent rivers and coastline grottoes, powdery ski-slopes and sunlit beaches, Genoese ruins and Napoleonic mementoes. There is game in the rough country including wild boar and still, but very occasionally now, wild mountain sheep, as well as woodcock and blackbirds which feed on *lentisque*, a cousin to the pistachio nut. These are flavoured with native sage to provide a regional delicacy. Among the flora are pale asphodels; wild strawberries; *morille* mushrooms; sweet, *cédrat* lemons (from which Cédratine liqueur is made) and the famous pines which have been known to reach a height of 200 feet (61 metres).

The Greeks, who knew a good island when they saw one, called Corsica 'the most beautiful'.

Opposite The rugged bulk of Monte Cinto looms up behind the little town of Piana, situated 1400 feet (427 metres) above sea-level. On the road from here to Porto, the red granite has been eroded and sculpted into fantastic shapes.

Top Ringed by fine old houses, the old harbour of Bastia is a mooring place for fishing and pleasure boats. This largest town and former Genoese capital of the island also has a busy commercial port.

Above Ramparts still surround the fortified citadel at Calvi, reminders of the island's embattled past. Here, as in other Corsican towns, dramatic ceremonies take place at Easter time, with hooded penitents carrying crosses to the cathedral.

Towns and Villages

This rocky island bears traces of the many peoples that have invaded it over the centuries: the prehistoric site at Filitosa with its menhirs and carved stones is at least 8000 years old; a Greco-Roman city at Aleria is being excavated; the Pisans left Romanesque churches, the Genoese fortifications.

The coast is ringed with fifteenth-century towers that served as fortresses and observation posts; some seventy remain today, romantically silhouetted against the sea. The towns themselves are fortified citadels. Bonifacio looks much as it did in the thirteenth century, a stronghold built on the edge of a plateau where a steep sheer wall of rock drops down to the sea.

Ajaccio, the capital of Corsica, is situated in the curve of a beautiful bay. An ancient citadel guards the town, with its spacious squares, wide avenues and picturesque fishing port. There are reminders everywhere that this was Napoleon's birthplace. The Musée Fesch has a major collection of Italian paintings, including works by Botticelli and Veronese. Bastia, the former Genoese capital, has many fine patrician houses and an imposing Governor's Palace that now houses a museum of Corsican ethnography. The fine Baroque church of Saint-Jean-le-Baptiste is one of hundreds of Baroque churches built throughout the island. The elaborately-decorated interiors with carved furnishings and gilded stucco contrast with the rather sober external architecture.

However, it is not for architecture that most people come to Corsica, this charming island. It is for the many resorts, like Ile-Rousse with its fine sandy beach; Calvi with its yacht harbour; and Corte with its attendant mountain villages. An inland town and fortress from the eleventh century, Corte retains its Corsican character and in fact is a stronghold of Corsican nationalism. This area is splendid for trout fishing and shooting, while on the high grassy plateau of Niolo there is fine mountaineering and the occasional company of semi-nomadic shepherds, whose musical prowess is exceptional.

The eastern part of the island is made up of fertile land which has been farmed since Roman times: the coast has been quite heavily developed to accommodate the tourist trade, and a string of rather unhappy holiday villages has sprung up in recent years. The southern plain is dominated by a mountain where two small and peaceful villages, Antisanti and Prunelli, command beautiful views.

There is a wild, rocky region situated between Calvi and Porto which also offers tranquillity. Here the river Fango flows to the sea through game-rich woods. Porto itself, set in what is said to be the most beautiful area of the island, is a little village situated on the curve of a deep-water gulf.

Curious Easter celebrations take place in several Corsican towns, when hooded penitents take part in candle-lit processions on Good Friday. In some places, such as Sartène, a heavy wooden cross is carried, representing the Calvary.

Left This stylish, early poster advertizes coastal flights linking popular resorts. Bastia has long been a favourite spot for tourists, with its long, sandy beaches and Genoese architecture.

Top Mountains dominate this tiny island, rising sheer from the sea in places, rolling away to the horizon. Here the villages cling to peaks or line the valleys in between.

Above Thick fleeces from mountain sheep are carded prior to spinning in a Corsican village. Weaving is a traditional craft in villages such as Corte, Antisanti and Saint-Florent.

Cuisine, Wines and Spirits

Rugged and mountainous, Corsica is the home of simple restaurants and simple, wholesome food. Fishermen ply the coastline and their catch is the mainstay of the diet: sardines freshly fried in batter (*sardines frites*); grilled red mullet with olives (*rougets grillés aux olives*); fish stew (*iminu*) and shellfish in abundance – cockles, limpets, winkles and sea-urchins, apart from the better known lobsters and crayfish.

From the foothills, where herds of sheep and goats are kept, comes a selection of tasty cheeses, like Brocciu or the blue-veined Bleu de Corse. Most of the sheep's milk is, however, made into 'white' Roquefort and sent to ripen in the famous caves (page 215). These herds also provide meat: two specialities are kid grilled with herbs (*chevreau grillé*) and saddle of lamb roasted with garlic (*selle d'agneau au four*). To complete your meal there are some delicious chestnut pastries (*fritelli* and *fiadone*).

Harbourside restaurants such as these in Ajaccio (**top**) and Bonifaccio (**above**) are excellent places to enjoy the local seafood, particularly *iminu*, a hearty local version of *bouillabaisse*.

Right Vineyards surround a farmhouse below the village of Sartène. The Corsican wine industry is rapidly expanding, and its products repay investigation.

Corsica as a vineyard area is in the process of exciting change. A century ago, there were 50,000 acres of vines producing 600 million bottles of wine. By the end of the last war, the vineyards had dropped to 13,000 acres; but today the vines cover 65,000 acres, with a production of up to 2,000 million bottles. Not all of this is great wine, but most of it is good and some of it is excellent. The particular regions to look for good wine are: Cap-Corse (especially for the dry, white wines and the sweet Muscats), Patrimonio (with its own *appellation*), Calvi-Balagne, Coteaux d'Ajaccio, Sartene and Porto Vecchio. Much of the difference lies in the hands of the wine-maker and it is evident that a wine from a *propriétaire-récoltant* will be more individual, if not at all times better than one from one of the *caves coopératives*. The main grapes, with the addition of the basic varieties from Provence and Languedoc, are the Nielluccio, a wonderful black grape now found to be identical to that used principally for Chianti; the Sciacarello, a light red grape always vinified with the other varieties; and the Vermentino, rather like the Ugni Blanc of Provence. Corsican wines are often every bit as good as their south-of-France counterparts and, in many cases, especially when drunk with the local *charcuterie* and cheese, much more individual.

Index

253

Wine Glossary and Acknowledgements

à la temperature de la cave cellar temperature, around 12° centigrade

appellation controlée the French system of controls on the origin of the wine, where it is grown and what it is made from

apéritif any alcoholic drink taken before a meal

brut very dry, usually used for sparkling wine

cachet style or distinctive individuality

caves cellars for storing wine, below ground

commune a defined area in an **appellation**, usually a village area such as Volnay or Saint-Julien

climat a subdivision of a **commune** denoting a plot of special character, i.e. Volnay 'Les Champans'

dégorgement 'disgorgement' of Champagne, to get rid of the sediment left by the fermentation in the bottle

eau-de-vie a spirit arrived at by distillation

épluchage selection of grapes by hand, after picking and before pressing, to eliminate the less good

goût de terroir having a special taste reminiscent of, and distinctive to, the area the wine is from

gros rouge cheap, blended wine generally of high alcohol content and little character

grand cru a name given to a plot of vines where the wine resulting is better than the others. Part of the **appellation controlée**

liqueur d'expédition mixture of old Champagne and cape sugar added to Champagne after disgorgement to top up the bottle and round out the taste

négociant person buying wine in bulk or in bottles for re-sale

la méthode champenoise method by which still wine is made sparkling, by an exaggerated secondary fermentation in the bottle

pastis an **apéritif** made on an alcohol base flavoured with liquorice

piqué a wine which has 'turned', giving an impression of vinegary sharpness

pourriture noble 'noble rot', a fungus that attacks the grapes in the Sauternes region

propriétaire-viticulteur owner of a vineyard usually responsible for the finished product

premier cru parcel of vines or **climat**, generally less than **grand cru**, but better than an **appellation communale**

récoltant-manipulant in Champagne, a grower who makes and sells Champagne from his own vines

remuage process in Champagne-making to consolidate the sediment prior to **dégorgement**

réglementé a Government control of spirits

route de vin an informative and scenic route through the vineyards

sec generally means dry, but in Champagne semi-dry

spritzig very slightly sparkling, 'lively'

sur lie a wine bottled off its lees which has a freshness and sometimes a touch of sparkle

vendage tardive late picking of overripe grapes to make a sweeter wine

vigneron person responsible for tending the vines

vin gris very pale rosé obtained by pressing but not macerating red grapes

vin doux naturels an **apéritif** or dessert wine where the sweetness is kept by stopping fermentation with the addition of alcohol

vin jaune very rare wine from the Jura, taking on a yellow colour after six years in the cask

vin d'ordinaire cheap blended wine of no particular origin

vin de paille very sweet wine made in the Jura by laying the grapes on straw mats to dry out and increase the proportion of sugar

vin sauvage old-fashioned expression usually relating to the white wine from the Sauvignon grape